Between Advents

Between Advents

Sermons for the Lectionary, Year C,
Advent through Eastertide

BRUCE L. TAYLOR

WIPF & STOCK · Eugene, Oregon

BETWEEN ADVENTS
Sermons for the Lectionary, Year C, Advent through Eastertide

Copyright © 2021 Bruce L. Taylor. All rights reserved. Except for brief quotations in critical publications or reviews, no part of this book may be reproduced in any manner without prior written permission from the publisher. Write: Permissions, Wipf and Stock Publishers, 199 W. 8th Ave., Suite 3, Eugene, OR 97401.

Unless otherwise noted, scripture quotations are from Common Bible: New Revised Standard Version Bible, copyright © 1989 National Council of the Churches of Christ in the United States of America. Used by permission. All rights reserved worldwide. Emphasis added.

Scripture quotations marked (RSV) are from Revised Standard Version of the Bible, copyright © 1946, 1952, and 1971 National Council of the Churches of Christ in the United States of America. Used by permission. All rights reserved.

Wipf & Stock
An Imprint of Wipf and Stock Publishers
199 W. 8th Ave., Suite 3
Eugene, OR 97401

www.wipfandstock.com

PAPERBACK ISBN: 978-1-6667-0251-4
HARDCOVER ISBN: 978-1-6667-0252-1
EBOOK ISBN: 978-1-6667-0253-8

05/11/21

In memory of
Dick Campbell and Marion Garrett

Contents

Introduction — xi

First Sunday of Advent—"Tomorrow, God"
Jeremiah 33:14–16; 1 Thessalonians 3:9–13; Luke 21:25–36 — 1

Second Sunday of Advent—"Whose Heart Will Be the First?"
Malachi 3:1–4; Philippians 1:3–11; Luke 3:1–6 — 7

Third Sunday of Advent—"Believing Is Seeing"
Zephaniah 3:14–20; Philippians 4:4–7; Luke 3:7–18 — 12

Fourth Sunday of Advent—"God's Revolution Has Begun"
Micah 5:2–5a; Hebrews 10:5–10; Luke 1:39–55 — 17

Christmas Eve (Early Evening)—"The Littlest Shepherd"
Isaiah 9:2–7; Titus 2:11–14; Luke 2:1–20 — 23

Christmas Eve (Late Evening)—"Between Advents"
Isaiah 9:2–7; Titus 2:11–14; Luke 2:1–20 — 30

Christmas Day—"Who Is Lying in Your Manger?"
Isaiah 52:7–10; Hebrews 1:1–4; John 1:1–14 — 35

First Sunday after Christmas—"The Most Natural Thing"
1 Samuel 2:18–20, 26; Colossians 3:12–17; Luke 2:41–52 — 40

Second Sunday after Christmas—"The Word beyond Words"
Jeremiah 31:7–14; Ephesians 1:3–14; John 1:1–18 — 45

Epiphany of the Lord—"When the Light Shines"
Isaiah 60:1–6; Ephesians 3:1–12; Matthew 2:1–12 — 50

Baptism of the Lord—"'You Are Mine'"
Isaiah 43:1–7; Acts 8:14–17; Luke 3:15–17, 21–22 — 55

Second Sunday in Ordinary Time—"A Sign of Things to Come"
Isaiah 62:1–5; 1 Corinthians 12:1–11; John 2:1–11   60

Third Sunday in Ordinary Time—"'Today, in Your Hearing'"
Nehemiah 8:1–4a, 5–6, 8–10; 1 Corinthians 12:12–30; Luke 4:14–21   65

Fourth Sunday in Ordinary Time—"The School for Loving"
Jeremiah 1:4–10; 1 Corinthians 13:1–13; Luke 4:21–30   71

Fifth Sunday in Ordinary Time—"A Letter Home"
Isaiah 6:1–8; 1 Corinthians 15:1–11; Luke 5:1–11   76

Sixth Sunday in Ordinary Time—"Strong Stuff, This Good News"
Jeremiah 17:5–10; 1 Corinthians 15:12–20; Luke 6:17–26   80

Seventh Sunday in Ordinary Time—"Like Parent, Like Child"
Genesis 45:3–11, 15; 1 Corinthians 15:35–38, 42–50; Luke 6:27–38   85

Transfiguration of the Lord—"On to the Cross"
Exodus 34:29–35; 2 Corinthians 3:12—4:2; Luke 9:28–43   90

Ash Wednesday—"The Christian Nation"
Isaiah 58:1–14; 2 Corinthians 5:20b—6:10; Matthew 6:1–6, 16–21   95

First Sunday in Lent—"Living in Sin, Living by Grace"
Genesis 2:4b–9, 15–17, 25—3:7; Romans 5:12–19; Luke 4:1–13   101

Second Sunday in Lent—"Beyond Touch and Sight"
Genesis 15:1–12, 17–18; Philippians 3:17—4:1; Luke 13:31–35   106

Third Sunday in Lent—"Water for the Spirit, Bread for the Soul"
Isaiah 55:1–9; 1 Corinthians 10:1–13; Luke 13:1–9   111

Fourth Sunday in Lent—"Return from a Far Country"
Joshua 5:9–12; 2 Corinthians 5:16–21; Luke 15:1–3, 11–32   117

Fifth Sunday in Lent—"What Are You Giving Up for Lent?"
Isaiah 43:16–21; Philippians 3:4b–14; John 12:1–8   122

Palm/Passion Sunday—"Conversation in a Workshop"
Isaiah 50:4–9a; Philippians 2:5–11; Luke 19:28–40   127

Maundy Thursday—"What We Do Here"
Exodus 12:1–4, 11–14; 1 Corinthians 11:23–26; John 13:1–17, 31b–35   131

Good Friday—"Beneath the Cross of Jesus"
Isaiah 52:13—53:12; Hebrews 4:14-16; 5:7-9; John 18:1—19:42   136

The Resurrection of the Lord (Sunrise)—"God's Flower Has Shattered the Stone"
Acts 10:34-43; 1 Corinthians 15:19-26; John 20:1-18   140

The Resurrection of the Lord—"Whom Do You Seek?"
Isaiah 25:6-9; Acts 10:34-43; John 20:1-18   143

Second Sunday of Easter—"Stubborn Faith"
Acts 5:27-32; Revelation 1:4-8; John 20:19-31   149

Third Sunday of Easter—"On the Other Side of Healing"
Acts 9:1-20; Revelation 5:11-14; John 21:1-19   154

Fourth Sunday of Easter—"Nothing Will Ever Be Quite the Same"
Acts 9:36-43; Revelation 7:9-17; John 10:22-30   159

Fifth Sunday of Easter—"Revelation"
Acts 11:1-18; Revelation 21:1-6; John 13:31-35   164

Sixth Sunday of Easter—"Water of Life"
Acts 16:9-15; Revelation 21:10, 21:22—22:5; John 5:1-9   170

Ascension of the Lord—"Witnesses of Hope"
Acts 1:1-11; Ephesians 1:15-23; Luke 24:44-53   175

Seventh Sunday of Easter—"Real Life"
Acts 16:16-34; Revelation 22:12-14, 16-17, 20-21; John 17:20-26   179

Appendix   185

"Peace . . .Our Hope for the Future"
Isaiah 55:10-13; Matthew 5:1-12   187

List of Sources Cited   191

Introduction

LUKE IS MY FAVORITE Gospel. While my appreciation of the particular features and emphases of all four Gospels has increased over years of seminary training, weekly encounters in the task of sermon preparation, and the lived scriptural insights gained through congregational life and pastoral care, the witness of Luke as good news has repeatedly insinuated itself into my spiritual consciousness (or, perhaps, the Holy Spirit has brought its themes and episodes more frequently to my mind than those of any other Gospel). Exegetes and interpreters have noted its rich multiplicity of special foci, including the attention given to the work of the Holy Spirit, the concern for the marginalized, including women and the poor and the foreigner, and its technique of explicating the Lord's Supper by way of presenting scenes of Jesus at a number of meals before and after the crucifixion. Here, of course, we find the poignantly memorable parables of the good Samaritan and prodigal son, or more descriptively, the prodigal *sons*. Here are the great canticles sung by Mary, Zechariah, and Simeon that have become inscribed on the souls of worshipers through the traditional liturgy of the church. And here is the most beloved version of the wondrous birth of the Son of God in the simplest of settings and among the humblest of people.

For me, the theological axis of the Magnificat and Jesus' programmatic announcement of his ministry in the synagogue at Nazareth define the core of the gospel and the core of this Gospel, and articulate the mission of discipleship in light of God's spoken valuation of creation in the first chapter of Genesis. It challenges any inclinations of the church and the clergy and laity alike to compromise the high calling to steadfast and sacrificial servanthood and humility, and the witness of Luke's second volume, the Acts of the Apostles, demonstrates to the church in every age that Christ's faithful trust in his followers to adhere to the ministry he has set before them remains not only vital but possible. The reason, of course, is the potent and genuine fulfillment of Christ's promise to his church in the provision and protection of the Holy Spirit, which is (I believe) blasphemed by anyone who denies the possibility of its power to move hearts to yield to the will of God.

Many commentators over the centuries have speculated that Luke, a protégé of Paul, must have been a physician. His Gospel discloses a unique interest in the ailments and maladies that Jesus cured, which had resulted in suffering that was not only physical, but social as well. Whether or not the author of the Gospel was trained in medicine, he certainly gave witness to Jesus' own attention to the condition of the people he encountered that went well beyond any purely spiritual interest. Indeed, acknowledging the Jewish inability to separate body and soul, or the Jewish refusal to do so, Luke's Jesus models for the church the practice of holistic ministry that regards feeding, healing, sheltering, and befriending to be just as important and necessary as forgiving, and provides a mandate for the church's engagement in peacemaking and what has been called the "social gospel." And Luke's Gentile identity may well have rendered him particularly sensitive to the status of "outsider" that Jesus' words and deeds are shown to transcend and overcome.

Although Luke is my favorite Gospel, it has proven to be the Gospel that I find most difficult to preach on, for the very reason that it is my favorite. In short, such a rich field of lilies resists homiletical gilding—at least, mine. How does one speak about the birth in the manger, the parental yearning for a wayward child's return and then profound joy when it actually happens, and the disregard of cultural and ethnic and religious barriers to meet the needs of the injured and excluded without obscuring or detracting from what is so beautifully self-evident? One can only stand alongside such stories and voice one's own wonder, rather than attempting to improve upon them by making them more complicated than they are and thus end up trivializing what is divinely profound.

I want to acknowledge my special indebtedness to three companions in the effort who, among my many published "consultants" on Luke who are serenely unaware of their roles in my ministry, have been particularly reliable assistants in the homiletical vocation: Fred Craddock, Eduard Schweizer, and Eugene LaVerdiere. Even more than other commentators, I have found their insights to be unerringly useful in the delicate task of leaving the center of the stage to the Gospel itself and, in the case especially of LaVerdiere, revealing the sacramental development unfolded in Luke's use of stories about Jesus at table with friends and even adversaries. A parishioner in one of my churches related to me the joyful multilingual dinnertime companionship at the end of a day of walking along the Camino de Santiago, and ended with the comment, "And it occurred to me, this is what you have talked about in so many sermons and class sessions about dining together in the kingdom of God!" I also want to thank the many writers of hymn texts who, over the centuries and particularly in the past few decades, have so enriched and adorned the church's meal to which "they will come from east and west, and from north and south, and sit at table in the kingdom of God"[1]—an image that lies at the heart of Luke's experience of life in Christ—often with new attention to the everyday conviviality of Jesus on his way from the cradle to the cross.

Once again, use of the lectionary and sermonic treatment of the whole range of its suggested scripture passages is useful and important to the faithful exposition of any of them. It is our commission, as preachers of the gospel, to introduce congregations to the fullness of scripture and discover for ourselves with fresh wonder the treasures that await whoever approaches the Bible prayerfully and trusting the Holy Spirit's readiness and ability to guide and reward the faithful reader, hearer, and doer of the word—truly a lifetime's vocation as we find ourselves between advents.

---

1. *"Book of Common Worship,"* 68.

First Sunday of Advent

Spanish Springs Presbyterian Church, Sparks, Nevada

November 29, 2009

Jeremiah 33:14–16

1 Thessalonians 3:9–13

Luke 21:25–36

"Tomorrow, God"

"So what has it gotten you, this 'good news'?" The voice came from the next cell. Raspy and mocking, it issued between fits of coughing and wheezing. The old man lifted his head slightly and drew his legs up close to his chest to preserve his warmth, which the cold stone floor had been sapping from his outstretched limbs. Somewhere, there was the sound of slowly dripping water. The jail was dank and smelled of human waste.

"He will not abandon me," the old man replied to the taunt from behind the stone wall.

A raspy laugh answered his statement, but it quickly disappeared into another fit of coughing.

"Nor *anyone* who turns to him in faith," the old man added.

To this, there came a snort from the next cell. "I heard him," the raspy voice said after a few seconds. "That Jew who spoke down by their meeting place. What do they call it? 'Synagogue,' that's it. I heard him. A lot of rubbish about the cross proving his point." Another snort, which led to more coughing. When he recovered, he added, "They sent him packing, fair enough—talking about a king on a cross, indeed." There was a thud. The man to whom the voice belonged had apparently been standing at the bars of his cell, and now had sat down on the hard floor. "Good news. Ha!" There was silence again, broken only by the sound of dripping water. Eventually, he asked, "What are you called?"

"Jason," the old man replied, his chin resting on his knees and his arms wrapped around his legs. "Some know me now as a follower of Jesus."

"Jesus, yes, that's the name that little Jew called him," the other man said with a slight chuckle. "The Christ, he said he was—the anointed one, whatever that means."

"It has to do with the Hebrew scriptures," the old man informed him. "He's the one the prophets of the Jews said would come."

"Bah," the voice from the other cell uttered.

"The Lord," the old man added.

"Have a care," the raspy voice replied. "Talk like *that's* what got you *in* here. So the guard told me. And not the first time."

"Friends put up my bail the first time," the old man admitted. "Then I was arrested again after some ruffians disrupted our worship."

"Worship of what? The Jewish God?"

"Yes, Jesus' Father—the God to whom Jesus prayed."

"You people are daft," the other man said. "Didn't learn your lesson the first time?"

"The truth is the truth," the old man responded. "My being threatened with arrest or not doesn't change that."

"The truth is that the world belongs to the emperor, and he's not interested in sharing it with your 'king.'" Now that the man had a theme, his cough was less persistent. "And what kind of a king wastes his time in a place like Palestine? And dies on a cross? From what I heard, he died like a criminal. *Gods* don't *die*. And *kings* don't die on a *cross*."

"Oh, he's not dead," the old man answered. "He's alive. He's here with me now."

"With you *now*? Sharing a *jail cell* with you? *I* hear no other voice. I saw you when they brought you in here. You're alone, my insane friend, you're quite alone."

Now the old man laughed softly. "Quite the contrary," he said in a low voice, not to convince the other man, and with a smile that the other man could not see. "And it's not the *first* time he's been in a jail cell."

"If someone bailed *me* out of here, *I* wouldn't go looking to be thrown back in again. That just *proves* how insane you are!"

"One day," the old man said, "none of this will be regarded as the disgrace the authorities intend. Even now, I count it a privilege."

There was an immediate burst of incredulous laughter that quickly gave way to another fit of coughing, then more laughter. "Rotting in jail a *privilege*? Being arrested '*good news*'? What has this God of yours done to your sense of values? Surely no one *else* in Thessalonica would think being in this stinking hole is an *honor*!"

"Being in *jail*, *no*. Being in jail because of *him*, yes. And his being *with* me here, *definitely*."

"You'd do better with a God who's strong enough to break these bars and show you the privilege of breathing clean air again, and not worrying about rats nibbling at your toes in the night."

"Whether out *there* or in *here*, I am *equally* free," the old man said. "And the fact that these things are happening only means that the day of his final triumph is drawing near."

"Bah," was the only response.

After a time, the old man began to hum to himself, and then to sing softly.

"What's that you're doing?" the raspy voice asked.

"What? Oh, I'm just singing."

"I *know* you're singing. What is the *song*?"

"It's a hymn. Something that we sing to the Lord in worship."

The other man snorted. The old man resumed his song, still singing softly, barely audibly, but still loudly enough that the song could be identified as a cheerful tune, not a sorrowful one.

"How can you do that?" the other man asked, his voice now angry. "How can you do that? I want you to stop. You're insane."

"I don't mean to distress you. But I assure you, I'm quite sane."

"How *can* you be? Singing like *that* in a place like *this*. Don't you know they could find you guilty of *treason*? Don't you know they could *kill* you?"

"What they do to me is of little account. They cannot do to me what they most *wish* to do. They cannot separate me from my Lord. And they certainly cannot do worse to *me* than they did to *him*. And he *lives*. And *I* shall live *with* him. Besides, it is little time now until he comes again and all this will be changed."

"I thought you claimed he was with you in your cell?"

"He is. In his Spirit. But he will return in a way that *all* people will recognize, and then every prison will be opened, as all eyes will see him."

"When?" the other man demanded.

"Soon," the old man replied. "When the time is right. When everything is ready."

"Dreams. Just dreams. Silly, stupid dreams. Nothing ever changes. If you're on the bottom, you *stay* on the bottom. The rich and the powerful make sure of that. They have the law in their pockets. Nothing ever changes." There was more coughing, loud this time.

When the coughing subsided, the old man said, "I think things changed quite a *bit* when Jesus was raised from the *dead*."

This time, the old man's words were met only with silence—no rebuke, no challenge. After a few moments, he asked, "Would you mind if I finished my song?"

"Go ahead," the other man answered weakly.

"I could teach you the words," the old man ventured. "Then we could sing it together."

"I don't want to sing," the raspy voice replied, now gruff again. "I don't feel like singing. Singing in here . . . that *is* insane!"

The old man started again where he had left off, and when he had finished, he started praying for his neighbor, out loud.

"What are you doing now?" the raspy voice demanded to know. "What are you saying?"

The old man continued with his prayer, abbreviating it from what he had intended, and then turned his address from God to the man in the next cell. "I was praying for you, asking God to comfort you and to open your mind to him and welcome you into his kingdom."

"Don't," the man barked. "I don't like it."

"I'm sorry," the old man said. "I didn't mean to upset you. I've *been* praying for you ever since I came *in* here."

"Why?"

"I've been praying for *all* who are here, and for all who have *ever* been here and all who ever *will* be here."

"Why?"

"Because *Jesus* would. And I think *Paul* would."

"Paul. That's the one who was forced out of town, along with some of his friends."

"Yes."

"You're insane!" the other man responded.

"Would you like to learn to pray?"

"What? To someone who was executed on a *cross*?"

"To God. To his Father."

"To the God who *allowed* him to be executed on a cross?"

"Yes. The God who may allow *me* to be executed on a cross."

"So he *will* abandon you?"

"No. He will not abandon me. Just as he did not abandon Jesus, but raised him from the dead."

"You're insane," the other man sneered, and then coughed again.

"Jesus told his followers that they would undergo all sorts of trials. Nations will be in turmoil. Even the forces of nature will seem to be at war. But the Son of Man will come with power and great glory. Then our salvation will be near its completion, *and* the salvation of the world. Now is the time to repent and to make ready."

"You're definitely insane," the other man said.

"No," the old man said. "It is the *world* that is insane, until it acknowledges that Jesus is Lord."

"And then what?" the other man asked, sarcastically.

"Then hatred will end. There will be no more prisons. There will be no more war. Idolatry will end. Everything that the prophets promised will come to pass."

"And when will this be? In time for me to be home for supper, perhaps?"

"Soon," the old man repeated. "When Christ returns. When the time is right. When everything is ready."

There was now silence for several minutes. The old man again became aware of the sound of dripping water. He began humming again, and eventually the hum gave way to words, as before, and shortly after he concluded his hymn, the raspy voice came again, this time without anger, without sarcasm, without pride.

"Teach me to pray."

The old man smiled. "Of course," he said. "When his disciples asked how *they* should pray, our Lord taught them these words . . . ." The old man spoke them phrase by phrase, with the other man repeating, coughing occasionally. "Do you think we can say them together now? Let's try it." The old man patiently voiced the prayer he knew so well, and the other, in a voice less confident but determined, joined in.

After a few moments of silence, the raspy voice asked, not with any trace of anger or impatience, "What happens now?"

"Now, we live in faith and act in hope."

"'Thy will be done.' Is he going to have us released?"

"If we are living in faith and acting in hope, he has *already* released us—has released us from fear, has released us from anger, has released us from hatred. Do you see how he has already released us from loneliness?"

The other man coughed quietly.

"Jesus is here with us. And God has also given us each other."

"I'm not sure I can have faith in something I can't see," the other man said softly from the other side of the stone wall, more in the way of a confession than an accusation.

"Can you see *me*?" the old man asked. "For me, faith is reflecting back on yesterday and understanding that God was faithfully caring for me then, experiencing whatever today has to offer and trusting that God is working his will through it, and knowing that tomorrow, God will be faithful to his promise of salvation, despite what I see or can't see. Every moment of life is a blessing, a gift. I can demand no more, have done nothing to deserve the good things that I have already received."

"And you never have doubts about your God?" the raspy voice asked in a tone that suggested a quest for understanding.

"Oh, yes. Well, not 'doubts' so much as impatience, wondering why things don't happen faster. But then, something happens that causes me to look back on events and see that God's timing was right after all. Over these months that I have been walking in the way of Jesus, his Spirit has helped me to be more patient, to be more trusting, to be more confident that God's will shall be done, that God will take care of tomorrow. I think of how bleak it must have seemed for the disciples when Jesus was crucified. And then I think of their joy when he was standing among them, talking with them, even eating with them after he was raised from the dead. And I know that tomorrow is secure in God's hands. And then, you know, the waiting becomes much easier."

It was quiet again for several minutes, except for the sound of the dripping water and the occasional muffled cough from the other jail cell. Finally, the other man asked in his raspy voice, "Perhaps you could teach me what you were singing."

Second Sunday of Advent

Spanish Springs Presbyterian Church, Sparks, Nevada

December 7, 2003

Malachi 3:1–4

Philippians 1:3–11

Luke 3:1–6

"Whose Heart Will Be the First?"

IT WAS NOT LONG into our history as Spanish Springs Presbyterian Church—I think we were still meeting for worship up at Bud Beasley Elementary School—when a young man came up to me one Sunday after the worship service with a question about my sermon. In commenting on the scripture passages for that day, I had apparently made some reference to God's concern that we feed the hungry and care for the poor, as the passages had said. The man said to me, "I have always been taught that, when the Bible talks about feeding the hungry and taking care of the poor, it's talking about their *spiritual* hunger and their *spiritual* poverty. It *doesn't* mean that the church is supposed to be concerned about giving people food or worrying about people's living conditions." A little startled, I don't remember exactly how I responded—probably something like, "Why shouldn't we suppose that Jesus and the prophets meant exactly what they said?" Anyway, the man never came back, and I assume that he found a congenial pew in some church—and there are a growing number—that *doesn't* consider the plight of the poor as a priority of the gospel and that *doesn't* regard tending to people's physical needs as a major part of the good news.

It is quite possible that the man had indeed been taught that the gospel isn't about taking care of *physical* needs, isn't about *sharing* God's creation, isn't about treating people with *respect* for anyone made in God's image, isn't about tending to our *neighbor's* material well-being. Throughout the Christian era, people who have benefited from the prevailing social order have encouraged the church to interpret the Bible as referring to purely spiritual matters and have defined "spiritual" so narrowly as not to touch at all directly on the earthly welfare and dignity of people who are of a different race, of a different gender, of a different nationality, of a different social class. One parishioner in a former church used to declare regularly that social conditions like poverty and hunger and discrimination and international issues such as war and human rights would improve only when people's hearts change. That's true enough. But *Christians* are people whose hearts are supposed to have changed *already*. It may be that *some* people come to church to hear how their *neighbors* are going to be judged. But the true disciple of Jesus Christ knows that the gospel is first and foremost a judgment upon *us* who *believe*—*our* attitudes, *our* allegiances, *our* desires, *our* priorities. Jesus directed his call for repentance first of all to those who were inclined to come and hear him, not to their neighbors who were ignoring him and hadn't the slightest interest in what he said or did.

Perhaps a better response to the man who questioned me about the spiritual nature of the Bible would have been to encourage him to consider the Gospel of Luke. In all of the New Testament, no book is so insistent on the need for repentance. Time and again in Luke, Jesus tells people to *repent*, for the kingdom of God is *at hand*. They are to change their hearts. They are to turn themselves around, to quit going in the direction they have *been* headed, and go instead in the direction that *God* requires. That's what "repentance" means, literally—"to change one's direction," "to turn around" and go a different way. The necessity of repentance is declared early in the book, even *before* Jesus began preaching. "The word of God came to John son of Zechariah in the wilderness," Luke tells us. "He went into all the region around the Jordan, proclaiming a baptism of repentance for the forgiveness of sins" (Luke 3:2b–3 NRSV). The baptizer told the crowds to "bear fruits worthy of repentance" (Luke 3:8a NRSV). Repentance is a very big deal in Luke.

But in all of the New Testament, no book shows so many occasions of Jesus ministering to the poor and the hungry and the sick and the outcast and those considered undesirable and alien and unclean and sinful as Luke's Gospel does. And when the crowds at the Jordan asked John what they needed to *do* to be *saved*, John said that they must share their clothes and their food with those who were without, and not be greedy in collecting what was owed to them, and not practice extortion or deceit. And all of John's instructions and teachings had to do, Luke says, with the fulfillment of the words of the prophet Isaiah:

> "The voice of one crying out in the wilderness:
> 'Prepare the way of the Lord,
>   make his paths straight.

> Every valley shall be filled,
> > and every mountain and hill shall be made low,
> and the crooked shall be made straight,
> > and the rough ways made smooth;
> and all flesh shall see the salvation of God.'" (Luke 3:4a–6 NRSV)

It seems to me that it takes some amazing theological handsprings to conclude that Christianity and the church and individual Christians, for that matter, have no obligation of faith to be concerned with things that aren't purely spiritual. The Jews, including Jesus, knew of no division between the body and the soul, the physical and the spiritual. They *did* know what *hypocrisy* was, however—saying that you love God and then disregarding the needs of your neighbor, confessing that God is merciful and then evicting the poor out of their homes, going through the rituals of worship and then ignoring God's call for justice and compassion. And in Luke's very introduction of Jesus and his ministry, the plight of the poor and the humble and the alien and the outcast are prominently set over against the prerogatives and privileges of the rich and the well-fed and the well-connected and those with a religious "in." "Bear fruits worthy of repentance," John said to the crowds at the Jordan. "Do not begin to say to yourselves, 'We have Abraham as our ancestor'; for I tell you, God is able from these stones to raise up children to Abraham" (Luke 3:8 NRSV). Pedigree—either spiritual or biological—is of no avail. Propriety—either religious or social—is irrelevant. *All* are called to repentance, and even *Jesus himself* answered John's call to the baptism of repentance that signaled his sympathy with the poorest, the most despised, the most sinful, and involved him in their lives of deprivation as well as their yearning for salvation.

Luke wrote his Gospel for the sake of the church, for the use of the church, to be read as congregations met to worship. Luke intended for his Gospel to be an avenue for Christ to speak to *Christians*. The call to repentance is for *you* and *me* even *before* it is for the *world outside*. It is a call for people who know what God demands and what God teaches to be the *first* to change their hearts from the habits and manners of selfishness and pride and greed and prejudice and to welcome the kingdom of God despite the world's stubbornness and the disobedience of *un*believers.

It was not to the *Gentiles* that the Old Testament prophets were speaking, but to those who considered themselves to be God's special people. What God's special people sometimes *forgot* was that, from *God's* point of view, their *specialness* had to do with their *responsibilities* every bit as much as their *blessings*. What God intended eventually for the *whole world, they* were to be doing *today*, modeling the attitudes and behaviors of faithfulness, being an example, a shining light, a city on a hill. And the prophets time and time again repeated God's emphatic demand for justice for the poor, food for the hungry, compassion for the widow and the orphan, hospitality for the foreigner and the outcast.

Jesus did not come to *overturn* the prophets, but to *fulfill* them. Jesus was not born to *excuse* inattention to people's physical needs, but to heal and feed and raise to dignity, even as he forgave sins, and to enlist *others* in healing and feeding and raising to dignity, even as *they* forgive sins. He called people to account for *ignoring* the prophets, he didn't excuse them from doing what the prophets had *commanded*. Malachi testified to God's judgment upon the people's slovenly and self-serving worship, approaching God so casually as to think that just about anything would do for an offering and that worship was more about satisfying human whims and congratulating human achievements and making themselves feel warm and self-satisfied than glorifying the majesty of God. God's judgment upon such practices wasn't *cancelled out* by Christ's coming. God's judgment upon such practices was *ratified* by Christ's coming. The prophet announced that God's judgment upon God's own people would be like fire that purifies gold and refines silver or like soap that scrubs clean every impurity. God's judgment wasn't *voided* by Christ's coming. God's judgment was on the way to being *satisfied*.

Later in the book, Malachi says that the difference between the *righteous* and the *wicked* is between the one who *serves* God and the one who does *not* serve God. The condition of our *spirit* is revealed by our *behavior*. "Return to me, and I will return to you, says the LORD of hosts" (Mal 3:7b NRSV). In other words, "Repent!" Make your worship once again a holy offering to God, Malachi said, and quit making it a lie by honoring God with your *words* and then *dis*honoring God with your *deeds*. In other words, make the physical consistent with the spiritual. They cannot be separated. "See, I am sending my messenger to prepare the way before me" (Mal 3:1a NRSV), God announced in Malachi. And generations of Christians have seen in that passage a promise fulfilled by John, the one who baptized at the Jordan, announcing the coming of the Lord, calling for repentance and saying exactly what that means: "Whoever has two coats must share with anyone who has none; and whoever has food must do likewise. . . . [Tax collectors, collect] no more than the amount prescribed for you. . . . [Soldiers, do] not extort money from anyone by threats or false accusation, and be satisfied with your wages" (Luke 3:11, 13, 14b NRSV). Turning the spirit toward *God*, John made clear, and then Jesus after him, means turning your heart, your hands, your purse, toward your neighbor, and especially toward your neighbor in need. And it isn't just Luke's Gospel that points us toward making our repentance tangible. Surely Paul had concrete works of faith in mind when he prayed that the Philippian Christians "may be pure and blameless, having produced the harvest of righteousness that comes through Jesus Christ for the glory and praise of God" (Phil 1:10b–11 NRSV). A "harvest of righteousness," Paul said, "fruits of repentance," as John put it—a crop of deeds done for those who are in need, including the least and the lowliest, in response to the generous and merciful love of God in Jesus Christ, the same generous and merciful love of God that makes it right to worship God in the sanctuary in the beauty of holiness, in singleness of purpose and purity of heart, offering God *not* what is easy or in vogue, but what is worthy and profound.

> In the fifteenth year of the reign of Emperor Tiberius . . . the word of God came to John the son of Zechariah in the wilderness. He went into all the region around the Jordan, proclaiming a baptism of repentance for the forgiveness of sins, as it is written in the book of the words of the prophet Isaiah,
> "The voice of one crying out in the wilderness:
>   'Prepare the way of the Lord,
>   make his paths straight.
> Every valley shall be filled,
>   and every mountain and hill shall be made low,
> and the crooked shall be made straight,
>   and the rough ways made smooth;
> and all flesh shall see the salvation of God.'" (Luke 3:1–6 NRSV)

"Hearts have to change before hunger and homelessness disappear, before wars end and everyone is treated fairly," my former parishioner kept saying. That is very true. Whose heart will be the first?

Third Sunday of Advent
First Presbyterian Church, Dodge City, Kansas
December 11, 1994
Zephaniah 3:14–20
Philippians 4:4–7
Luke 3:7–18

"Believing Is Seeing"

WE LIVE IN AN age of short sayings—bumper stickers, slogans, zingers on church marquees. Unfortunately, in the past several years, it has become more common to see and hear mean-spirited quips, and vulgar ones. Much of what I spot on T-shirts these days is pretty disgusting. But occasionally, someone comes up with a witty phrase or pithy motto. One of my favorites is on a sign that hung in my mother's kitchen for many years: "Life is short. Eat dessert first." Also in my mother's kitchen was a framed drawing of a rocking chair on which there was a tall pile of round-bottomed crockery, with the caption: "Life is just a chair of bowlies." Sometimes, a well-known saying is inverted like that just to shake us up a little bit. It is a common advertising technique used to get our attention among the daily dose of commercials and ads that most of us instinctively ignore.

Occasionally, though, profound truth is revealed when we twist a common phrase. A few years ago at Christmastime, I saw in a store and purchased for my son, Jesse, a little metal Christmas box, on the lid of which is the painting of a little boy sitting in his bed looking in gleeful amazement at one of Santa's elves perched on the bedpost at the foot of his bed, and dangling from the bedpost behind the boy's head is a Christmas stocking with a long list to Santa stuffed in it. And the lettering at the top of the picture says, "Believing Is Seeing." As a Christian, as a minister, as a theologian, that captures profoundly for me the emphasis of the Advent season and the perspective of Christian hope throughout the year.

Now, none of you knew what the sermon title was before you came to worship today; perhaps you came to find out what anyone could preach on from Zephaniah, although I hope that your motive was the *best* one, of wanting, like every Sunday, to give thanks to God and sing praise to God and listen for God's word of what God wants you to do as a faithfully obedient disciple of Jesus Christ. "Believing is Seeing." But in our highly rationalistic world of science and logic, it may be that you have difficulty believing what you do *not* see—like peace and mercy, even love—and have decided that you will only believe in what your senses confirm. If so, you are not alone, of course; most modern people take the same approach to reality. What is surprising is that that attitude is so prevalent in the church of Jesus Christ, which should be different. After all, in the twentieth century, the church includes no one who actually saw and heard Jesus as the crowds did when he was teaching and healing, and includes no one who saw and touched Jesus as the disciple Thomas was invited to do after the resurrection, yet the church still insists upon belief in Christ's teachings and healings and resurrection nevertheless. The Christian doctrine still includes matters that cannot be proven and that run contrary to instinct and experience—for instance, that God created all people to live in harmony and to share the bounty of creation with one another, while in fact there are very few congregations that are not segregated in some fashion—racially, ethnically, by clan, by class; and that Christ said that if we are to save ourselves, we must give ourselves away, while in fact that message is not always taken to heart in the *church* any more than in the corporate *board room*. Many of us are unwilling to act upon our professed belief until we *see* the evidence with our own eyes. By that time, of course, it is no longer really *belief* so much as provable *experience*.

Most people in biblical times were much the same as we. And when, twenty-six centuries ago, a prophet named Zephaniah promised comfort and consolation to those who wait patiently upon the Lord and who serve the Lord devotedly, the people of Judah probably decided they would believe it when they saw it. Enemy armies were massing to the north, threatening invasion and destruction.

> I will utterly sweep away everything
> from the face of the earth, says the Lord.
> I will sweep away humans and animals;
> I will sweep away the birds of the air
> and the fish of the sea. . . .
> I will stretch out my hand against Judah,
> and against all the inhabitants of Jerusalem. (Zeph 1:2–4a NRSV)

The people could see the danger for themselves—a threat to their nation which Zephaniah interpreted as the Lord's judgment for their failure to worship properly the one true God. What they could *not* see, and therefore had a difficult time *believing*, was how the Lord was going to overthrow the threatening armies as he *promised* whenever the people of Judah should *return* to worshiping God.

> I will deal with all your oppressors
>   at that time.
> And I will save the lame
>   and gather the outcast,
> and I will change their shame into praise
>   and renown in all the earth.
> At that time I will bring you home,
>   at the time when I gather you;
> for I will make you renowned and praised
>   among all the peoples of the earth,
> when I restore your fortunes
>   before your eyes, says the Lord. (Zeph 3:19–20 NRSV)

The reason for this encouraging word was that the Lord was dwelling with his people in their midst as a warrior who was powerful enough to save Jerusalem from her enemies. Jerusalem would be purified and God would be so proud of the holy city that he would rejoice and exult over it. Not only that, declared Zephaniah, but the time would come when there would be no alien lands, no strange peoples, and no ungodliness. Then every knee would bow and every living thing and all creation join in a great swell of praise and worship of the God of life who created and rules everything that is.

"Yeah, right," the person in the street might have thought when he or she heard Zephaniah. And, of course, the city eventually fell to her enemies and the temple was destroyed. Fancy *anyone* thinking that God was going to rejoice and exult over Jerusalem!

It is no coincidence that the Christmas holiday period is a time of increased suicide and family violence. It is the time of year when *everyone* is supposed to be joyful and carefree and in good spirits, but it is actually the time of year when almost everyone suffers from stress and anxiety. For many, of course, all the jolliness is artificial and cruel, for *their* Christmas will be lonely, or will intensify memories of lost loved ones and thoughts of what might have been. Our culture is not very sensitive to that, nor, frankly, are our churches. Even if most of us, thankfully, do *not* have great personal sadness at Christmas, most of us *do* have the frustrations of trying to create Norman Rockwell memories out of long lines at the check-out counter and socializing with people we hardly know and trying to get squirrelly kids dressed and to their church functions and flinching at the thought of the year-end mountain of bills. We look up, many of us, and can see only the armies massed on our borders ready to swoop down on us, and wonder what there really is to rejoice about in life, not just at Christmastime, of course, but throughout the year.

There were probably more than a *few* people in the Philippian congregation who wondered if Paul was in touch with *reality* when he wrote to them saying, "Rejoice in the Lord always; again I will say, Rejoice. . . . Do not worry about anything" (Phil 4:4, 6a NRSV). They, too, saw threats on their horizon; it was a time of persecution for the church and for individual Christians, many of whom had been cut off from their families and ridiculed by their friends. Some, perhaps, had lost their jobs because of their faith. Most remarkable of all, Paul himself was in prison and in danger of execution for preaching the gospel when he wrote those words. Like the landscape blackened with massing armies during Zephaniah's day, like the gloomy prospect of persecution faced by the Philippian Christians, the view of Paul's worldly future from his jail cell must have been very bleak indeed.

But through the eyes of faith in God's promises, through the comforting thought of God's invisible hand on his shoulder, through his belief that as God had miraculously sustained him in days past, so God would care for him in days to come no matter what might befall, Paul could see ample reason to rejoice despite the walls of his prison, for he was experiencing even in that miserable and threatening place the peace of God, passing all human logic and understanding, keeping his heart and his mind in Christ Jesus. He did not expect *human happiness*, but even *then* he *was* experiencing *divine joy*. The *object* of his worship was not a rosy future, but the eternal God. For Paul's faith was in the Lord, and he believed, with all his heart, that the Lord was at hand, on the incomparable evidence of Jesus' own promise, no matter what discouraging things Paul saw or heard. It was not a matter of living in a fool's paradise, as some might think. It was a matter of living in thankful dependence upon God.

Injustice and trouble are *not* the last word, for the Lord is coming. And any human-made happiness that we can conceive cannot compare with the joy of those who wait patiently upon the Lord. Paul's words about the peace of God were *not* addressed to well-fed people who live in warm homes and can worship without fear of injury. The peace of which *he* spoke is not *deliverance* from the trials and tribulations of this world, but joyful trusting contentment in the *midst* of the trials and tribulations of this world. It is not irrational daydreaming, although it *does* defy human reason and it is based on *hope*; it is a quiet trustfulness which comes not from what we read in the headlines or hear on television, but from the perception of God's reality established in his purpose of salvation and which includes *our* salvation.

Do you look about you and see only human tragedy in a chaotic world, or do you see God's promised salvation unfolding in your life? Believing is seeing. Little children know it, although adults often forget it. How much we are likely to *miss* if we confine ourselves to the truth we can *prove*; in fact, we will miss seeing the most important truth of all. I do not mean Santa's elf on our bedpost. I mean the peace of God, which passes all understanding, life eternal here and now. As Zephaniah first promised a people long ago, God *is* present in our midst in *spite* of the loneliness and chaos of modern life—do you sense his presence when we gather as his people around this table? God's judgments against us *have* been removed in *spite* of our persistent woes—do you experience the peace with God which is offered us in the outstretched and nail-scarred hands of our Lord? Our enemies *have* been cast out in *spite* of the daily *threats* that we experience—do you understand the empty tomb as seal of God's promise that even our final enemy, death, has been destroyed? Can you see that—a peace in your life that is more profound than just the cessation of conflict, a generosity in our world that is more complete than annual holiday food drives, an abundance of life that cannot be confined even by the grave? Not through the working of reason and logic, not through the giving of any *human* pledge, not even through the fullest measure of any *earth*-bound happiness, but through faith in God as God has revealed himself in Jesus Christ. Believe. And see.

Fourth Sunday of Advent
Spanish Springs Presbyterian Church, Sparks, Nevada
December 21, 2003
Micah 5:2–5a
Hebrews 10:5–10
Luke 1:39–55

"God's Revolution Has Begun"

"Which kind do you want?" asked the postal clerk across the counter from where I stood. I did not have my glasses on, so I couldn't see clearly all of the possibilities. But I knew what I was looking for, so it wasn't necessary for me to inspect all of the other ones. "That one," I said, and put my finger on the image of a woman holding a baby. "That'll be twenty-seven dollars," he said, "for one hundred fifty stamps."

There are very few people in the world who wouldn't recognize an artistic rendition of the Madonna and child, whether in a painting, or sculpted into a statue, or printed on a stamp, for that matter. In fact, I don't think that I had ever seen this particular painting. But even through the fuzziness of my close-range vision, I knew what I was looking at. The details may vary from artist to artist, the style may vary from culture to culture, the pose may vary from century to century, but the story is so familiar that few of us wouldn't recognize a portrayal of Mary and the infant Jesus, even without our glasses. And although we Protestants do not regard Mary with the same veneration that Roman Catholics do, we recognize that great respect is appropriate for God's chosen vessel of our redemption, and are certainly willing to put her picture on our Christmas card envelopes. Still, many of us may regard the first chapter of Luke, which is so much about Mary, as an irrelevant preamble to what we are *really* interested in—the journey to Bethlehem, the shepherds, the baby in the manger—and may not know quite what to make of Mary's meeting with Elizabeth, or why Luke (and *only* Luke) starts *his* story of *Jesus* by telling us at length about the words and actions of people *other* than Jesus.

Long before she was in a frame or on a pedestal or affixed to Christmas card envelopes, Mary was a young woman—most likely in the first half of her teenage years—who had been born into an undistinguished family in an insignificant hill town in Galilee, a very ordinary maiden without prospect of *fortune*, let alone *fame*. If you and I were to script God's entrance into human affairs, we most likely would not have selected a country girl (peasant class, it seems) from a place few people had ever heard of (Nazareth isn't mentioned anywhere in the Old Testament or in any history book of the period, certainly not in any travel brochures) who conceived a child out of wedlock (Jesus' birth had gossip and scandal written all over it). But perhaps it was just such a mother that was necessary in order for faith's attention not to be on *her*, but on *God*. The birth of the Son of God by the working of the Holy Spirit wasn't about the miracle of *motherhood*, but about the miracle of *salvation*.

And the miracle of salvation has a lot to do with our sin and our undeserving. It has a lot to do with our need and our powerlessness in the face of wrongdoing—our *own* wrongdoing, and the effects of the wrongdoing of *others*. And the messiahship of Christ isn't about *our* notions of what we *want* in a Savior, but about *God's* way of working the great drama of redemption. And to help us *understand* God's way of working the great drama of redemption, Luke takes us back before Christ's birth to an episode of a meeting between two unlikely players in such a drama—a childless old woman and a teenage unwed mother-to-be. And Luke discloses in that encounter what people can expect from the Savior that God is sending into the world: a blessing of those who are of low esteem in popular assessment, a humbling of the arrogant and the privileged, a championing of all who have suffered grief and humiliation at the hands of others, a filling to satisfaction of folk who have been empty in *this* world, and a toppling of those who have treated the world as their oyster, and the people in it as their underlings and slaves.

The song of Mary when she receives Elizabeth's blessing—the song known to generations of Luke's readers as the "Magnificat"—wasn't just speculation on Mary's part, or an idle wish of a poor and frightened girl to exchange her shameful dilemma for a life of ease and plenty. Luke is setting the stage to help us understand just exactly what happened in the stable in Bethlehem, the beginning of God's great revolution captained by a Messiah who never led an army, who never drew a sword, who never issued an imperial decree. But already, sensitive spirits knew his divine origin and earthly mission and honored him with their allegiance, even before birth. For "when Elizabeth heard Mary's greeting, the child leaped in her womb" (Luke 1:41a NRSV). And Mary's faithfulness, so pivotal to the salvation that

God was bringing to pass, was worthy of divine favor and earthly praise. "Blessed is she who believed that there would be a fulfillment of what was spoken to her by the Lord" (Luke 1:45 NRSV), Elizabeth testified.

> And Mary said,
> "My soul magnifies the Lord,
>   and my spirit rejoices in God my Savior,
> for he has looked with favor on the lowliness of his servant.
>   Surely, from now on all generations will call me blessed;
> for the Mighty One has done great things for me,
>   and holy is his name." (Luke 1:46–49 NRSV)

There could hardly be a scene so remote from popular notions of importance and privilege. *Elizabeth*, past middle age, the wife of a priest who had been mysteriously struck mute in the temple, pregnant after long years of childlessness; *Mary*, to all appearances just another "bad girl" whom many families would have disowned and cast out into the street where she would have been taunted and ridiculed and perhaps stoned. These two women, pushed so far to the margins of power, living so far beyond the notice of emperors and kings, seem an unlikely start to a revolution. Their meeting in joyful bewilderment at their selection by God to be instruments of the world's salvation seems hardly a strategy session for overturning the prevailing order and restoring creation to its original pure innocence. But, then, the birth of a baby in a barn because no one was willing to make room for him in more appropriate surroundings wasn't very impressive by worldly standards, either. Yet, if we believe that the birth of Jesus in the cattle shed was indeed the coming of God into the world in human flesh, then what Elizabeth, and especially Mary, had to *say* about it all isn't just a tiresome *footnote*. For Luke, it is key to understanding the importance of the incarnation.

> "[God's] mercy is for those who fear him
>   from generation to generation.
> He has shown strength with his arm;
>   he has scattered the proud in the thoughts of their hearts.
> He has brought down the powerful from their thrones,
>   and lifted up the lowly;
> he has filled the hungry with good things,
>   and sent the rich away empty.
> He has helped his servant Israel,
>   in remembrance of his mercy,
> according to the promise he made to our ancestors,
>   to Abraham and to his descendants forever." (Luke 1:50–55 NRSV)

Not only would the powerful and mighty of the world not have recognized in the birth of a baby in a cattle stall the pivotal event of human history, but they would hardly *welcome* the sort of salvation that that baby was going to bring. And, in fact, the powerful and mighty of the world *still*, by and large, do not acknowledge that a *revolution* has begun and is under way—God's own revolution, God's own turning upside down the world's values and the world's expectations and the world's notions of what is good and right and acceptable and true. But a revolution began, nevertheless, early one morning in a cattle stall in Bethlehem, and the decisive blow was struck several years later early one morning in a cemetery outside of Jerusalem just three days after it seemed like any revolution had been decisively crushed, and it is only those whose vision of reality is clouded by greed and fear and suspicion and lust and vengefulness who think that everything is going to remain the same as it has always been, for that revolution continues with every deed of mercy and kindness and compassion and confidence and hope done in the name of Jesus Christ.

> But you, O Bethlehem of Ephrathah,
> > who are one of the little clans of Judah,
> from you shall come forth for me
> > one who is to rule in Israel,
> whose origin is from of old,
> > from ancient days.
> Therefore he shall give them up until the time
> > when she who is in labor has brought forth;
> then the rest of his kindred shall return
> > to the people of Israel.
> And he shall stand and feed his flock in the strength of the LORD,
> > in the majesty of the name of the LORD his God.
> And they shall live secure, for now he shall be great
> > to the ends of the earth. (Mic 5:2–4 NRSV)

So the prophet expressed the long yearning of the people of Israel for a *revolution*, an *overturning* of the *accustomed* ways, a *change* from oppression and sorrow, by the coming of a king such as they had had in David, born in Bethlehem, a champion of the people, one who tended to their needs as a shepherd tends the sheep. But king after king had disappointed them, and then the nation had been crushed by the armies of Babylon, and even when the exiles were returned to Israel, they never again had a real king of their own, never again were given any real say in their own destiny, never again prospered, never again were free. Injustices continued as before—the rich grew more arrogant and oppressive in their wealth, the poor became more numerous, and their rulers and their judges neglected their needs. The blessings of God were forgotten or taken for granted. But the hope for a messiah did not die.

And then, one night, at that very same Bethlehem, still small and unimportant in most people's eyes, God *fulfilled* the promise made to the people—fulfilled it in a most unlikely way. In the feeble glow of a crude lamp, amidst the smelly straw and drafty chill of a barn out behind the local inn, far from the palace of Caesar, totally unbeknownst to Herod, long *after* the *respectable* people had gone to bed heedless of the fears and hardships of the poor and the hungry and the homeless and the oppressed, a baby was born. And at that instant, the whole world changed.

> "He has shown strength with his arm;
>   he has scattered the proud in the thoughts of their hearts.
> He has brought down the powerful from their thrones,
>   and lifted up the lowly;
> he has filled the hungry with good things,
>   and sent the rich away empty.
> He has helped his servant Israel,
>   in remembrance of his mercy,
> according to the promise he made to our ancestors,
>   to Abraham and to his descendants forever." (Luke 1:51–55 NRSV)

Outside the stable, perhaps, nothing *seemed* to have changed; in the little village of Bethlehem, a stray dog still barked in the distance, the sounds of snoring drifted out from shuttered windows, cats prowled the garbage; on faraway battlefields, soldiers still prepared to kill their king's enemies; in the cities, lenders still planned to foreclose on mortgages and evict the poor; in the temple and in the synagogues, priests and rabbis still prepared to perform their rituals and recite their prayers as usual, just as had been happening for years on end. The rich, by and large, were still haughty, and the poor, by and large, were still hungry. But God's *judgment* upon such business as usual was pronounced in a startled cry from a baby as it emerged from the womb into the lamplight, and it echoed in an anguished cry of pain from a cross, and it thundered in a whispered cry of despair from women who thought that the tomb of their friend had been vandalized, and it reverberated in a cry of joy from a band of followers whose fear and confusion turned suddenly to wonder and praise when he who had *died* stood before them *alive* again. And all of that happened right under the noses of the very ones who thought that *they* were in charge of the way the world was headed, that *they* were the decision-makers about what was important and what wasn't.

What God has *declared*, God will *accomplish*. What Mary said God *had done*—shown favor to the lowly and the humble, cast out the proud and toppled the powerful and raised up the lowly and fed the hungry and turned away the bloated—was a song of the timeless certainty of God's promise and the sureness of God's purpose that will be fulfilled as assuredly as if it *has already happened*. God's choice of Mary, poor and lowly and subject to shame and ridicule, even, is *itself* graphic evidence of the very reversal of values and fortunes of which Mary sang.

> "My soul magnifies the Lord,
>   and my spirit rejoices in God my Savior,
> for he has looked with favor on the lowliness of his servant.
>   Surely, from now on all generations will call me blessed;
> for the Mighty One has done great things for me,
>   and holy is his name." (Luke 1:46–49)

God's revolution continues, although some, *many*, even, do not acknowledge it, would scarcely credit the notion, scoff at the very thought of such a profound result coming from such an insignificant beginning. Where are God's armies? Where is God's artillery? Where are God's battlegrounds? Where are God's prisoners of war? Where are God's generals—an elderly mother off in the hills someplace, and a pregnant country girl, unmarried and poor and destined, probably, to be poor and disdained all her life? "That one," people are saying in post offices. They may not all know, but *some* do, that, in putting their fingers on the image of a woman holding a baby, they are pointing to an artist's portrayal of a revolution.

> And he shall stand and feed his flock in the strength of the LORD,
>   in the majesty of the name of the LORD his God.
> And they shall live secure, for now he shall be great
>   to the ends of the earth;
> and *he* shall be the one of *peace*. (Mic 5:4–5a NRSV)

Christmas Eve (Early Evening)

Spanish Springs Presbyterian Church, Sparks, Nevada

December 24, 2003

Isaiah 9:2–7

Titus 2:11–14

Luke 2:1–20

"The Littlest Shepherd"

"Aw, gee," Tobias had grumbled, kicking at the dirt with the toe of his sandal. "Why do *I* always hafta?"

"You don't 'always hafta,'" his mother responded, doing her best to look stern despite the comical aspect of her youngest son acting the part of the youngest son. "Your brothers Elias and Jacob take turns with you."

"But *I* do it more than *they* do," Tobias continued to whine. "It'll be cold."

"They do it when their studies permit. Now that they are in the synagogue school, they can't be spending every night out with the sheep."

"Why did *I* have to be born last?" the young boy said with a groan.

"Because you're *special*," said his mother, "just like *David* was born last in *his* family and God chose *him* to be *king*, didn't he? Because he was special and his older brothers wouldn't do."

This answer broke the cadence of the conversation outside the front door of their modest little house on the outskirts of Bethlehem, which was the town where King David himself had been raised and where Samuel had anointed him king to replace Saul those many years ago. Tobias had to consider how to respond to his mother's case that he go out to tend the sheep through the night. Saying that he was afraid of the dark—which was partly true—had never worked. Needing his rest so that he could grow big and strong had never worked—his *brothers*, who had each had the task before him, were bigger and stronger than *he* was. And it looked like the coldness of the night wasn't going to work, either; he knew that his brothers before him had spent winter nights out on the hillsides, too, and had obviously survived. He thought of something new.

He coughed. "I . . . I think I must be getting sick."

"Then you had better stay in bed all day tomorrow when you get home and not go to the market with me or go out with your father on his rounds."

Well, that one didn't work. And Tobias could think of nothing worse than staying indoors all day long, missing out on a trip to the sights and smells and bustle of the market, or missing out on accompanying his father, who was the town's recognized doctor of horses and cows and goats and sheep, and who allowed his son to accompany him on his visits to farms and houses where some prized specimen of livestock or other was ailing. "Aw, gee," he repeated.

"Now, take some blankets and your water and run along to the flock." He would be replacing Mordecai, and would be joined by Simeon, who was replacing Enoch. Four families pastured their flocks together, and had worked out a system of trading off responsibilities so that there were always two shepherds on duty. Each family also had a dog to help keep the flocks together and ward off predators. Tonight, Tobias and Simeon would take turns sleeping while their dogs would patrol the perimeter of the flock and stay alert for any wolves that might be plotting mischief. Simeon was two years older than Tobias, and considered himself two years *smarter* than Tobias, and wasn't interested in befriending his younger counterpart. In fact, Tobias was the youngest of all the boys who shared the shepherding duties, and was bossed about by all of the others, which is what made spending the night on the hillside so unbearable. It wasn't so much the lumpy ground, which was no harder to sleep on than the mat on the floor of his house. It wasn't really the dark or even the cold—it was still something of a bit of adventure to be out all night long in the country. It was being the *youngest*, and the *littlest*, and the easiest to order *around*. That was what made Tobias object every time it was *his* turn to tend the sheep, night or day.

There had been a time, of course, when he had *pleaded* to be able to do what his older brothers were privileged to do. Finally, as he grew older, he had been allowed to accompany them on their sheepherding shifts to learn what was going to be required of him. But when he had come to be considered old enough for the responsibility of staying with the sheep by himself, it had taken only a couple of outings before he decided he would rather be doing *other* things.

"Aw, gee," he said again as he entered the house. He put the roll of blankets under his arm and reached for his canteen, a pottery jug on a leather thong that he would lower into the community well as he passed by on his way to where the flocks were being pastured. As he shuffled past his mother, she bent over and kissed him on the cheek. "There's a good boy," she said, just loudly enough for him to hear, as he plodded down the street toward the well.

The days were short now, and the air chilled noticeably as soon as the sun set. Tobias wore two tunics under his cloak to stay warm. He lowered his canteen into the well, and had to lean over the side before hearing the echoed splash and the gurgling of the air escaping as water flowed into the jug. The water level was lower than usual for winter because more people had been drawing from the wells around the town. There were a lot of travelers visiting Bethlehem—something to do with a *census*. He didn't know what that was, except that it had something to do with *taxes*, and his father always grumbled about taxes, and *they* had something to do with *Rome*, and his father always grumbled about Rome, *too*. From some of the people he passed on the streets the past few days, he had heard different accents and dialects from the one he was used to. His parents had been talking about how people were coming to Bethlehem from all over the country, and how some of their friends and acquaintances in Bethlehem had had to travel to *other* places because of the census.

Tobias had been to Jerusalem, which was not very far away, on festival days, but he had never been anywhere else away from Bethlehem, and it was a little difficult for him to understand why people needed to travel, or why they would *want* to, or where they went when they *did* travel. But there were a lot of strangers in town, and the businesses that served visitors, like taverns and the inn, were crowded, as well as the streets. In fact, as he was walking out of town toward the field where the flock was, he passed several travelers headed toward the city, including entire families, apparently, some on horseback, but not many, some on donkeys, some just walking, even a pregnant woman on a donkey being led by a man on foot. He remembered this especially, because the woman groaned a little as he passed them.

"It's about time," said Mordecai, as Tobias slowly trudged up the hill to where the flock was grazing. "Simeon's been here for a long time already." Simeon threw a glance in Tobias's direction, a look full of contempt and disapproval. "I'm going to be late for supper," Mordecai huffed as he brushed past Tobias, his own canteen, now empty, slung on his shoulder.

"Sorry," Tobias mumbled, almost inaudibly.

"You sleep now," Simeon barked at Tobias. "I'll take the first watch, until midnight."

This meant that Tobias, as usual, would have to be up and awake during the coldest part of the night. Now, it wasn't yet dark and he wasn't a bit sleepy, so he would be lying on the ground unable to fall asleep for a couple of hours yet, and then be shaken awake just as he had finally drifted off to slumber, to sit up and shiver the rest of the night until dawn. But it was useless to protest this injustice, and he spread out his blankets and laid down without a word in answer to Simeon. His dreams, when they came, were of a place that was warm and lighted, where he was eating his fill of his favorite foods and nobody was ordering him around. But the pleasurable scenes were cut short by a violent nudge to his shoulder. "Your turn," Simeon's voice thundered in his ear out of the darkness.

Simeon's face was indistinct in the darkness, just a blur through Tobias's sleepy eyes.

"Get up."

Tobias sat up with a yawn and started shivering as the blankets fell from his shoulders.

"Nothing's going on," Simeon said, already lying down and covering himself with his blankets, curled up under them to ward off the chill.

"Nothing *ever* goes on," Tobias thought to himself. And, in all of his turns at watch over the flocks, nothing ever *had* gone on—no danger had ever befallen them, no threat had ever even presented itself, certainly not in the form of thieves or wolves or anything else that the boys were out in the fields to protect against.

Tobias stood up, clutching his blankets around him, and walked gingerly to where he could see the flock, and sat down again, his back against a boulder, cold and hard. He was hungry, but he didn't want to expose his hands to the cold air to retrieve the bread that he had wrapped up in a cloth and had stuck inside the roll of blankets when he left home that afternoon.

He counted the sheep, which were all visible from where he was sitting—and he came up one short. He counted again. And, again, he was one short. He stood up, and counted a third time. Still the same result. His heart started beating faster as a chill went through him that wasn't caused by the cold air. "Oh, no. No, it can't be," he said to himself. He walked forward toward the flock, and through it, and still he could not see the missing animal. But he heard one of the dogs barking over the brow of the hill. Now he ran in the direction of the barking, and began to hear the panicked bleating of a lone sheep off in the same direction. Eventually, he came upon the missing animal, wedged between two rocks, the dog standing guard just a few feet away. It stopped its barking when Tobias appeared, now wagging its tail as Tobias petted it and said, "Good boy, good boy." The sheep was heavier than he was, but with a gentle lifting tug under its belly, the animal scrambled free from the rocks and ran off toward the rest of the flock, the dog proudly trotting along after it.

As Tobias plodded back toward his sentinel post, he became conscious again of the cold. But now his hunger was greater than his discomfort from the cold, and he paused to bend over and unwrap the cloth in which he had placed his bread. He was surprised to see three dark round objects alongside it—figs. His mother had put figs in as a treat for her little shepherd boy. He ate them with relish, and the bread, too, and sat down again, drawing the blankets around him.

And just then, he heard a noise. It was a noise of wind, like the fluttering of a bird's wings, but louder. And there was suddenly a bright light behind him, like the sun, but brighter even. And he jumped up in surprise, and his surprise suddenly turned to fear as he saw a man bathed in the light. "Who . . . who are you? And what do you want? Simeon! Simeon!"

Simeon was already sitting up in his bedroll, and, though quite a distance away from him, Tobias could see that his face was ashen and his eyes were full of terror.

"Don't be afraid," the man said. "I'm here to tell you about something wonderful, something that everyone is going to rejoice in. You, too," the man said, turning slightly and looking toward Simeon.

Simeon slowly propped himself up on his hands and knees, and crawled across the hillside, too weak from fright to stand up.

"Listen," said the man, turning back toward Tobias as Simeon neared. "You've heard about the Messiah. The Messiah, the Lord, is being born this very night in the city yonder. Go and see for yourselves, and you'll know that you've found him when you find a baby wrapped up in swaddling clothes and lying in an animal's feeding trough."

Simeon was beside Tobias now, still on his hands and knees. As soon as the man finished saying this, there was a great wind sound again, louder than the first, and they heard voices singing down from the skies, "Give glory to God in the heights of heaven, and on earth, let there be peace and good feeling among everyone." Simeon had closed his eyes by now, still shaking on all fours alongside Tobias, but Tobias stood still, open-mouthed and wide-eyed. And then, as quickly as the man had appeared, he was gone, and the light and the sound and the singing had departed with him.

Tobias stood still a moment, trying to understand what had just happened. "Come on," he shouted suddenly, and started running across the hill through the field. "Come on," he shouted again, not even looking back, but racing toward Bethlehem, the collection of buildings just visible on the horizon, dimly outlined by the light of the stars.

Bethlehem was asleep now, or most of it. There were some dogs barking in the distance, and now and then the sound of a cat searching through the garbage left outside an occasional door, but very few lamps lit at this time of night. All the way over the hillside and across the fields, Tobias had been thinking about the woman on the donkey and the man leading it.

Surely they would be at the inn. But what was this about a feeding trough? No one would put a baby in a *manger*! He raced through the streets to the inn, and saw that it was all dark inside, but he was feeling emboldened by what had happened in the field, and he pounded his fist on the locked door.

"What?" came a grumble from inside. "Who is it? What do you want?"

He pounded again.

"Stop, stop, you'll wake the guests." After about a minute, Tobias heard the door being unbolted and the proprietor, in his nightclothes, cracked the door open and peered out. "What is it?"

"Is there a woman here?" Tobias asked breathlessly. "A woman about to give birth to a baby? She would have arrived just this evening."

"What? Who are you? Why did you wake me up in the middle of the night?"

"Is she here? Please tell me!"

The proprietor snorted, and grumbled, "She's out in back, in the barn." And he slammed the door shut. Tobias could hear him slide the bolt back into place as he turned to sprint around the corner of the inn. By now, Simeon had just caught up with him, panting too hard to ask any questions, and he followed the younger boy by a few paces back toward the barn.

A light peeked out from the crack of the barn door, and it grew larger and brighter as Tobias shoved the door open wide enough to squeeze inside, Simeon just behind him. The barn was surprisingly warm from the presence of an ox and a couple of donkeys. At first, Tobias couldn't see any people, but he heard a rustling of straw from one of the stalls. "Hello," he said softly, tiptoeing toward the noise. "Is anyone here?"

"Yes," came the voice of a man from the stall. "Who is it?" And as the man stood up, Tobias could see his head and his shoulders over the edge of the middle stall.

"My name is Tobias, and this is Simeon," Tobias said as he inched forward. "We . . . we live here—in Bethlehem, I mean—and we were out with the sheep, and a man told us to come here." It sounded sort of silly in his ears as he heard himself tell the story.

Just then, he heard a woman's voice. "What is it, Joseph? Who is there?" And there came the muffled whimper of an infant from within the stall.

"It's alright, Mary. It's some shepherds. A man told them about us—about the baby." He turned toward the boys who were now rounding the side of the stall. "Come over here, boys, and see a miracle."

"The tomb was empty, I tell you. I heard them say so. And then his disciples saw him, talked with him, *ate* with him! He *is* the Messiah, just like I told you when he was healing all of those people and feeding them and when he was telling off the Pharisees." Matthias sat back in his chair and crossed his arms, looking justified but waiting for a response from Micah. The two men had just returned from Jerusalem, where they had gone for the Passover. Matthias had heard all about the strange events from a cousin of one of the dead man's disciples.

Micah turned to a third man sitting in the shade, and who was watching his son far out on the hillside, just a speck among the sheep. "What do you think? Is such a thing to be believed, Tobias?"

"Oh, yes," the third man answered after a long pause, nodding to himself, his eyes misty with some long-ago memory. "Oh, yes."

Christmas Eve (Late Evening)
Spanish Springs Presbyterian Church, Sparks, Nevada
December 24, 2000
Isaiah 9:2–7
Titus 2:11–14
Luke 2:1–20

"Between Advents"

> The people who walked in darkness
>   have seen a great light;
> those who lived in a land of deep darkness—
>   on them light has shined. (Isa 9:2 NRSV)

TIME AFTER TIME, THE people of Israel hailed a new king upon the throne. Time after time, the people of Israel hoped that this was finally the one who would be perfect in righteousness, the one who would bring peace and justice. Time after time, the people of Israel were disappointed—*none* of their leaders proved to be the messiah, the anointed one, a leader faithful enough to be considered the son of God. And so they waited. And they waited. And many of them finally grew *weary* of waiting, gave up any real hope that there would *ever* be a ruler in Israel worthy of the title Wonderful Counselor, Mighty God, Everlasting Father, Prince of Peace—even the priests and the scribes. They still held on to the tradition. They still gave lip service to the old prophecies. But the ideal had become too big for any earthly ruler to fulfill, and so no one really expected anything so wonderful to happen in *their* lifetimes, in *their* neighborhood, among common people like *them*. God would never turn on the spotlights and draw back the curtains and present the perfect king to *them*.

So the shepherds weren't sitting on the hillside that night two thousand years ago thinking to themselves, "*This* could be the night that something *wonderful* will happen. *This* could be the night that the *messiah* comes." They were with their sheep like they were always with their sheep, in pretty much the same fields as always, guarding against the same dangers as always, alert to keep their livestock out of the same troubles as always. But lo and behold, it *was* the night! Suddenly, "an angel of the Lord stood before them, and the glory of the Lord shone around them" (Luke 2:9 NRSV). They didn't slap each other on the back in self-congratulation, saying, "We knew all along that something like this was going to happen." The Bible says that they were *terrified*. "'Do not be afraid,'" said the angel; "'for see—I am bringing you good news of great joy for all the people: to you is born this day in the city of David a Savior, who is the Messiah, the Lord'" (Luke 2:10–11 NRSV).

At first, they probably couldn't comprehend what the angel was saying. To *them*? In *their* neighborhood? The *messiah*? They must have been not only terrified, but bewildered. That *ancient* hope? Even if it were *true*, where were the bright lights and the trumpets and the spectacular parade? But the angel told them what to look for to verify the truth of what the angel was saying—a child wrapped in bands of cloth and lying in a manger. And when they had gotten over the shock—not only of the angel appearing, but appearing to *them*—they went into town and found the child lying in the manger, as they had been told. Then it must have begun to sink in. The shepherds told everyone there what had happened out in the field. And then, after looking at the little newborn king, they returned to their task, "glorifying and praising God" (Luke 2:20 NRSV).

They had heard about the messiah coming so often, but without it ever happening, they had grown numb to the possibility. But then it actually happened! And it happened to *them*, and so it happened *for* them! The promise that God had made repeatedly through the prophets over the long centuries had come true, and they were some of just a handful of people who had been let in on the good news, seen it with their own eyes, though it was meant for sharing with *all* the people. The long, long wait was over. The time for rejoicing had begun. Jesus the Christ, Jesus the Messiah, was born.

Feeling somewhat alone and, perhaps, forsaken, on the island of Crete, out in the middle of the Mediterranean, the work of trying to organize a church must have seemed tedious at times for Titus and his comrades. Titus had been a companion of Paul, who always seemed so assured and confident, but now Paul had left. It must have been slow work; the first excitement of making plans for the mission had begun to fade or had vanished altogether, and now the daily realities had set in of trying to support themselves while the church grew slowly, off the beaten path and having only infrequent communication with fellow missionaries and with Paul or any of the other apostles. There must have been many days of drudgery and many nights of discouragement. And then there came to Titus and his helpers a letter, declaring again what they knew in their minds but had begun to discount in their experience—"For the grace of God has appeared, bringing salvation to all" (Titus 2:11 NRSV)—and urging them to be steadfast in their faith while awaiting what had begun to seem like a more and more distant hope, "training us to renounce impiety and worldly passions, and in the present age to live lives that are self-controlled, upright, and godly, while we wait for the *blessed hope* and the *manifestation* of the *glory* of our Great God and Savior, Jesus Christ" (Titus 2:12–13 NRSV). Titus and his companions had been preaching truthfully that the Messiah had come—they had undoubtedly met some people who had known Jesus personally, or had seen him after the resurrection, had heard from Paul's own lips of his encounter with the risen Christ on the road to Damascus—but waiting for Christ to *return* was so difficult, and the work was so slow, and Crete seemed so, well, *ordinary*, nothing special about it, that they were probably questioning the *value* of what they were *doing*—preaching, teaching, perhaps healing the sick and feeding the hungry.

Chances are, these Christian missionaries of Gentile background had never heard the details of Jesus' birth—the decree of Caesar Augustus and the journey to Bethlehem, the story of the shepherds and the angel. But they were probably beginning to suffer from some of the same spiritual monotony that the shepherds and many generations of Israelites before them had. When fulfillment is delayed, when days turn into weeks, and weeks turn into months, and months turn into years, *expectant* waiting can become *complacent* waiting and eventually not really *waiting* at all. We stop anticipating anything new or different happening today in *our* neighborhood among people like *us*. But if the angel's appearance to the shepherds tells us nothing else, it means that God *can* and *does* appear in unexpected moments and in unexpected places and among *people* one would not expect, and that God in fact chose just such an *un*expected time and place and family situation to introduce the Messiah into the world. God is faithful to the promises that God makes. God had *promised* the people Israel that the Messiah would come. And God has promised *us* that Christ will come *again*.

The tenderness of the manger scene, the beauty of Luke's rendition of the story of Jesus' birth, has captured the imagination of generation upon generation of Christians, and even non-Christians. The wonder of this night, the joy of this birth—every Christmas reawakens us to the great love of a God who stoops to put heavenly glory on such a human scale. Luke was such an effective teller of such a marvelous event—we can imagine ourselves there on the hillside with the shepherds, there in the stable with Mary and Joseph, there at the manger looking at the baby Jesus. Who is so cynical or self-consumed that they don't thrill at those words?

But by itself, Christmas is a sentiment, a whiff of evergreen in the desert, a sprig of mistletoe in a hard-nosed world. The *manger* isn't the *whole story*. Unless this wondrous appearance of God's grace convinces us of the importance of *trusting* God's promises, unless it awakens us to the *authority* of the Messiah, unless it trains us "to renounce impiety and worldly passions, and in the present age to live lives that are self-controlled, upright, and godly while we wait for the blessed hope and the manifestation of the glory of our great God and Savior, Jesus Christ" (Titus 2:12–13 NRSV), then we've missed the importance of Christmas altogether. Christmas—the goal of that first long period of waiting—gives us hope for the goal of our *own* long period of waiting—for the coming of Christ in glory at the end of the age, to bring a close to history and to inaugurate the kingdom of God in all of its fullness. On a Middle Eastern night two thousand years ago, in the company of a few shepherds and peasants, amid the dust and the smells of a cattle stall, God fulfilled the promise God had made for centuries—Christ was born in the gentleness of innocent childhood! And God has made another promise—and it may be fulfilled tomorrow, or it may be fulfilled ten thousand years from tomorrow—that Christ will come again in glory, and all people will recognize him as Lord, and everything will be set right, and the wicked and the unfaithful will be dealt with, and the righteous, those who have faith in Christ and *live out* their faith in Christ, will find that their faith has not been in vain.

We live between advents, you and I and all this present generation. We live between the coming of Jesus Christ who was born, who ministered, who was put to death, and who was raised from the tomb, and the coming of Jesus Christ at the end of time to complete the creation and present it to its Creator. "He it is who gave *himself* for *us* that he might *redeem* us from all iniquity and purify for himself a people of his own who are zealous for good deeds" (Titus 2:14 NRSV). And so "we wait for the blessed hope and the manifestation of the glory of our great God and Savior, Jesus Christ" (Titus 2:13 NRSV). And in the meantime, we do the good deeds that Jesus has taught us to do—the ministry of caring for the poor and the sick and the bereaved, the ministry of proclaiming truth and encouraging faith and witnessing hope, the ministry of prophecy against the tyrannies and injustices and oppressions of the *world's* order, the ministry of praying constantly for the world in faithful vigil. And we do these things because we trust the promise of a *second* advent, a second coming, in a timeliness that only God knows but which you and I have a hand in preparing and hastening with our faithful living today.

Is it far off on some island that you are called to labor while awaiting that glorious day of Christ's return? Is it at a school desk? Is it in an office or a shop? Is it in the cab of a truck or in the cockpit or cabin of an airplane or on the back of a tractor or a horse that is *your* place to await the blessed hope and the manifestation of the glory of our great God and Savior, Jesus Christ? The days may seem very much one like another, sometimes discouragingly so. But the day is coming when *all* people will know what was made known first to shepherds out in the field long ago, ordinary folks in an ordinary place on a night that seemed like any other night: God keeps every promise that God makes. And you and I are reminded *this* night of the wonderful and joyous reason that we can *trust* God's promise that the kingdom is *already* dawning, and that the King is coming again just as he said: "See," said the angel,

> "I am bringing you good news of great joy for all the people: to you is born this day in the city of David a Savior, who is the Messiah, the Lord. This will be a sign for you: you will find a child wrapped in bands of cloth and lying in a manger." . . . So they went with haste and found Mary and Joseph, and the child lying in the manger. . . . The shepherds returned, glorifying and praising God for all they had heard and seen, as it had been told them. (Luke 2:10b–12, 16, 20 NRSV)

The Messiah has come! And he is coming again!

Christmas Day
First Presbyterian Church, Dodge City, Kansas
December 25, 1994
Isaiah 52:7–10
Hebrews 1:1–4
John 1:1–14

"Who Is Lying in Your Manger?"

HE DIDN'T LOOK MUCH like God—helpless, yawning, crying, eyes drifting and unfocused, uncertain how to go about nursing, sleeping, mostly. He didn't *sound* much like God—shouting nonsensical verse back and forth with playmates in the village streets until it all dissolved into giggles, asking his mother, "What's for dinner?" as he came through the door, asking his father why the sky is blue and why some people are so mean. He didn't even *act* much like God, some people thought—he toiled on the sabbath and permitted his followers to do likewise, he ate with every despicable character he could find, he went to parties at the tax collector's house and conversed freely with Gentiles and women and, just as freely, criticized the pillars of religion and society. And he died just like a *human being*. But generation after generation has made much of the day which has traditionally been designated as the anniversary of his birth.

In the commercial scheme of things and on the family social calendar, there are many occasions for celebration and feasting and gift-giving and party-going. But none of them, not even the annual celebration of the birth of our nation, comes *close* to generating the level of activity and interest that Christmas does. Entire national economies seem to revolve around Christmas Day, and many family calendars do, too. Of course, not everyone who celebrates the occasion really thinks much about *him*, although almost every holiday television special has some song that mentions him, and almost every store has some display picturing angels, and almost every Christmas tree has a nativity scene under it, including a baby in a manger. Just consider the amounts of human energy and material resources that are annually spent because of December 25th—all somehow reflecting a vague feeling or strong belief or absolute *faith* that, lying in the manger behind the inn at Bethlehem, was someone quite extraordinary.

The writers of the New Testament tried in different ways to capture his uniqueness, Matthew and Luke telling of Jesus' conception by the Holy Spirit, but ancient literature claims supernatural conception for a *number* of mythic heroes. Matthew wrote of the appearance of an unusually bright star, but such signs in the heavens were thought sometimes to portend the birth of earthly kings—there was nothing singular in that. In Luke, angels appeared to shepherds in the fields proclaiming the birth of a Savior, but the Hebrew people were used to the notion of angels delivering messages, and they had hailed *many* infants as saviors of Israel before Jesus came along.

But from the very beginning of their writings, two authors in the New Testament give unambiguous testimony that the man who, as a child, lay in a manger at Bethlehem was more than simply someone favored by God, or someone who would be God's soldier, or someone who would be God's priest. They added *their* testimony to the testimony of *others* that Jesus was God's own Son. But John and the writer of Hebrews went on to explain that Jesus was appointed by God to inherit all things, God's own agent in creating the universe before time began and even now upholding the universe from collapsing into nothingness, reflecting God's own nature stamped indelibly on his soul, eternal with God, of the exact same substance as God, inseparable from God, but born among us, living among us, dying among us, living again within us in the Holy Spirit.

Jesus was the perfect revelation of God, because in fact he *was* God, God reaching out from eternity into human history, God bending down from heaven to bless the earth with his laughter and his tears, God embracing human joys and sorrows with the passionate love of his own great heart, God claiming the world for himself not by triumphant conquest but by selfless service, God having cosmic power at his command but choosing to exercise it in humble sacrifice, God the radiant light patiently searching out every dark recess until all of creation is bathed in its supernal brightness and warmth. And in the beautiful phrases of John's Gospel and the letter to the Hebrews, a mystery which is beyond human understanding is given that human expression which is the closest we can come to probing the mind and heart of God.

With his eyes of faith, Robert Southwell, a young English priest of the sixteenth century, peered into the manger and wrote of the wondrous and paradoxical mystery revealed there of God entering the world through human infancy, the Word of God incarnate:

> Behold the father is his daughter's son,
> The bird that built the nest is hatched therein,
> The old of years an hour hath not outrun,
> Eternal life to live doth now begin,
> The Word is dumb, the mirth of heaven doth weep,
> Might feeble is, and force doth faintly creep.
>
> O dying souls, behold your living spring;
> O dazzled eyes, behold your sun of grace;
> Dull ears, attend what word this Word doth bring;
> Up, heavy hearts, with joy your joy embrace.
> From death, from dark, from deafness, from despairs,
> This life, this light, this Word, this joy repairs.[1]

The testimony of the gospel is that in hearing and seeing Jesus of Nazareth, we have experienced the fullness of God. The God who was shrouded in mystery and unseen from the beginning of time—who, in his divine glory, could not be looked upon without the beholder being struck dead, he is so holy—chose to become known and accessible to us in Jesus Christ, very God of very God. God in the great divine wisdom came not in a coercive way, not like yet another conqueror or another emperor or another self-indulgent celebrity of any sort, but first in the helplessness of an infant and the simplicity of a stable, then in the deeds of a servant and in the company of common folk, finally in the shame of rejection and the ignominy of the cross.

It is not surprising that, to many people who look sentimentally upon the manger at this season, Jesus seems good and kind, but is not the ultimate authority in the universe or in their lives. The winsomeness of the nativity tugs at the heartstrings, to be sure. But childbirth in general does that. The child lying in the manger of their minds never achieves the proportions of being the creative and sustaining power of everything that is. And so, in the construction and maintenance of their own lives, their heartaches and their triumphs, their despairs and their victories, they hardly think to turn to him in confidence and trust and thanksgiving, for what has a little baby born two thousand years ago to do with them today? *What has Jesus to do with my job?* they ask. *Or my marriage? Or my relationship with my children or my parents? Or my illness? Or my blessings?* With no more understanding of the connection between Christmas and the other 364 days of our year, of course we never even get to the question of what claim that baby in the manger might have upon our affections and our allegiances and our attitudes and our actions, remote as his birth two thousand years ago was from our lives today.

---

1. Southwell, "Nativity of Christ," lines 1–12.

But the testimony of scripture is that the baby in the manger has *everything* to do with our lives today, that the birth we celebrate at Christmas was the most unique moment in all of history, when heaven touched earth and God became human, not metaphorically only in the form of a pleasant child who grew to be a decent man and so was rewarded by God for his goodness by being raised from the grave, not just a casual suggestion about what we might want to consider as we plan our social calendar from week to week, not merely one among a galaxy of other philosophers or charitable causes, but the creator of the universe, the upholder of the stars in the sky and the designer of every flower petal and atom, packaged in real human form, feeling real human pain and ministering to *our* real pain, knowing real human anxiety and ministering to *our* real anxiety, blessing real human hope and giving substance to *our* real hopes.

And suddenly, when we finally grasp that truth, or grasp it again for the umpteenth time, there bursts forth from that manger in Bethlehem a light which will not be extinguished, a light that illumines every dark corner of the world and every dark recess of our heart, and every moment of our life and the whole history of our race becomes charged with the eternal splendor of God: "In the beginning was the Word, and the Word was with God, and the Word was God. . . . And the word became flesh and lived among us . . . , full of grace and truth" (John 1:1, 14a, c NRSV). "We have seen his glory, glory as of a father's only son" (John 1:14b NRSV).

Who is lying in your manger this Christmas? Does the manger that you see contain a cute and cuddly baby who holds your attention for a little while, as any baby would, but then Christmas passes, and you go on about your business and your amusements and your disappointments and your frustrations and your relationships, good and bad, pretty much without thinking about the manger again until *next* Christmas? Or does the manger you see contain someone you would like to think holds the goodness and power of God, for he grew up to say and do some things that you admire, but in the end, after all, he just did not look or sound or act quite the way that you think God should, and so you will continue your search for truth and purpose someplace else—philosophy, job, addictions of various sorts? Or does the manger you see contain the wonder of the creation of the universe repeated in the simple miracle of childbirth, and that becomes for you a clue to the very nature of God, and you see in the child grown to adulthood the truth of God stamped upon every gracious word and the power of God stamped upon every forgiving assurance of Jesus Christ, and so there is no moment in your life and no event in this world that is not somehow touched by the illuminating rays streaming from that manger and you must offer yourself a continual thank offering to God so that every day of the year is transformed by the trust and joy and hope and love of Christmas?

"Long ago God spoke to our ancestors in many and various ways by the prophets, but in these last days he has spoken to us by a Son, whom he appointed heir of all things, through whom he also created the worlds" (Heb 1:1–2 NRSV). "The true light, which enlightens everyone, was coming into the world" (John 1:9 NRSV). "He is the reflection of God's glory and the exact imprint of God's very being, and he sustains all things by his powerful word" (Heb 1:3a NRSV).

Who is lying in your manger? The answer to that question determines how each of us will respond to Christmas. If it is truly Jesus Christ, God giving himself completely to us in his Son, what response can there be but a hopeful life of joyful obedience and confident trust? Robert Southwell continued his poem:

> Gift better than himself God doth not know.
> Gift better than his God no man can see.
> This gift doth here the giver given bestow;
> Gift to this gift let each receiver be.
> God is my gift, himself he freely gave me;
> God's gift am I, and no one but God shall have me.[2]

---

2. Southwell, "Nativity of Christ," lines 13–18.

First Sunday after Christmas
Spanish Springs Presbyterian Church, Sparks, Nevada
December 31, 2000
1 Samuel 2:18–20, 26
Colossians 3:12–17
Luke 2:41–52

"The Most Natural Thing"

THERE IS PROBABLY NOT a parent in this room who wouldn't like for Luke to have inserted another sentence in this morning's Gospel reading. Assuming at first that their adolescent son was back somewhere in the crowd—it wasn't unusual for whole villages to travel together to attend the Passover in Jerusalem, so children probably mingled quite freely in and among the throng—Mary and Joseph ultimately realized that no one had seen Jesus. They raced back to Jerusalem to try to find him, and spent three days looking in every possible place, retracing their steps, no doubt, to all of the spots they had visited on their pilgrimage. Finally, they spied him in the temple, sitting among the teachers there, listening to his elders and asking questions now and then, even answering well the questions they put to *him*. It would not have seemed extraordinary that he was with the teachers—he undoubtedly attended the synagogue school back in Nazareth, and he had obviously paid attention and thought about the things he was being taught. We can sense the relief that Mary and Joseph felt at having found him safe and sound. But when Jesus' mother said to him, "Child, why have you treated us like this? Look, your father and I have been searching for you in great anxiety" (Luke 2:48b NRSV), and he said to *her*, "*Why* were you searching for me? Did you not know that I must be in my Father's house?" (Luke 2:49 NRSV), the parents among us would like to know what Mary and Joseph said or did next. But the Bible isn't a book about parenting, and Luke was apparently not interested in finding out or giving us guidance about how to deal with similar situations in our own families, and so we have no divinely approved advice for how to keep from losing our little ones in the grocery store or shopping center, or what to say or do to them when they go wandering off on their own.

Can you imagine the panic of small-town parents thinking that they had lost their child in the big city? Several years ago, when we were living in Dodge City, my wife and I took the children to Wichita for a pre-Christmas shopping excursion and decided to make a real occasion of it rather than simply a one-day trip. Instead of driving three hours each way on a Saturday, having to contend with the weekend crowds, we would go as soon as Christi got out of school on Friday (Jesse was not yet in school), spend the night in a motel next to the Towne West shopping center, and drive back home after lunch and maybe a trip to the zoo on Saturday. I don't know what the population of *Jerusalem* was in Jesus' day, but Wichita is the biggest city in Kansas, and Towne West is the biggest shopping mall in Wichita, with more than a hundred stores and all of them crowded in December. After a couple of hours of shopping on Friday evening, the plan was to see a holiday movie at the theatre inside the shopping center.

We had deposited the evening's purchases in the car or taken them back to the motel and returned to the shopping center to stand in line at the ticket window. The children, of course, were all excited, hard to keep still, and, looking around, drinking deeply of the sights and sounds of the shopping emporium that was so much more grand than anything Dodge City had to offer. The movie was entertaining, but the children got fidgety, especially Jesse, who asked to be allowed to go down and sit in the front row. When the movie was over, I helped my wife put Beth, then less-than-a-year-old, in the "snuggly" and attended to gathering the paraphernalia of coats and a few additional packages that we had with us. We pushed against the crowd of exiting moviegoers that was sweeping up the aisle, watching for Jesse and aiming for the door at the front of the theatre that led directly to the parking lot. We finally found ourselves outside the one-way door with some other people who had also come out that way, counting heads and finding that we had only two of our children, both girls, no boy.

We ran around to the shopping center entrance, back to the theatre. We explained briefly to the usher our problem and asked whether he had seen Jesse (he hadn't), searched the empty theatre auditorium, came back out into the mall concourse, fearful that he had been kidnapped or was wandering the shopping center frightened and crying, our*selves* now frightened and near tears, retraced our steps through the crowds going into every store we had visited, thinking that he might have looked for something familiar. Twenty minutes, maybe thirty, and no Jesse. Back to the theatre, just at our wits' end, and I looked across the concourse and noticed a video arcade, complete with flashing lights and the sounds of bells and guns and speeding cars blaring from the machines. Something made me go in there on a desperate hunch. I pushed through the teenagers, looking this way and that, and finally, in the farthest corner of the room, there Jesse stood, transfixed by a screen, his little hand on controls that weren't doing anything without a coin being dropped in the slot, dazzled by the colors and the motion. And if we hadn't found him, he'd probably *still* be there, frankly, six years later, oblivious to time and to the fact that his family was missing. We had wasted almost half an hour to profound anxiety. Of *course* Jesse was in the arcade. *Jesse* being *Jesse*, going in there was the most natural thing for Jesse to *do*. How he had gotten past us in the theater, pushed along with the crowd that we *thought* we were inspecting so *carefully*, his mother and I still don't know. But when our words gave vent to our worry, Jesse's expression, and perhaps even his words, said to us, "Why were you searching for me? Did you not know that I must be in the video arcade?" Probably almost every parent has some such story to tell.

"Why were you searching for me?" Jesus asked, with perhaps as much sincere bewilderment as *Jesse* had at our panicky hunt for *him*. Neither Jesus nor Jesse knew that he was lost; in fact, they *weren't* lost, from *their* perspective. They knew *exactly* where they were, and where they *were* was exactly where they *wanted* to be. "Did you not know that I must be in my Father's house?" (Luke 2:49 NRSV). Of course, that statement is the whole reason for Luke reporting to us this single incident out of Jesus' childhood—to confirm up front, in the earliest pages of his Gospel, that Jesus had not just *fleshly* parents, reckoned in the normal biological way, but a *spiritual* parent to whom he bore a unique relationship. The *rest* of the family had been on their way back to *Nazareth*, to *Joseph's* house. But *Jesus* was *already* at home in his *Father's* house in the temple in Jerusalem—was *already* in the place where *God* was considered to be specially present.

In the first thing that the Bible records Jesus as saying, he spoke about *God*, and he spoke about God in terms of an intimate relationship that, while not totally *different* from *other* people's relationship to God, was nevertheless *unique*. God is the heavenly parent of us all. But when *Jesus* referred to God as "my Father," he signaled an awareness that *his* relationship to God was not one that was open to other people. His parents did not understand what he said—did not catch the nuances, did not recognize the implications. But Jesus was already gaining an awareness of God's purpose for his life that made it imperative for Jesus to fulfill certain responsibilities, perform certain deeds. Again, it is not unlike the awareness that should eventually come to each one of us that our life is not our *own*—our life belongs to *God*, and we need to be sensitive to the Holy Spirit's guidance in making choices in our lives about things like education, marriage, career. But *Jesus'* path in life would be *uniquely* in tune with God's will—revealing God to the world in every word and every act—and uniquely destined for the cross of our redemption. So, indeed, Jesus "must" be in whatever *belongs* to God, whatever *involves* God, whatever *reveals* God—the temple, yes, and also the world of joys and sorrows, of triumph and defeat, of exuberant life and sometimes tragic death. For Jesus, who was completely faithful to the will of God, it was the most natural thing for him to do. His parents would never really understand, as the Gospel glimpses of Mary on this and later occasions make plain. That word "must" would distinguish *Jesus'* life from the life of every *other* person who has ever lived. How *could* they understand?

Samuel's mother had dedicated her son to God to make sacrifices at Shiloh for people's sins long centuries before Mary had to watch her son die on the cross, a sacrifice for the sin of all. In a sense, parenting is about realizing and working out the fact that our *children* don't really *belong* to *us*. They aren't something we bring home in a shopping bag and put on the shelf, plug in or turn on when we want to, neglect at other times, keep forever in our home, unchanging and forever subject to our control. That is especially and supremely true if we parents are *Christians*. What *Hannah* did *formally* at *Shiloh*, what *Mary* did *tragically* at *Calvary*, was to acknowledge that *God's* parental rights are paramount over our *own*. It must be a bittersweet moment when a Roman Catholic couple surrenders a child to become a priest or a nun. But it is no less momentous an occasion when *we* give *our* children over to receive the sacrament of baptism, if we *really mean* what we *say* when we pray that God will graft them into the body of Christ and pour out the Holy Spirit upon them, that they may have power to do God's will and continue forever in the risen life of Christ. Baptism should be the anvil upon which one's life in this world is forged into the life of the kingdom, the key that unlocks any doors between what we *actually* do on our *weekdays* and what we *promise* to do on *Sunday morning*. When the Passover festival had come to an end, and most people were going back to the places where they raised their families and performed their occupations, the temple was *still* the most natural place for Jesus to be. Listening and questioning and responding to the lessons of God was still the most natural thing for Jesus to do. "Did you not know that I must be in my Father's house?" (Luke 2:49 NRSV). Of course we should.

When I was in law school, I had a class from a crusty old fellow who was one of the most insensitive people I have ever met, who also happened to be my advisor. He kindly invited all of his advisees to his house for dinner one night, many of whom were Jewish, and then served ham as the only main course. One of the students in the class that I had from this professor was blind, but the professor told several jokes over the course of the quarter that ridiculed blind people. Another of my classmates one day was passing out flyers in the hall outside our classroom about an upcoming evangelistic gathering as we were waiting for the classroom to come free. The professor got hold of one, and commented to several of us, "What is someone his age doing spending his time on stuff like this? When you're young, you ought to be *breaking* commandments, not *preaching* them." The young man's flavor of Christianity was different from mine, but I was appalled by the professor's comment. Where in scripture does it say that being faithful to God is a matter for *adults only*, middle-aged and beyond? Why *shouldn't* a person training for the practice of human laws be attentive to the priority of God's commands? Just who *was* this guy to criticize the Holy Spirit's stirrings within my classmate's soul? Shouldn't *every* human endeavor be carried out within the framework of *God's will* as we have come to know it in *Jesus Christ* and *God's purpose* for our lives as we have come to discern it through the power of the *Holy Spirit*? To yearn to know God better while we are preparing for our vocation—surely that ought to be the most natural thing in the world! In fact, any *Christian* had better do just that! Otherwise, we are denying the practical implications of the truth that we proclaim. In life and in death, we belong to God.[1] And God calls each of us to live in a way that takes that truth seriously, that exempts no activity or conversation from that truth, that from our mother's arms blesses us on our way to maturity as servants of God, our Father.

The most natural thing for a Christian is to be with Christ, to be where he is, listening to the preaching and teaching of scripture, praising God with the community of the faithful, walking amongst and ministering to people who are in need, traveling the way of the cross. Why would anyone expect us to be anywhere else?

---

1. See *Constitution of the Presbyterian Church*, 4.001.

Second Sunday after Christmas
Spanish Springs Presbyterian Church, Sparks, Nevada
January 3, 2010
Jeremiah 31:7–14
Ephesians 1:3–14
John 1:1–18

"The Word beyond Words"

"For God so loved the world that he gave his only Son, so that everyone who believes in him may not perish but may have eternal life" (John 3:16 NRSV). Martin Luther called that beloved passage of scripture "the gospel in miniature," it is so profoundly rich in meaning. So suggestive and evocative, it communicates on a number of levels, has inspired millions of sermons. But notice that this "gospel in miniature" says, "For God so loved the world that he gave his only *Son*" (John 3:16a NRSV), not an encyclopedia, not a theological textbook, not a test of orthodoxy, not just a bunch of words. And yet, over the centuries, and in fact starting very early in the history of the church, we human beings have felt compelled to try to reduce the focal event of the universe—the birth, life, death, and resurrection of Jesus—to a formula, to a prescription, to a recipe, to a definition that people can be tested and graded on, and one that has sadly been repeatedly fought over, even to the point of men, women, and children being killed, singly or in whole communities, for the purpose of keeping certain sets of words intact.

Perhaps it is inevitable, this human concern over words and the special preoccupation that we have with reducing the central truth of all existence to something that can be written on paper. That opens the door to the danger of thinking that the truth of Christ is something to be *learned* about, something to be *memorized*, something to be *recited*, and which *others* can be compelled to learn, memorize, and recite. Or that it is a commodity that can be possessed, and from which other people, those we don't think measure up, can be cut off or excluded. But the truth of the incarnation, of God coming among humankind to pitch a tent in our midst, so to speak, is not first and foremost something that is to be *defined*, but something to be *experienced*. And that truth, though so fundamental, is something that can be appropriated only by *faith*, not by memorizing facts or perfecting definitions or claiming ownership.

The Bible itself is evidence of that, though it contains thousands upon thousands of words. In the Spirit-guided wisdom of the early church, the New Testament contains *four* Gospels, each with a different perspective that highlights different facets of the mystery of God-in-Christ. So the Bible itself testifies to the insufficiency of words alone, or any one set of words—a single Gospel was not adequate. We are fortunate, indeed, that the Bible developed in a time before projection screens and bullet points. And the Fourth Gospel, the one that is most clearly a *reflection* on the teachings and actions of Jesus, begins by identifying Christ not with a set of *words*, but with the *Word*, the intention and fulfillment of God, God's self-expression. Immediately in the first chapter, John lets us know that everything Jesus said and did had an origin beyond the boundaries of calendar and geography; by recalling the imagery of the story of creation itself, John leads us to understand that Jesus' teaching had cosmic importance, his activity had eternal significance. Matthew and Luke give us the stories of the virgin birth, Jesus' conception by the Holy Spirit, as *their* way of expressing that Jesus was not just another person whose life could be described by statistics and itineraries and calendars. John has taken a step back from the baby photos to show us the bigger picture of Jesus' importance for all existence: "He was in the beginning with God. All things came into being through him, and without him not one thing came into being. What has come into being in him was life, and the life was the light of all people" (John 1:2–4 NRSV). And then John's Gospel goes on to show instances of how the Word—Jesus—was and is the exact expression of God's creating, sustaining, and reconciling power—a truth too wonderful for words, for those who have faith to perceive it. John is inviting us to experience ourselves the truth that can only be known by faith—what it means that Jesus is the Word of God, an experience that will not be for *me* exactly what it is for *you*.

Most of us, though, like things tidy and precise. We are impatient with truths that require imagination. We want to reserve making a commitment until we have been convinced with facts and figures, until the case has been proven by simple equation and all risk has been eliminated, and even then, our commitment may be temporary. Two thousand years after the birth and death and resurrection of Jesus, and many centuries after the formulation of theological doctrine about it all, we have the *words* before us—creeds and confessions, terms, phrases, hymns—and the temptation is to approach the incarnation as an intellectual exercise, to learn it as a lesson in some academic subject. And if we approach it that way, we are very lucky indeed if we come to appreciate Christ as the Light that illuminates the full dimensions of eternal life. We are so used to measuring, to quantifying, to assembling facts and judging them according to the scientific method. And our prosaic approach to just about everything binds us to customary standards of space and time. So we ask, for instance, if the Word became flesh and dwelt among us on earth, did heaven have a "vacancy" sign on the gate for those thirty-some years, because God was *here* and not *there*? Most of us, if not all of us, are stuck in the same habits of literalism as Nicodemus, who thought that being born anew meant emerging a second time from his mother's womb. The affirmation that "the Word was God" is not so much a statement about the *identity* of being between Jesus and God as about the *quality* of being. Heaven was not emptied when the Word became flesh. God was not the Father for all those years, and then temporarily switched to being the Son. When Jesus spoke to God, he wasn't just talking to himself. And when the Bible says that *we* can become children of God, it is not by some alteration of our family tree. It is not our *bloodline* that identifies us as God's own, but our *faith* that when Christ shed *his* blood on the cross, he sealed our relationship with him in self-giving and obedient love, and drew us into the same parent-child connection with God that *he* had. The early believers who reflected on Christ's love and obedience and authority and faith could only explain it by saying that he was the Son of God. They were grasping for human words and familiar concepts to testify that Jesus, in *all* that he said and did, was the perfect expression of God, in fact the very Word of God, the truth *through* which and *for* which everything that is was brought into being.

Over the years, a lot of Christians have come to think that it is more important to proclaim certain things *about Jesus* than to allow their lives actually to be transformed *by Christ*. So, for instance, many Christians can recite the Golden Rule and then turn around and treat other human beings, or some of them, as inferior to themselves and beneath God's notice. Every Sunday school child must learn that Jesus is the Prince of Peace, yet only a few sects, considered by most other Christians to be peculiar and fanatical, actually require their members to refrain from taking up weapons. Christmas is all about the truth that the Messiah has come, but most of us who talk about keeping Christ in Christmas nevertheless remain vulnerable to modern hero-worship and political demagoguery. Can true children of God really tolerate the waste of war and the neglect of the poor and the prevalence of disease and the fouling of God's earth?

"In the beginning was the Word" (John 1:1a NRSV), creative and truthful, bringing about God's loving and gracious purpose. And when the

Word became flesh and lived among us, we were privileged to see what the glory of God really is: transforming the *ordinary* into the *extraordinary*, being satisfied not with what is merely *good* but evoking the *best*, worshiping God purely and rightly and lifting the burden from the poor, forgiving freely even while calling to righteousness, feeding the hungry and curing the sick, opening eyes and ears and summoning the dead from their tombs, setting aside privilege and kneeling to serve others, loving others even to the point of dying for them. So fully did Jesus conform his life to God's priorities that his followers cast about for words and concepts to express the unity of will and outlook that bound Jesus and God, and concluded that nothing short of sonship would do, drawing on Jesus' own references to God as his Father.

But even that familiar human analogy is too limiting, cannot convey the eternal dimension of the relationship. Just so, arguing about them, fighting about them, insisting that everyone use the exact same words, is not only pointless, but, I think, must be an insult to God and strongly suggests that we have missed the truth of the Word coming to live among us at all. Yes, we have creeds and confessions and catechisms. That is how we recognize and acknowledge our unity in Christ aloud and in public, and we do so every time we worship together, in words taken from one of the creeds or confessions or catechisms that, we have agreed, together constitute an authentic witness to God. But not one of them is perfect. Not one of them exhausts the ways the truth of God can be expressed. Not one of them should be the basis for excluding anyone who has faith in Jesus Christ but finds that the official formulas don't express accurately what he or she has experienced of the living God. And to spend our energies and resources on debating the words, as Christians have historically done, is to demonstrate that our spirits are, in fact, untouched by the Word. After all, councils and synods are not the way the glory of the Word is shown forth, but living daily as if Christ has indeed come and is surely going to come again.

We must resort to human words when sharing the Christian faith; speech is a gift of God. But the coming of the *Word* shows that *words* are not the substance of our faith. The Word could not be expressed in a memo, or even an entire Bible full of commandments. It is a truth to be lived out, a relationship to be experienced. Our lives, thus, are to be sacramental, as baptism and the Lord's Supper mysteriously involve us in the fullness of the Word beyond what mere words themselves can do. And so, the Word became flesh and lived among us, and we have beheld his glory, the glory as of a father's only son, full of grace and truth, seen in the face of a baby as can only be hinted at in a treatise, seen in a sacrificial death on a cross as can only be suggested in a hymn. To respond to the Word is to live as God's children, which is to reflect that grace and truth in what we do and what we say, well beyond the doctrines we can affirm or the creeds we can recite.

Beyond all the beautiful words in Matthew and Luke about the birth of Jesus, beyond all the theologically correct words that have been written in creeds and confessions and commentaries and hymns and sermons, even, lies the Word, incarnate in Christ, to which, alone, we must decide whether and how we will respond, and our decision determines whether we, too, will become children of God. It is not a matter of biology or genealogy. It is a matter of faith that Christ was, is, the fullest and truest expression of *who* God *is* and *what* God *wills*, and what God wills every *human being* to be. God wants us to be God's own children, in the same way that Christ showed himself to be. And that means going well beyond affirming and reciting all the words that anyone could ever say *about* Jesus. It means *abiding* in the Word that, in the person of Christ, God sent to live among us, that we may be transformed by his grace and truth and so reflect God's glory in everything that we do and say—the glory of the cross. "To all who received him, who believed in his name, he gave power to become children of God, who were born, not of blood or of the will of the flesh or of the will of man, but of God" (John 1:12–13 NRSV). Do you hear in that testimony the invitation, the necessity even, of going beyond all the words we can say *about* Jesus to experiencing and responding to the creative and redeeming Word that became flesh and lived among us in Christ? If so, you know the meaning of Christmas.

Epiphany of the Lord
Spanish Springs Presbyterian Church, Sparks, Nevada
January 6, 2010
Isaiah 60:1–6
Ephesians 3:1–12
Matthew 2:1–12

"When the Light Shines"

"THAT'S JUST LIKE US!" the early Christians for whom Matthew was writing must have thought when they heard about how Jesus, even as a baby, had been forced to flee from Judea and find refuge in the hills of Galilee—"Galilee of the Gentiles" (Matt 4:15 NRSV), as Matthew quotes the reference from Isaiah. As far as Matthew was concerned, Jesus was born in *Bethlehem* because that's where Mary and Joseph *lived*. Unlike in *Luke's* Gospel, in *Matthew*, they didn't *start out* from Nazareth; they *fled* to Nazareth, in Galilee, a border region whose population was a mixture of Jews and Gentiles, by way of Egypt, in order to escape the threats against the baby Jesus made by King Herod in Jerusalem. Just so, the Christian church that Matthew knew had been forced to flee into the border region of Galilee and even to Syria beyond, in order to escape the persecution that the Jews mounted against it in and around Jerusalem. At the end of Matthew's Gospel, it is to *Galilee* that Mary and Mary Magdalene are instructed to direct the disciples, first by the angel who meets them at the tomb, and then by Jesus himself, appearing to them in his resurrected body, and it is in *Galilee*, far from the savagery of *another* King Herod, that the risen Lord Jesus makes rendezvous with the eleven and commissions them to go and make disciples of all nations, baptizing them and teaching them what Christ commanded.

    In those early years of the church, the followers of Jesus were suffering threats and hardship even as the *Lord* had suffered. If there had been any thought that the resurrection would make life *easier* for the disciples, it had quickly evaporated. The disciples' joy at seeing Jesus again must soon have been tempered by the realization that the world had not yet changed, was rejecting the news of the resurrection, still refused to acknowledge Christ's lordship. There must have been considerable disappointment and sadness that faith in Christ left them *more* vulnerable to the world's hatred, forced them to leave their jobs, rendered them homeless in their own land. They could not miss the irony that, when Jesus was born, according to Matthew, he was greeted and presented with expensive gifts fit for a king not by his *own* people, who had *claimed* to be *awaiting* a messiah, not by the priests of the Jewish temple and the scribes of the Jewish law, but by *Gentiles*, religious leaders from *afar*, the *magi*, who had their *own* sacred writings and spiritual traditions, but discerned, nevertheless, that a great cosmic event was happening in Bethlehem and they must go and pay homage. Fearful of Herod, they, too, had thought it best to slip out of Judea unnoticed. Would those who believed that Jesus was the Son of God *always* be unwelcome in the land God gave to his people, just as Jesus *himself* had been rejected? Would the church have to *remain* in hiding, in the shadows, shunning exposure so that it could survive? And, if so, survive for *what*? What was the point of it all, if the followers of Christ had to live all the time like scared rabbits? How could they "go . . . and make disciples of all nations, baptizing them in the name of the Father and of the Son and of the Holy Spirit, and teaching them to observe everything" (Matt 28:19–20a NRSV) that Jesus had commanded the *first* disciples?

Just at precisely the time we would have expected the early Christians to be most enthusiastic and inspired to evangelize, they were being turned out of the synagogues and harassed by family and friends. Would the church shrivel up and die in the face of adversity and the disadvantage of having to operate, as it seemed, in exile? The light that God had introduced into the world's darkness, scholars tell us, very nearly sputtered out of existence, buffeted by the winds of opposition. Were it not for the insistence of Paul and his associates that the gospel must be taken to Cyprus and Asia Minor and Greece—were it not for the work of the Holy Spirit to enlarge the church's horizon of mission and evangelism to preach to the Gentiles and enfold *them* into the covenant that God first made with Abraham many centuries before—you and I and many millions of others over the past two thousand years would never have heard that God thought so highly of us that he came into the world in the form of a baby who grew up to teach and heal and befriend and forgive and then was put to *death* for his ministry of inclusive love, but afterwards was *raised* from the dead and appeared again to his followers. We would have nothing to celebrate, and the world would still be in profound darkness, without hope of salvation, without assurance of God's mercy.

God has a habit of choosing the least likely channels for the flow of his redemptive grace. "But you, O Bethlehem of Ephrathah, who are one of the little clans of Judah, from you shall come forth for me one who is to rule in Israel, whose origin is from of old, from ancient days" (Mic 5:2 NRSV). Israel had itself not seemed such an obvious choice to be God's beacon of light to the nations—a small player in a world dominated now by Assyria, now Babylon, now Egypt, now Persia, now Greece, now Rome. And after she had been conquered by Babylon, and a large part of her population was taken into exile and then allowed to return again after several decades, she had seemed to be brought so low that she could not rise up again from the canvas of history's boxing ring. The last chapters of Isaiah are addressed to an Israel despondent and discouraged. The exile was over, but the people still felt defeated. The achievements of Kings David and Solomon seemed far distant, and God's favor seemed but a dream. The very purpose for which God had chosen Abraham and his offspring—to be a blessing to the nations, to the Gentiles—was now nothing but a mocking insult. How could beat-up, ground-down, despised, and forgotten little Israel be a credit to God? To what sort of faith and obedience could she inspire *anyone*? Only a fool could think she had any future even remotely as glorious as her past. History had chewed her up and spit her out and gone on to celebrate other peoples and other nations, worshipers of idols and doers of brutality and builders of empires.

Against this gloomy assessment, Isaiah trumpeted the call of God, who had a long history of turning impossible situations into the fulfillment of his promises. Contrary to appearances, it was not *Israel* that was steeped in darkness, but the *rest* of the world. God had not abandoned Israel, and God's purpose that Israel be a light to the world had *not* been defeated. Would Israel respond faithfully and fulfill her destiny, not to be an empire to win worldly acclaim, but to be God's servant and show forth God's truth? "Arise, shine; for your light has come, and the glory of the Lord has risen upon you" (Isa 60:1 NRSV). This was not the time for God's chosen people to discredit their calling. "For darkness shall cover the earth, and thick darkness the peoples; but the Lord will arise upon you and his glory will appear over you" (Isa 60:2 NRSV). What? How could that be? "Nations"—the word could also be translated "Gentiles"—"shall come to your light and kings to the brightness of your dawn" (Isa 60:3 NRSV). The people must have thought the prophet was out of his mind. What in the world would attract foreigners to Zion?

The answer, of course, was *nothing*—at least not so long as Israel remained in her own dark mood of defeat and despair, thinking that greatness could lie only in a mighty army and a robust gross national product and all the other standards by which the world usually judges success but continues to fall short of God's righteousness. No, by all those measures, Israel was a poor bit-player in the world. But Israel's *true* treasure and strength and significance had never been in such things. Her *true* greatness had been that she worshiped and obeyed God, a unique distinction that had made her a light in the midst of the world's spiritual darkness. And, as light always draws people's attention, as people wandering and groping in the dark are relieved and hopeful to see a light shining before them, so Israel, when she returned to faithfulness, would fulfill God's age-old intention for his chosen people by drawing others to him. And all those who had been scattered in exile would return, and everything that was removed would be restored. Even kings would come in pilgrimage from the nations, bringing their offerings. But Israel's blessing would not lie in the other nations' belated acknowledgment of Israel's worthiness. Rather, their coming and bringing offerings would be the consequence of Israel's return to confident faithfulness. "Then you shall see and be radiant; your heart shall thrill and rejoice. . . . They shall bring gold and frankincense, and shall proclaim the praise of the Lord" (Isa 60:5a, 6b NRSV). Because Israel was once again allowing the light of God to shine forth through her own righteousness, other nations would *see* the light and come to worship and obey the one true God who yearns for all people to yield to his embrace.

The apostles perceived that the prophecy had been fulfilled, at long last, in God's most complete revelation of himself in the birth of a baby in Bethlehem—revelation even to the Gentiles who traveled a great distance, drawn by the shining of a new star, to behold the one who himself is the world's true light. Would those early Christians, persecuted and uprooted, remain faithful to Christ the light, to whom the nations had come in the persons of the wise men from the East, bearing gifts of gold and frankincense and myrrh, by themselves reflecting the light that had shown forth in their own worship of God and obedience to his Son, despite privations and hardships? Would they remember that *God* is the scorekeeper, and that the *world's* judgments of what is successful and impressive are always false and misleading? Would they be steadfast in striving to be faithful, though the world mock their praise and reject their love? Forced to flee from Jerusalem and Judea into the Galilean hinterland and beyond, had not Jesus promised to meet them precisely there, in Galilee, and had he not given them a commission to fulfill from just such a place? Why, then, were they discouraged and fearful and thinking of giving it all up? And indeed, as the Bible shows, the most extraordinary thing happened: the church found its way forward not through the Jews, but through the Gentiles, a handful of whom, after all, had been the very first to recognize that Jesus was a king and to honor him accordingly. And as the gospel spread, nations did indeed turn to the one true God, all as a result of the faithfulness of believers who ignored the judgments of the world and concentrated on giving themselves to worship God rightly and serve God obediently.

Shall we concentrate on the obstacles rather than the pledge, on the hardships rather than the certainty? To the degree that we do, the light burns low and can barely be seen through the gloom that pervades so many people's lives and seems to distort the present and cloud the future and offers no clear path to God. *Or* shall we, in our words and actions, reflect the conviction that the light of God is no longer just a *promise*, but that it has *come*, that it has shone forth in Jesus Christ, and still does? You and I and all the church are to reflect that light by worshiping God and being faithful as Jesus was faithful—teaching, healing, forgiving, feeding, befriending. And if we are faithful, when the light shines through the church clearly and brightly, it will be irresistible, and people of every condition and background, every nation and race, will turn away from the darkness and come to the light, which is Christ. A new day in the history of the world will dawn, and everything that has been in shadows will be illuminated. Wars will cease, poverty will be eradicated, sins will be forgiven, the former things will be forgotten. And when everything will be seen as it truly is, the glory of the Lord will appear over all.

Baptism of the Lord
Spanish Springs Presbyterian Church, Sparks, Nevada
January 7, 2006
Isaiah 43:1–7
Acts 8:14–17
Luke 3:15–17, 21–22

"'You Are Mine'"

IF YOU COULD SUMMARIZE the contents of the Bible in a single sentence, it would be, "The Bible tells the story of God's ceaseless efforts to redeem the world that God created and that God loves." From beginning to end, it is about God's stubborn insistence that human beings and all creation turn from the paths by which they are wandering away from him and return to the One who brought them into being, who sustains them, who yearns for them. God's ultimate act to accomplish his purpose, of course, was the sending of his own Son into the world, Jesus the Messiah, and the establishment of the church through which Christ is still present and at work in the world to bring peace and wholeness and forgiveness and hope by the power of the Holy Spirit. "Do not fear," God spoke to the exiles in Babylon, forcibly removed from the promised land because of their disobedience to God's commands and their disloyalty to *him* who had *made* them a *people* and given them *everything* they *had*, "for I have redeemed you; I have called you by name, *you are mine*" (Isa 43:1b NRSV).

Their disobedience and disloyalty that had resulted in the defeat of their nation and their being carried off into exile were *ultimately* matters of *identity*—they had forgotten who they *were*, or had misunderstood it. Now, their doubt and discouragement were *also* matters of identity—they had forgotten who *God* is, or had misunderstood it. *God* was *still* the One who had brought their nation into being and who was faithful to his covenant, fully capable of redeeming them from their captivity and powerful to save them from their predicament, and not only *capable* and *powerful*, but *determined*. But it required them also to remember who *they* were—God's own, God's chosen, God's precious, God's delight.

> When you pass through the waters, I will be with you;
>   and through the rivers, they shall not overwhelm you;
> when you walk through fire you shall not be burned,
>   and the flame shall not consume you.
> For I am the LORD your God,
>   the Holy One of Israel, your Savior. . . .
> Because you are precious in my sight,
>   and honored, and I love you,
> I give people in return for you,
>   nations in exchange for your life.
> Do not fear, for I am with you;
>   I will bring your offspring from the east,
>   and from the west I will gather you;
> I will say to the north, "Give them up,"
>   and to the south, "Do not withhold;
> bring my sons from far away
>   and my daughters from the end of the earth—
> everyone who is called by my name,
>   whom I created for my glory,
>   whom I formed and made." (Isa 43:2–3a, 4–7 NRSV)

A second, very important affirmation of the Bible's one story of God's redeeming work is that it is accomplished by *gathering*. Salvation is not about so many *individuals*. *God's* redemption, restoration, is about bringing individuals *together*, forming a *people*. God's salvation takes place in *community*. Indeed, salvation is for the *sake* of the community that God has purposed from the beginning of time. And that community is God's own people.

Matthew, Mark, and Luke all testify that when Jesus, many centuries after Isaiah, came to the Jordan to be baptized by John, a voice from heaven declared, "You are my Son" (Luke 3:22 NRSV); God was *again* making a declaration of identity, this time about the special and unique identity of Christ. Indeed, in all likelihood, that is the primary reason that Jesus had sought out John to *be* baptized—not because Jesus had committed any sins for which he needed to repent, but to seek confirmation of his identity, and his mission, and to receive the power of the Holy Spirit that would be necessary for him to perform his ministry, his miracles, and, ultimately, his sacrifice. The Gospel writers differ as to whether the voice from heaven was heard only by Jesus or was heard by the entire crowd, but the significance of the baptism as showing God's claim upon Jesus' life is unmistakable. And Jesus *remained* mindful of God's claim upon his life, *remained* mindful of who God had declared him to be, all the way to the cross. And his faith was vindicated, and his identity was manifest to all who would open their eyes to the truth, when God raised him from the tomb.

Just so, in *our* baptism, God has declared who *we* are, has given us our *identity*, has proclaimed that we belong to *him*. Some Christian traditions place emphasis upon baptism as being about the individual's decision to follow Christ. There is that element, of course, for any adult who asks to be baptized, or the parents of any child who ask to have that child baptized. But baptism *itself*, in the context of scripture, is not about *our* approval of God, but about God's choice of *us*, not about *our* decision recently made, but about *God's* purpose determined long before we were even born, about God's intentions for all of creation, about God's many deeds of salvation, quite a few of which were worked through water. So baptism is very much about identity—the identity that God has bestowed upon us. Baptism is a visible expression of the words "You are mine" (Isa 43:1 NRSV). As God promised his people of old that he would be with them even as they passed through threatening waters, so God embraces us in the waters of baptism, threatening, but also life-giving, cleansing, renewing.

Psychologists and human development experts say that identity is one of the chief issues that every person with a healthy psyche deals with in adolescence—"Who am I?" Many adolescents, and even some older people, try to *manufacture* an identity, or emulate someone *else's*, whom they admire. Do you remember doing that? For the Christian of any age, the baptismal font should be a reminder that the question "Who am I?" is ultimately answered only when we confess the response to the question "*Whose* am I?" And the answer to *that* question, for anyone who has been baptized, is, "I am God's own." And the meaning of that answer is *best*, perhaps *only*, discovered as an *entire people* confess together, "*We* are God's own." The people whom God was calling together from the ends of the earth in Isaiah were created for God's glory, the prophet declared. That is the purpose that stands behind all living beings. God's declaration that we are precious in God's sight, even honored, and, indeed, *loved*, elicits as its only fitting response the fervent desire on our part to submit obediently to God's will, and to find there our genuine fulfillment. Honoring the covenant relationship sealed at our baptism is the only context for human happiness and genuine contentment. The sole ground of anybody's real confidence in this world, the sole ground of Israel's confidence in the time of Isaiah, is God's promise to be with us, loving us radically and unconditionally, vowing and acknowledging that we are *his*, bought and paid for against all other claims by the death and resurrection of his Son. "What is your only comfort, in life and in death?" the Heidelberg Catechism begins. "That I belong—body and soul, in life and in death—*not* to *myself* but to my faithful Savior, Jesus Christ, who at the cost of his own blood has fully paid for all my sins [read "for all my disobedience"] and has completely freed me from the dominion of the devil [read "from all other claims upon me"]; that he protects me so well that without the will of my Father in heaven not a hair can fall from my head; indeed, that everything must fit his purpose for my salvation. Therefore, by his Holy Spirit, he also assures me of eternal life, and makes me wholeheartedly willing and ready from now on to live for him."[1]

There are many voices being heard from places *other* than heaven in our society, claiming that we belong to *them*, trying to buy our allegiance and our loyalty, ultimately our souls. There are the claims of nationalism, along with the rhetoric that we're not patriots unless we do *this* and vote for *that*. There are the claims of political parties, of economic theories, of family and clan, of race and ethnicity, of brand loyalty and team loyalty, and every one of them wants us to find our identity in *them*, *their* perspectives, *their* salesmanship, *their* promises that they can't possibly keep. And every one of them is a poor substitute for the voice that comes from heaven as, water dripping from our head, the sign of the cross is made with oil on our brow, and we are marked as Christ's own forever, bound firmly in the covenant that God has established from of old and to which God has remained steadfast over the centuries despite every provocation and which God continues to honor to this very day: "I have called you by name, you are mine" (Isa 43:1c NRSV).

The Christians at Samaria had already received the sign and seal of their inclusion within God's covenant when Peter and John came to them. They had already been baptized. And that had a *double* significance for people who had long been considered by the *Jews* as being *excluded* from the covenant God had made with Abraham because they failed to worship at Mount Zion in Jerusalem, because they failed to embrace the sacred writings other than the Torah, because they were a racially mixed people. Now, in the waters of baptism, they had been welcomed into the covenant from which human prejudice had excluded them. Now, God's affirmation "You are mine" applied to *them*. But, for some reason that no one has ever satisfactorily explained, they had not received the Holy Spirit to empower them for ministry and for life together as a community of faith. And so, their baptism was not quite complete. Peter and John remedied this, not by baptizing them again, but by laying their hands upon them, a gesture that we see repeated over and over again in Acts, by which the Holy Spirit is given with the result that the gifts of the Spirit are distributed within the community

---

1. *Constitution of the Presbyterian Church*, 4.001.

as needed. God's declaration "You are mine" is to be followed immediately by "Receive my Spirit," and again and again as people are empowered for particular works.

This morning, we ordain four people who, having already received the sacrament of baptism, have already received gifts of the Holy Spirit. Today, however, we lay hands upon them invoking the Holy Spirit to empower them for the particular work of leading and serving this congregation and the community beyond as elders and deacons. None of them has sought the office to which she or he is being ordained; it is our belief that God has chosen them for their service, and has spoken through the voice of the congregation, "You are mine, and I give you my Spirit to fulfill this task." None of them owns his or her ordination any more than we can be said to own our baptism. Emphatically, ordination is not a way of staking a claim on *God*, but acknowledging and affirming God's claim upon *us*. May all that they, and we, do, think, and say be a testimony to the identity that has been given to us from the beginning of creation and sealed in our baptism—the identity declared in words that thunder from heaven and rend the waves, creating a way to freedom, and cause rivers to flow from rocks, giving life to all, and whisper in the gentle gurgling of the baptismal font, "You are mine."

Second Sunday in Ordinary Time
First Presbyterian Church, Dodge City, Kansas
January 18, 1998
Isaiah 62:1–5
1 Corinthians 12:1–11
John 2:1–11

"A Sign of Things to Come"

WHILE BROWSING OVER A bargain book counter a few weeks ago, I was impressed by the number of book titles that have to do with ranking various things—colleges, vacation spots, management tools, recipes. Our culture seems to be so obsessed with competition just now that we have to compare everything with something else and determine which is "better" or "the best." Long before David Letterman's "top ten list," there was *Consumer Reports*, ranking everything from tennis balls to toasters. Now we annually have lists of the best places to live, the best-dressed people, the best barbecue sauces. And we pay money for them. It's silly, really; no two people have identical criteria about things like places to live. No two people have exactly the same taste or value things the same way. Beauty is surely in the eye of the beholder. It is all really quite subjective. But the way things are going, I would not be at all surprised to see on the bookshelves, someday, a book titled "The Best Spiritual Experiences." Only, that one would not be at all original.

Some of the Christians in ancient Corinth already wrote *that* one, almost two thousand years ago. And it seems that they ended up ranking speaking in tongues at the top of their list—even above the spiritual gift of being able to work miracles. Anybody who happened to *have* the gift of speaking in tongues seems to have looked upon anyone who *didn't* happen to have the gift as an inferior Christian. And that caused quite a bit of consternation in the pews and controversy in the fellowship hall among those who not only *didn't* have the gift, but didn't trust those who *did*. It must have seemed to them that it was creating an exclusive club, and of course the notion of boundaries was totally contrary to the broad, inclusive welcome of Jesus Christ into his church. The goal of being a follower of Christ was being misconstrued as being able to point to oneself as specially gifted by the Holy Spirit.

When the apostle Paul heard about it, he wrote to the Corinthian church to make clear that there are *many kinds* of spiritual gifts, that they *all* come from the *same* Holy Spirit, and that they are *given* for the purpose of contributing to the *good* of the *whole body* of the one Lord Jesus Christ. None of them is an end in itself, not even the gift of working miracles, not even the gift of healing. So it isn't a question of one gift being *better* than another. It is not a matter of *ranking*, but, if they *were* to be ranked, speaking in tongues would certainly *not* be at the top of the list.

Somehow, the gift of tongues has always caused controversy and division in the church. The spectacular nature of glossolalia, as it is called, tends to focus attention on the experience itself, to idolize one manifestation of God's Holy Spirit. In fact, the Holy Spirit is present wherever the work of God is being done, wherever Jesus Christ is acknowledged as Lord, wherever the kingdom is being revealed. The gifts of the Spirit are *tools*, not *goals*. The church in which I grew up started a mid-week prayer group. It quickly became a showcase for a couple who spoke in tongues, and the ability to speak in tongues quickly became promoted as the test for whether or not you were a truly spiritual person, and *that* soon became extremely disruptive in the life of that church. It was not the fault of the Holy Spirit for *bestowing* the gift, of course. The problem was the human disposition to focus on what is of only *secondary* importance and so entirely miss the *point* of it all.

Something like that happens with many of us when we read about the miracles of Jesus. We are not quite content to accept the miracles of Jesus on the grounds that he performed them—events that engender faith. Instead, we celebrate them as ends in themselves. They seem to be what Christianity is all about, and any *real* Christian—any person with enough *faith*—ought to be able to perform a spectacular miracle of his or her own. So we have snake-handlers in the Appalachians; occasionally, one gets bit and has to go to the hospital. There are people who promise this or that specific blessing through prayer; if it doesn't come about, you're obviously not praying hard enough or you don't have faith enough. And there are entire congregations, some of them huge, organized around healing illness solely by the means of prayer. We continue to have the urge to *rank* our Christian experiences, and the spiritual spectacular still seems the most impressive experience of all.

In John's Gospel, Jesus reluctantly began his ministry in a setting where he was actually only a minor participant in what was going on—at a wedding feast, to which he and his disciples had been invited. The focus that day in Cana was the newlyweds—the bride and the groom. Jesus had apparently not planned to do anything that would put the spotlight on himself. Like all the other guests, he was there to toast the happy couple and to help make it a memorable occasion for them. But then, an unfortunate thing happened. The host ran out of wine. He had badly miscalculated the amount necessary to keep the guests convivial for seven days, or he had seriously underestimated the number of guests who would attend. Jesus' mother was there, too, and when she learned about the crisis, she told Jesus. She must have informed him of the problem in a way that suggested he ought to do something about it. But it wasn't his party. It wasn't his responsibility. And it wasn't his "hour." It is notoriously difficult to translate Jesus' reply accurately, but it seems to have been essentially, "That's none of our business; it's not our concern."

Mothers, as we know, can be persistent. Here, Jesus' mother ignored what the Son of God actually said to her, and told the house servants who were standing nearby, "'Do whatever he tells you'" (John 2:5b NRSV). Can't you just hear Jesus sighing with an exasperated, "O, Mom!" "Now standing there were six stone water jars for the Jewish rites of purification, each holding twenty or thirty gallons" (John 2:6 NRSV)—I mean, these were big jars. "Jesus said to [the servants], 'Fill the jars with water.' And they filled them to the brim. He said to them, 'Now draw some out, and take it to the chief steward.' So they took it. When the steward tasted the water that had become wine, and did not know where it came from (though the servants who had *drawn* the water knew), the steward called the bridegroom" (John 2:7–9 NRSV); and the steward said to him, "Why have you been holding back the good stuff?"

Nearly a couple hundred gallons of wine might be the entire yield of a small vineyard. John wants us to know that this was an impressive miracle, not just a card trick or a disappearing coin or a rabbit out of a hat. John wants us to know that Jesus ruptures the envelope of everything we have known or imagined, exceeds the bounds of all our previous experience, requires us to leave behind our ordinary way of thinking and our customary expectations and our normal concerns. From the heart of the old righteousness—even from the water of the Old Testament purification rites—springs forth something entirely new and something much better, even like wine far superior to anything that we have tasted before. The most *ordinary* is transformed into the most *extra*ordinary. The vessel of the *old* covenant, John tells us, has served as the womb of God's *new* covenant. The empty Jewish jars are filled with an unprecedented, wonderful, and abundant gift. The Messiah long-awaited by the Jews has arrived in a totally unexpected way. And now

God's greatest blessing for humankind breaks forth on a most unexpected occasion. The *steward* is still concerned with the familiar categories of wine and the ordinary customs of wedding feasts. All *he* can suppose is that the *good* wine was there all along in the cellar. But the servants who drew the water at Jesus' bidding knew the true source of the wine. Jesus had worked a miracle. It was the first sign that revealed Jesus' glory. It had the effect of engendering faith. "And," John tells us, "his disciples *believed* in him" (John 2:11b NRSV).

John wants us to know that the significance of the miracle does not rest in the miracle itself. The miracle is not the goal. It is merely a sign that points to the person who *performs* the miracle—Jesus. Throughout the Old Testament, good wine, abundant wine, is a feature of the promised new age, the kingdom of God, the time when God's will shall be fulfilled and God's rule will be established and acknowledged by all peoples. The miracle at Cana was the "first of his signs" (John 2:11 NRSV) not just because Jesus hadn't performed any others yet. It was the "*first* of his signs" because it was only the *beginning* of what was to *come*—the abundant gifts of grace that God provides in Jesus Christ. This is the inauguration of God's long-promised salvation. Jesus' turning water to wine at a wedding feast at Cana is *the sign of things to come*. And for those who have eyes to see and ears to hear and minds to understand and hearts to love, Jesus' miracle is not just a spectacle that dazzles, but a sign that leads to faith. Many will stop at the spectacle. Perhaps that is why not everyone who heard of Jesus' miracles and then sought him out to perform a miracle for *them* came to stand beside Jesus at Calvary. Not everyone perceives that Jesus is the *true* bridegroom who invites us to his *eternal* wedding feast. But Jesus' disciples, then and now, perceive in the graciousness of Jesus' abundant gift of good wine a glimpse of the identity and character of God himself. And so *they know who Jesus is*. And after this epiphany, says John, there were also many other things that Jesus did. If every one of them were written down, John says, probably the world itself could not contain the books that could be written.

The essence of *any* miracle is that it shatters *conventional* explanations and expectations. The steward was perplexed by the sudden appearance of so much wine of such quality. He was *impressed*, but *his* interest was only in the *wine itself*. He assumed what conventional reasoning told him, and he totally missed the mark. He had no idea that he was being blessed with a foretaste of the heavenly banquet. He had no clue that he was in the presence of the Son of God. He had no inkling that he was standing at the threshold of salvation, and that *that* was an infinitely greater thing than even six stone jars full of fine wine.

What water is to wine, so is any other experience of life compared to the fullness, the color, the adventure, the vibrancy of living in the company of Jesus Christ. But we aren't living as disciples who love Jesus for himself if our Christianity stops at the *threshold*, if we get stuck on the *signs* of his glory as the *goals* of our faith, if we suppose that Christianity is a contest to see who is the most spiritually endowed of all, if we compare our religious temperature with that of other people on some supposition that we *deserve* the Holy Spirit's miraculous gifts. One of the most beautiful scenes in Franco Zeffirelli's *Jesus of Nazareth* is when Mary Magdalene, whom Zeffirelli, like many others, interprets as a harlot, happens into the large crowd that pursued Jesus to the other side of the Sea of Galilee. Jesus worked another miracle on that occasion—a miracle of feeding the multitude with five loaves and two fish. In Zeffirelli's portrayal, Mary Magdalene takes some of the bread, tastes it, and sinks to the ground shaking and in tears. Undoubtedly, like the others, she is hungry and grateful to have the bread. But in that scene, Zeffirelli communicates to us that, through the wondrous miracle, Mary suddenly understood who Jesus *was*.[1]

John wrote his Gospel, with the reports of the miracles of Jesus, to help bring us to faith, which happens when we believe the signs and the testimony that Jesus Christ is God himself in human flesh. And then *we know* just how loving, how gracious, how merciful *God* is, and that God unconditionally loves *us*, and that God is graciously generous to *us*, and that God mercifully forgives *us*. And whatever miracle has introduced us to the true identity of Jesus is only the first of the cornucopia of blessed gifts awaiting us and all people in Christ as our faith and our trust and our discipleship grow and mature, and wonder leads to praise, and praise leads to devotion, and devotion leads to new life. Do *you* see God shining through the miracles of water become wine, of broken people made whole, of selfishness being transformed into generosity, of hatred yielding to understanding, of doubt giving way to trust? Each of these miracles is only a sign of things to come.

---

4. Zeffirelli, *Jesus of Nazareth*.

Third Sunday in Ordinary Time
First Presbyterian Church, Dodge City, Kansas
January 22, 1992
Nehemiah 8:1–4a, 5–6, 8–10
1 Corinthians 12:12–30
Luke 4:14–21

"'Today, in Your Hearing'"

It was not unusual to ask a guest to read and comment upon the scriptures during the synagogue service. The Jewish men of the community would gather together for blessing and prayer, for hearing a reading from the law and a reading from the prophets, for collecting alms, and we can well imagine that day in Nazareth when the carpenter's son came back to town—the one who had been performing miracles and had been teaching about other parts of Galilee—that he would be invited to exercise the privilege. The customs of the synagogue had developed during the period of the exile in Babylon, when the Jews could no longer make offerings and observe their ritual at the temple and the shrines of their homeland.

Jesus was participating in a well-established tradition of his people that sabbath at Nazareth. Luke says that regular worship in the synagogue was his custom, for Jesus was a Jew and thought like a Jew and honored the Jewish practices—something that we Christians occasionally forget. So, it was as a Jew among Jews, as a rabbi among a congregation well-schooled in the law and the prophets, that Jesus, the famous hometown boy, was asked to read from Isaiah the lesson chosen for that sabbath:

> "The Spirit of the Lord is upon me,
>   because he has anointed me
>   to bring good news to the poor.
> He has sent me to proclaim release to the captives
>   and recovery of sight to the blind,
>   to let the oppressed go free,
> to proclaim the year of the Lord's favor." (Luke 4:18–19 NRSV)

After reciting these words of the servant in Isaiah, he would have sat down among the others gathered there in the synagogue, as was customary, and would have commented upon the scripture that he had just read. It was then that he spoke those words that startled his listeners, and, if we think about them, must startle us, too: "Today this scripture has been fulfilled in your hearing" (Luke 4:21b NRSV).

We would not be here gathered in Jesus' name, most of us, if we did not believe that Jesus was anointed by God—endowed with the Holy Spirit to proclaim God's salvation from bondage of every kind. The very word "Christ" means the anointed one, the Messiah. And we call him Savior. But some of us may be a little uncomfortable about that first word of ministry that Jesus speaks in Luke—"today." We may have difficulty recognizing that Jesus is addressing *us*, as well as those ancient Nazarenes, when he says, "in *your* hearing." Perhaps we have been led by teachers or preachers or others to believe that the kingdom of God is something that will come only in the future, either at some vague time or as the culmination of specific identifiable events. Perhaps we cannot imagine, with wars and poverty and disease and death and heartaches and headaches, that the kingdom has already arrived. "Today, in your hearing." Is what we have *now* all there is to it—recession, drugs, crime, terrorism, AIDS? Is this the good news that Jesus was talking about?

Just as likely, and for the very same reasons, Jesus' listeners there in the synagogue at Nazareth probably did not at first apprehend what Jesus was saying about the fulfillment of scripture, or about himself—that *the Messiah has come*, and with him has begun the new era of the Lord's favor, the kingdom: the reversal of fortunes for the poor, opening the gates of every sort of prison and opening the eyes of those who cannot see, relieving the burdens of injustice and the yoke of affliction, declaring the forgiveness of God, which cancels the heavy debt of sin. Not just another restatement of God's promise for the *future*, not simply another vision of the way things *will* be in the world to come, but the truth that exists *now*, *today*, even as we hear the words. And that means there's no time to postpone *our decision* about the authority of Jesus and *our response* to God's command, no luxury of waiting until it is more convenient or less costly, no excuse for lack of commitment.

Just as what he read at the synagogue in Nazareth was nothing new to the people gathered there—they had heard the passage from Isaiah before, many times—so Jesus taught nothing new as he preached in the fields and villages of Galilee. The people realized long before Jesus came that God demands of us more than the *ritual* of sacrifice, more than simply *honoring* the *letter* of the law. What *was* new was Jesus' emphasis upon God's fulfillment of his promise of salvation and wholeness and peace in *himself* "today." And not everybody was open to understanding. Were the chickens laying any more eggs? Were the goats giving any more milk? Was the landlord charging any less rent? Were the Romans treating the Jews with any greater respect? When they could see it and touch it and feel it, *then* they would *agree* that a fundamental change had taken place. But *until* then, nothing was different—certainly not just because the carpenter's son returned to his hometown, read the same passage they had heard many times before, and said, "Today this scripture has been fulfilled in your hearing" (Luke 4:21b NRSV).

What the Nazarenes and countless of their attitudinal descendants could not perceive, of course, was that the fundamental change wrought by the coming of the Messiah must be a change in the human heart—an opening up to the love and forgiveness of God and then a thankful obedience to God's command. This is what will produce the kingdom in full flower. What they missed was the clear vision of faith which motivated a Mother Teresa out into the dark and grimy and dangerous streets of Calcutta each day—streets which to all appearances got no brighter or cleaner or safer for her having been there. What they missed was the clear vision of faith which emboldened a Rosa Parks to get onto a "whites only" bus in Montgomery, Alabama, and refuse to get off simply because of the color of her skin, thus inspiring many people to reconsider the basic dignity of the human creature—an act which, on the face of it, showed no promise of helping to break down the wicked walls of segregation. What they missed was the clear vision of faith which prompted a Clarence Salisbury and a Duncan Spining each to carry their medical bags to the Navajo hogans around the Presbyterian mission at Ganado, Arizona, and which transformed their brief assignments into long careers of applying modern medicine to the treatment of ancient diseases—dedicated service which produced only a *few* curious questions about Christ and even *fewer* baptisms into the Christian faith. Or perhaps the streets of Calcutta *do* glisten for the feet of a saint having walked them. Perhaps human dignity *is* advanced for all people of every color because of the undaunted spirit of one black woman. Perhaps the angels sing not only for the *handful* of Navajos converted to *Christianity* but also for the *thousands* of children cured of measles and flu and tuberculosis—diseases which once accounted for a horrendous infant mortality rate among the Navajo people.

"Today [the scriptural witness that God has appointed one to bring good news to the poor and to proclaim release to the captives and to set at liberty the oppressed and to publish the year of the Lord's favor] has been fulfilled in your hearing" (Luke 4:21b NRSV). *Has* the Messiah come into the world? It seems that there is very little sign of his presence in the headlines of the daily newspaper. But the loving, compassionate, daring, and joyful hearts of people like Mother Teresa, Rosa Parks, Dr. Salisbury, and Dr. Spining, and the thankful faces of the people to whom they ministered in the name of God's anointed one, constitute an emphatic testimony to the reality of God's kingdom *today*.

The message of Epiphany, in whose light we are worshiping this season, is that the "someday" of human yearning, the "someday" of fondest hope, is now the "today" of God's fulfillment. And the fulfillment is in *our hearing*—the Jesus Christ about whom we read, about whom we preach, for whom we have gathered here, in whom we confess our faith, is he *to* whom all the scriptures point, is he *for* whom the world has waited so long, is he *in* whom every promise of God is kept. This was the good news to which Luke was pointing so dramatically when he showed us Jesus in the synagogue that day, unrolling the scroll, reading from the prophet, saying, "Today, in your hearing." And Jesus speaks thus to people today, to hurting and longing folk in every age: "Do not suppose," says Jesus, "that you must do anything to *qualify* for good news, to *earn* release from your bondage, the restoration of clear vision, relief from affliction, acquittal for your guilt. I am he who will lift your every sorrow and shoulder your every burden and forgive your every sin, if you will but turn to me and believe."

And Jesus speaks thus to the church today, to Christians in every age and place: "Do not suppose that threats to national security must be past before *you* speak out for peace, that *your* larder must be full before *you* attack the scandal of hunger, that *your* job must be secure before you root out the prejudice and inequality that persist in the workplace, that the solution to a problem must be in full *view* before *you* take even the *first step* toward its *correction*. Today the scripture has been fulfilled in your hearing," says Jesus. "I am God's anointed one. I have endowed you with every useful gift for the work that must be done; you lack no resource, only the courage and the will, and if you will only open yourself fully to my Spirit among you, the courage and the will also shall be yours. Do not be discouraged, but neither be dissuaded by the values of a selfish world and a cynical age. There are poor and starving and homeless people who need good news—not merely words, but deeds of unconditional compassion. There are people bound in prisons of despair and abuse and injustice who are waiting for release—they need tangible reasons to hope. There are those who see nothing but darkness all around them, the gloom of cheerless day following cheerless day in monotony and the shadow of suspicion that no one cares about them—they need the bright spark of something to live for *beyond* themselves and a clear vision of how *every* person is dear to God and needed in the joyful task of bringing creation back to its proper order. There are victims of other people's pride and fear and jealousy and insensitivity, some of them existing in refugee camps, some of them made to carry passports in their own homeland, some of them ridiculed and threatened because of the color of their skin or the accent of their speech—they need strong witnesses on their behalf to the truth that *all* people are entitled to dignity because *all* people were created in the image of God. There are those who have sinned against God and in the process have sinned against you or against society as a whole, who are longing now for acceptance and return to fellowship and renewal of trust—they need forgiveness from folks who are truly thankful every day for their own forgiveness through my death on the cross. Do not close your ears and your heart and your mind to the fact that the time of fulfillment is today, not tomorrow, not next year, not some indefinite *future*, but *now*."

This is the year of the Lord's favor—*this* is the day of jubilee—the kingdom of God is *now*. An old nun helps an emaciated man from the streets of Calcutta onto a cot and feeds him rice and broth with a spoon. A middle-aged woman grits her teeth and steps onto a bus and sits down, feeling the disapproving eyes of everyone trained upon her because of her defiance on behalf of her people. A surgeon completes his fourth operation of the day in the mission hospital, and his mind takes him back twenty years to how he once had to *beg* sick Navajos even to take an aspirin. As she clears out her desk, a young executive ponders how she will tell her out-of-work husband and her children that she has quit her job rather than comply with her boss's demand that she falsify a safety report. A schoolboy sits in dread of the closing school bell and his likely encounter with the bully whose nose he bloodied with a lucky punch at recess when the brute picked on a friend of his simply because he was black, or brown, or yellow, or red, or a Jew, or a Muslim. A grief-stricken father finds the generosity of heart to visit the jail cell of the young driver who, when drunk the night before, smashed head-on into the car his son was driving, not to *curse* the killer, but to say, "I forgive you" to a young man who is some *other* father's son, alone and frightened. A teenager goes into a supermarket to buy fingernail polish, and she comes out of the store instead teary-eyed but smiling, with cans of food to put in the church parlor for donation to a needy family that the congregation has adopted.

> When [Jesus] came to Nazareth, where he had been brought up, he went to the synagogue on the sabbath day, as was his custom. He stood up to read, and the scroll of the prophet Isaiah was given to him. He unrolled the scroll and found the place where it was written:
>
> "The Spirit of the Lord is upon me,
>   because he has anointed me

> to bring good news to the poor.
> He has sent me to proclaim release to the captives
> and recovery of sight to the blind,
> to let the oppressed go free,
> to proclaim the year of the Lord's favor."
>
> And he rolled up the scroll, gave it back to the attendant, and sat down. The eyes of all in the synagogue were fixed on him. Then he began to say to them, "*Today* this scripture has been fulfilled *in your hearing*." (Luke 4:16–21 NRSV)

Fourth Sunday in Ordinary Time
Spanish Springs Presbyterian Church, Sparks, Nevada
February 1, 2004
Jeremiah 1:4–10
1 Corinthians 13:1–13
Luke 4:21–30

"The School for Loving"

THE EPISTLE LESSON FOR today is familiar to many of us. Indeed, the thirteenth chapter of 1 Corinthians may be one of the most-read, best-known, and well-loved passages in all of the Bible. And rightly so—Paul was at the top of his form when he wrote it. It is beautiful literature; it is strong imagery; it is appealing truth. Most of us, when we hear it, may find our minds taking us back to the setting in which we have perhaps most frequently heard it—weddings. When I give a list of scripture suggestions to couples for the selection of texts to be read and preached on in their wedding service, most of them ask for 1 Corinthians 13 as one of the readings. But many of them—I would judge a majority—aren't aware that the passage really isn't about romantic love (theirs or anybody else's), the sort of affection and emotion and desire that we think of as existing especially between an engaged couple. The Greek word for *that* sort of feeling is *eros*, from which we get the English word "erotic." The Greek word that we translate as "love" in 1 Corinthians 13 is *agape*, a word that connotes a deep caring about the welfare of *another* person as much or more than one cares about him- or her*self*. Such *agape* sort of love is not out of *place* in a marriage—indeed, any marriage that is based on *eros* only and not on *agape* won't last very long. But Paul's subject here simply has *little* to do with *Valentine's Day* and a whole *lot* to do with *Christmas* and *Good Friday* and *Easter*. And when I preach on this passage in a wedding service, I always try to put it in the context of the sort of love that Paul was actually concerned about.

A marriage should be a school for learning to love. It should be a nursery in which the love that one feels toward a sweetheart-turned-spouse grows and stretches to extend far *beyond* the special care spouses very properly feel toward each other, until it embraces all of humankind with genuine sympathy and deep compassion. Having become practiced with one special person in living for the sake of another, we then can offer ourselves more generously to *all* others. That is one important and very practical reason for planning to spend some years in a marriage before having children. A Christian marriage does not exist for its own sake, but as a part of God's plan for the benefit of all of creation. A marriage isn't about just two people. It's about *all* of us. That comes as surprising news to some couples in premarital counseling, when I ask them, as I routinely do, what difference it will make to the *rest* of us that the two of them are *married*. Often, they are totally stumped. But I firmly believe that a wedding in the church, and in fact *any* wedding at which a minister officiates, should reflect in its readings, in its music, in its sermon, in its prayers, an understanding of marriage that is as broad as God's purpose for it.

Paul addressed 1 Corinthians not to a wedding party, but to the congregation of a church—one that was dysfunctional in the extreme, deeply divided, not at all fulfilling the purpose for which Christ died. In fact, the Christians in Corinth were scandalizing the body of Christ. They had become prideful, factious, competitive, jealous, rude. They boasted about their wisdom, they boasted about their knowledge, they boasted about the spiritual gifts with which *some* of them, at least, had been endowed and which they were using arrogantly to draw distinctions between one another, not for the common good as spiritual gifts were *supposed* to be used. They behaved shamefully toward one another, men toward women and women toward men, they humiliated their poorer members by the way they pushed them aside at the Lord's Supper, they kept catalogues of slights and snubs, and they made a habit of looking for the *worst* in one another and then, undoubtedly, *gossiping* about it. In response to all of this, Paul wrote his lyrical lesson about love, what it *is* and what it *isn't*, what it *does* and what it *doesn't* do.

Paul, like most educated people of his time and place, valued the ability to speak well. He esteemed knowledge, he praised wisdom. He regarded himself as having been endowed by the Holy Spirit with various gifts, and, quite obviously, he *had* been. He frequently pointed to his own life as an example for others, of how Christians were to live—not in a prideful way, for he was just as often the first person to admit that whatever good he did was not his *own* achievement, but the achievement of *Christ* at work *in* and *through* him. He was keenly aware that others would be *attracted* to Christ or *turned off* of Christ by the way they saw *Christians* living and treating each other. So he wanted the Christians in Corinth, and in all the other churches that he had helped establish, to know that faith in Jesus Christ requires a new way of life—that salvation must mean living with new values and new allegiances and new hope, and with a new attitude toward our fellow men and women. *Central* to that new way of living, and the motive *without* which it is *not* genuine life in Christ, is *agape*—love. Whatever Paul had achieved, whatever Paul *hoped* to achieve, was no true witness to *Christ* unless it was done *with* and *because of love*—caring for the welfare of *other* people as much or more than he cared for *himself*, wanting only the *best* for them, and doing everything he *could* for their sake, even if it meant setting aside his *own* rights and privileges, even it meant inconveniencing himself, even if it meant suffering for their sake. Kindness, mercy, forbearance, mutuality, humility, patience—these were characteristics of the Christian life, the more *excellent* way than even the *highest* virtues of ancient philosophy and pagan religion. The motive force of the Christian life is *love*. The love of which Paul spoke, in fact, is the *same* sort of love that Jesus Christ had, and *continues* to have, for you and for me and for all people.

So it is not at all inappropriate that, as two people enter into a covenant of lifelong partnership and intimacy, perhaps of bringing new lives into the world, they should ponder the ways in which what they share should prepare them to live more compassionately and generously for *others*. But as much as we expect Christian *marriage* to be a school for learning to love more broadly, so the Christian church *itself* should be the school in which, practicing the Christian virtues with each other, we become equipped to love even total strangers in the same way that Christ does. Our Confession of 1967 says that we are to cultivate a life together within the church—gathering to praise God, to hear God's word for humankind, to receive the sacraments, to pray for the world and enjoy fellowship with one another, and to receive instruction and comfort. But it *also* says that the church exists for the purpose of loving others—of dispersing to serve God wherever we may be by *ministering* to others and giving witness to what we believe not only in what we *say*, but, emphatically, in what we *do*. The quality of our relations with *others*, the Confession says, is the measure of the church's fidelity to *Jesus Christ*. The degree to which we *share* with others, the degree to which we *forgive* others, the degree to which we *stand up* for others, the degree to which we *sacrifice* for others, is the measure in which we love *God*, and the measure in which we are thankful for God's love for *us*.[1] The Confession of 1967, which reminds us of all these things, is based upon and reflects the teaching of Paul to the Corinthian church, that fractious bunch of self-righteous and self-consumed peacocks.

---

1. *Constitution of the Presbyterian Church*, 9.20–22, 31–33, 35–38, 44, 46.

Some of you have seen and inquired about an object that sits on a shelf in my office—a framed peacock feather. My mother gave it to me as a memento of the charge that Rev. Wayne Sebesta delivered to me at my ordination a little over twenty years ago. He related something written by Flannery O'Connor—a single peacock, with its beautiful feathers spread wide in proud display, is a glorious thing, but when you get a bunch of peacocks together, you have a *situation*. "Bruce," he said, "a congregation is a bunch of peacocks." Well, I would be pleased to inform my friend Wayne that the congregation of Spanish Springs Presbyterian Church is the least peacock-like bunch of people that I have ever known, and for that, I am very thankful. But what Paul saw in the church in Corinth was a bunch of peacocks, strutting, crowing, asserting their preeminence, protecting their turf, spreading their feathers in each other's faces, the very *opposite* of the love which compelled Jesus Christ to heal others, to feed others, to forgive others, to encourage others, to protect others, to allow himself to be nailed to a cross, and to die for the salvation of the very people who ridiculed and mocked him, who denounced and rejected him, who judged him unworthy to live.

The task of being a congregation that fulfills Christ's purpose for the church has never been an easy one. And it is every bit as difficult today, in our culture of competitiveness and one-upsmanship, of brevity and haste, of loud shouting and in-your-face communication, of whatever-makes-me-feel-good and get-out-of-my-way, as it was the in the days of pagan Greece and Rome. Our culture would have us learn to be selfish and proud, rather like the people in the synagogue at Nazareth, who thought that Jesus should have been doing miracles for the folks of his own hometown rather than running off and healing and feeding and forgiving *sinners*. We won't develop the habits of generosity and mercy and humility and compassion out *there*, that's for sure. But if we *don't* school ourselves in them, if we *don't* learn the lessons with *one another*, we, as Christians, will have nothing important to offer the world into which Christ has sent us, will have nothing to contribute to its redemption. For whatever we will have accumulated or achieved in the way of spiritual treasures and religious insight will have no value at all to us, or to God, or to anyone else, if it hasn't been done *with* and *by means of* love, *agape*—love that cares as much about the *other* person, *any* other person, as it cares about *itself*. And so the church must *never* be a place of empty sacrifice or noisy self-promotion, of over-stuffed prayers or clanging competitiveness, of judgmental preaching or brassy self-assertion. The church is the school for loving.

> If I speak in the tongues of mortals and of angels, but do not have love, I am a noisy gong or a clanging cymbal. And if I have

prophetic powers, and understand all mysteries and all knowledge, and if I have all faith, so as to remove mountains, but do not have love, I am nothing. If I give away all my possessions, and if I hand over my body so that I may boast, but do not have love, I gain nothing.

Love is patient; love is kind; love is not envious or boastful or arrogant or rude. It does not insist on its own way; it is not irritable or resentful; it does not rejoice in wrongdoing, but rejoices in the truth. It bears all things, believes all things, hopes all things, endures all things.

Love never ends. But as for prophecies, they will come to an end; as for tongues, they will cease; as for knowledge, it will come to an end. For we know only in part, and we prophesy only in part; but when the complete comes, the partial will come to an end. When I was a child, I spoke like a child, I thought like a child, I reasoned like a child; when I became an adult, I put an end to childish ways. For now we see in a mirror, dimly, but then we will see face to face. Now I know only in part; then I will know fully, even as I have been fully known. And now faith, hope, and love abide, these three; and the greatest of these is love. (1 Cor 13:1–13 NRSV)

The church is the place to learn to love as Christ loves, and to practice it with each other, so that we can then take what we have learned among each other out into the world wherever we go and with whomever we come into contact, whether in the schoolyard or in the board room, whether in the bedroom or in the marketplace, whether in the council chamber or in the homeless shelter, whether among fellow believers or among people who do *not* profess faith in Christ. After all, we're not *peacocks*. We're *Christians*.

Fifth Sunday in Ordinary Time
First Presbyterian Church, Dodge City, Kansas
February 5, 1995
Isaiah 6:1–8
1 Corinthians 15:1–11
Luke 5:1–11

"A Letter Home"

My Dear Wife,

By now you will know that I have come with Jesus. I hope that you haven't been worrying about me, why I didn't come home the other day from fishing. I suppose that I should have gotten word to you sooner, somehow, though I trust that someone who was at the docks must have told you. I thought about writing a note to you several times, but just didn't, for some reason. You have often commented how impulsive I am, and I suppose that is so. I got caught up in the spirit of things, I guess. No, no, that is not quite what happened. It wasn't the mood of the *others*. It was *Jesus*. When he looked at me and told me not to be afraid, that from now on I would be catching not *fish*, but *people*, I simply *had* to follow him, and the others came, too—James and John and the rest. And I guess I was a little afraid I might not come at all if I paused even to say goodbye.

I'm taking for granted that you know everything that happened, but perhaps I should tell you exactly how it was. We had had a discouraging morning, casting and hauling nets, and nothing! Not a thing! You know me—my boast that if there wasn't but a sardine in that whole lake, I would be snacking on sardine by breakfast! So you know what kind of a mood I must have been in when we reached the docks. For all my skill (for all my boast), the nets kept coming up empty. We finally gave up—sometimes, you know, that's all you can do, and hope that things go better the next day.

While we were washing the nets and spreading them to dry, Jesus came walking along, and immediately a crowd gathered. You know how it's been ever since the incident at the synagogue—the man with the demon. And of course, there was your mother's fever, and all the other cures that people have heard about. Everyone was wanting to get close to Jesus, pressing him down to the very edge of the water. So, when he saw that we had come in from fishing, he climbed into my boat and asked me to take him just off shore. Tired as I was, I did what he asked—little enough of a favor after what he did for your mother and others we know. A few yards out, we threw out the anchor, and just sat in the boat and listened as he talked to the crowd for a while, telling about what he calls "the kingdom of God." It sounded so wonderful—so different from the selfish sort of king that we have, and the hard sort of life that we live. Joyful it is, the way Jesus described it. At first, I thought it was just talk—hmph! "The kingdom of God." But slowly, I began to understand—it's always "slowly" that I begin to understand, isn't it? But, as I listened, the burdens of our daily toil seemed not to matter so much anymore—even the frustrations of having nothing to show for a day's work but empty nets and still the lenders breathing down your neck and the tax collector demanding his payment. I began to see that that's just the way it is, but that isn't all that life is about, and not even the most important part of life. You know that fishing has always been my life, plus you and the children, of course, and a celebration now and then.

Jesus had been speaking for some time when he stopped and told me to put back out onto the lake and cast my nets again. You can imagine my surprise. Had I, the best fisherman in Capernaum, not just dragged the lake from one end to the other and found nothing? And here was a carpenter's son telling me to go back out into deep water and cast the nets again! "Master," I tried to explain to him (politely, of course), "we have worked all morning long but have caught nothing. We've just washed the nets and spread them to dry." But he just looked at me, smiling. He must have known how tired we were. I guess he knew how discouraged we were as well. But he just kept looking at me, expecting me to do it. So we all hauled the nets back into the boats and went out again, grumbling as you can imagine. We got out into the deep water and cast our nets and after a few minutes began to pull them in again—what was the point of waiting? We knew it was hopeless. We *thought* we knew it was hopeless.

Dear wife, I am absolutely telling you the truth when I say that the nets were full to breaking when we hauled them back in! Such a catch as none of us has ever seen, more fish than you can begin to imagine. We filled both boats until the water was up the sides and we seriously feared of sinking. But I was less fearful of drowning than of being in the presence of a worker of God's own miracles! You know best, of all people, how I am given to rough temper and rash speech. I overreact to things, I speak when I should listen, I work with my hands and I curse with my lips, I sometimes drink too much, I sometimes break the laws of the sabbath. I dream big, I plan big, I talk big, but what has ever come of my big dreams and my big plans and my big talk? What was I doing in a boat with Jesus? I told him that I'm a sinner, that he shouldn't be with someone like me, dirty, coarse, stubborn, bad-mannered. I'm just a fisherman. But he had provided the catch! He was the only reason we caught anything that day. It had to be a miracle. It *was* a miracle, such as only a prophet of God could produce. He brought me to my knees—something that no man has ever done before. "Go away from me," I pleaded, as if, in the middle of the lake, there was anywhere for him to go. But he just sat there, looked at me a few moments, still smiling, unphased by what I had said.

I think I was trembling by then. Who was this man? How could he stand to be with me? What did he think of me? What was he going to do to me—he who had the power to fill my nets with fish where there were no fish before? Why shouldn't he curse me to hell? But he didn't say anything about my past. He just told me not to be afraid, can you believe it? And then he said something that made me feel different about it all: "From now on," he said, "you will be catching people." And I knew that my life on the lake was over. And, dear wife, I sense that my life in Capernaum may be over as well. To follow him, to serve him, to do what pleases him . . . . I don't know how, but, yes, from now on, I will be catching people.

I can't explain my feelings. I just know that I must go with him, even though it means leaving our home and being away from my dear family, I don't know how long. He hasn't said, and none of us has dared to ask. Somehow, that seems like a small thing for such joy and peace as I feel. It isn't that I dislike our life together, you and I. Please believe that. I love you and the children. And I love you no less today than I loved you before I took him out on the lake. Can you understand that? How can I make you understand something that I don't understand myself? But I have no choice but to follow Jesus now—at least I can't *not* follow him and have any peace in my soul. And I *do* have peace. Yet this peace I have is a surging thing—not the peace of comfort and security, wine in the storeroom and money in the bank, but a feeling of having found myself, of opening my eyes to see things as they truly are, and as I have never seen them before, a peace that comes not in *rest* but in *doing*. And, on this, I must follow through. Yes, you are quite right that I am impulsive. Who in their right mind would do what I have done—leave home and family and the only job I know how to do? The others, I think, feel the same way. I can read it in their eyes. But I can read in their eyes also the conviction that they *must* be here with Jesus, and follow wherever he bids us go. And, somehow, I'm not afraid anymore. Jesus still smiles at me.

Please kiss the children for me. Tell them that I love them, and that I am thinking about them, and that I'll be back. No, better not tell them that, not just yet, anyway. Perhaps you and the other wives can draw strength from each other, and consider that your husbands were all affected the same way by Jesus and what he said and by our miraculous catch. Recall what he did for your mother. You yourself have commented on the power of Jesus' kindness, that he seemed truly sent to us by God. I *believe* that now, I really do. And I believe that God really cares about *us*, and what happens to people like you and me. So I must do this for him. Please try to understand. It may be that your prayers for me all these years have brought a result you did not expect.

God be with you, dear wife.

Your loving husband,
    Simon

P.S. You may sell the boat.

Sixth Sunday in Ordinary Time
First Presbyterian Church, Dodge City, Kansas
February 12, 1995
Jeremiah 17:5–10
1 Corinthians 15:12–20
Luke 6:17–26

"Strong Stuff, This Good News"

EVERY FALL, ON THE fourth Thursday of November, our nation, by congressional decree, pauses to give thanks for its blessings, recalling the prayers of our civic ancestors when they first came to these shores from Europe. Those *first* observers of thanksgiving to God in America were grateful merely to have survived the ocean voyage and to have landed in a verdant landscape, either Massachusetts or Virginia, depending upon whichever chamber of commerce you choose to believe. By the time President Lincoln proclaimed the first *national* Thanksgiving Day in 1863, the fruitfulness of the land had been proved by two and a half centuries of harvests—surely ample reason for a nation to give thanks to God. Yet, considering the bloody war which was ripping the United States apart in 1863, one might think that it was the most *illogical* of times for a president to proclaim a national day of thanksgiving. And the student of history cannot miss the irony that the first national Thanksgiving Day fixed by *Congress* fell on the fourth Thursday of November, 1941—less than two weeks before America was drawn into the terrible war that had already engulfed Europe and Asia.

Most of us are likely to think of blessings, after all, as life's *good* things—wealth, health, prestige, peace. Whom have we ever heard give thanks for their poverty, for their brokenness, for their obscurity, for their turmoil? So it seems strange, doesn't it, to find Jesus teaching "a great crowd of his disciples and a great multitude" (Luke 6:17 NRSV) of others gathered on a level place, saying to them that it is the people who are now poor, hungry, weeping, and reviled that are blessed? Surely it was strange at the time that it happened. It was generally believed that wealth and health and celebrity and harmony were signs that a person or a nation was favored by God. But here was Jesus, telling them just the opposite—not only were the poor, the hungry, the weeping, and the reviled *blessed*, but, in fact, Jesus said that the rich, the full, the laughing, and the admired were in for tribulation and misery! The fortunes of the meek and the mighty, Jesus was explaining, are to be reversed, just as *Mary* had proclaimed before Jesus was born. And if the Son of God has declared it, then it is so—the end-time is already here.

In fact, it wasn't only the *ancient* peoples who thought that creature comfort and material prosperity were signs of God's pleasure. Most of *us* think the same way today, or at least we talk and behave as if that were true. Even though we might have the Beatitudes memorized and silently recite them in times of misfortune and distress, I doubt that any of us really considers poverty, for instance, to be a blessing. I'm not sure that *Matthew* could bring *him*self to conceive of poverty as a blessing—he changed "Blessed are you who are poor" (Luke 6:20b NRSV) to "Blessed are the poor in spirit" (Matt 5:3a NRSV), and changed "Blessed are you who are hungry" (Luke 6:21a NRSV) to "Blessed are those who hunger and thirst for righteousness" (Matt 5:6a NRSV). *Matthew blunted* the sharp illogic of Jesus' teaching which *Luke preserves*. Equally to the ancient and the modern must the chant of St. Francis of Assisi seem incomprehensible: "For sister poverty / We give thanks."[1] And yet, there are the words of Jesus, as plain and direct as any in the Bible:

> "Blessed are you who are poor,
>   for yours is the kingdom of God.
> "Blessed are you who are hungry now,
>   for you will be filled.
> "Blessed are you who weep now,
>   for you will laugh.
> "Blessed are you when people hate you, and when they exclude you, revile you, and defame you on account of the Son of Man. Rejoice in that day and leap for joy, for surely your reward is great in heaven; for that is what their ancestors did to the prophets." (Luke 6:20b–23 NRSV)

"To tell the truth," the poor and hungry and mournful and reviled might say, "I'd be perfectly willing to be a little less blessed."

But if Jesus' catalogue of *blessings* surprises us, see what a shock we are in for with Jesus' catalogue of *woes*!

> "Woe to you who are rich,
>   for you have received your consolation.
> "Woe to you who are full now,

---

6. In the portrayal of St. Francis in Zeffirelli, *Brother Sun, Sister Moon*.

> for you will be hungry.
> "Woe to you who are laughing now,
> for you will mourn and weep.
> "Woe to you when all speak well of you, for that is what their ancestors did to the false prophets." (Luke 6:24–26 NRSV)

And who of us—citizens of the wealthiest nation in the history of the world, almost all of us capable of eating three nutritious meals a day and seldom with cause for tears, nearly all of us able to recall instances when we enjoyed being flattered in some regard—who of us doesn't honestly fit more rightfully in Jesus' list of woes than in Jesus' list of blessings? And, perhaps, our nation? How about our church? Is this the good news that Jesus came to preach? And if so, how is it *good* news for people like you and me?

If anyone thinks that Christianity means simply applying a varnish of Sunday sentiments and platitudes about the sweet by-and-by to a life of self-centered material gain, Jesus destroys the notion right here. Being a follower of Jesus Christ means *not* following the worldly-wise down paths of pride and idolatry, of comfort and security. That is the road to woe. Being a follower of Jesus Christ means for disciples *now*, as it meant for disciples *then*, surrendering all claim to independence and all pursuit of self-interest, living in total trust and reliance on God, and living in faith all the more in times of poverty and hunger and mourning and rejection—precisely at those times when the *world* would say, "Abandon your God, who rewards your goodness with poverty and repays your faithfulness with others' contempt." Only those who live in such total trust in and reliance upon God can say with purity of heart that everything they have is truly a blessing from God. Perhaps only those who have been seriously ill know what it is not to take good health for granted; perhaps only those who have been unable to purchase a meal know what it is not to take food on the table for granted; perhaps only those who have known the senseless destruction and cruel misery of war know what it is not to take peace for granted. In such cases, yes, they are surely blessed beyond those who have never known illness or hunger or war. Those who have everything that they think they want or need in the way of material things, or even such intangibles as health and family and friendship, may indeed have a hard time hungering after God. Poverty, illness, oppression might be the *only* price at which *some* people can acquire the blessings of *really trusting* in God. Simplicity of heart and the capacity to find happiness in oneself are rare commodities in a culture built on abundance and amusement (not that any civilization should take this as an excuse for returning to the days of orphanages and sweatshops, the silliness of recent political debate aside). We cannot redeem society by subjecting the *powerless* to a virtuous discipline of poverty to which the rest of us would never think of subjecting *ourselves.*

But there is more to Jesus' teaching than romanticizing the plight of the poor. Jesus was speaking to those whom he had called to be his disciples, and especially those whom he had appointed to carry the gospel to the far corners of the earth. And by reporting that, Luke was speaking to the church of his own day, decades after Jesus was crucified and raised from the tomb. The Sermon on the Plain is Jesus' call of his followers to the life of discipleship. The promises of blessing are to those who know that they are utterly dependent upon God, who trust God completely in life and trust God completely in death, and who are free from pride and self-interest to live in service to Christ now by serving others in his name. The target of the woes is that attitude, whether demonstrated by miserliness or by materialism, by glumness or by gaiety, of not needing God, or that says, dramatically or subtly, "God cannot be trusted." Thus are poverty, hunger, mourning, and slander the experience of the disciple. But the paradox is that it is in *discipleship* that we have blessings beyond all riches, beyond all feasting, beyond all gaiety, beyond all celebrity. And the fact that the disciple of Jesus *shares* with him the experience of poverty, of hunger, of mourning, and of being reviled means that the disciple shares the deep and special concern that *Jesus* has for the poor, the hungry, the sorrowful, and the excluded—the special concern to minister to them in practical ways and to be steadfast *advocates* for them in whatever forum is available to us.

Strong stuff, this good news. The teachings of Jesus, the promises of blessing and the certainty of woes, are not just suggestions about how to be happy or how to avoid unpleasantness. The words of Jesus, including these few powerful and unambiguous verses, are God's word to us, and God's word is not empty, it is not casual, it is not to be cast aside with such self-assurance as "Well, Jesus can't mean that exactly," or "Jesus doesn't expect that of me," or "None of my friends takes it all that seriously, so why should I?" The good news which Jesus brought to the poor, the release which he proclaimed to the captives and the recovery of sight which he proclaimed to the blind, the freedom which he was sent to bring to the oppressed, the year of the Lord's favor which he was appointed to announce—these things are not just for some *future* time and for a few monkish super-Christians, and they are certainly not just some pitiful hope to help keep people content in their present misery. These things are the agenda of the followers of Jesus Christ today.

Are we excused from doing everything that we can to minister to the poor today because Jesus once observed that there will always be poor people? No. Are we justified in not doing everything that we can to promote peace and justice because Jesus predicted that there will be wars and rumors of wars? No, not if we are disciples of Jesus. For that is not the manner of disciples, but the manner of people who are attached to their wealth, those who have piled up against the possibility that God will not be faithful tomorrow, those who laugh when there is plenty about which they should weep, those who enjoy public regard too much to endure the scandal of standing by Jesus as he is put to death like a criminal.

"Cursed are those who trust in mere mortals and make mere flesh their strength" (Jer 17:5a NRSV), proclaimed the prophet. "Blessed are those who trust in the Lord" (Jer 17:7a NRSV). Jesus said: "Woe to you who are rich. . . . Blessed are you who are poor. . . . Woe to you who are full now. . . . Blessed are you who are hungry now. . . . Woe to you who are laughing now. . . . Blessed are you who weep now. . . . Woe to you when all speak well of you. . . . Blessed are you when people hate you, and when they exclude you, revile you, and defame you on account of the Son of Man" (Luke 6:24a, 20a, 25a, 21a, 25b, 21b, 26a, 22 NRSV). How blessed are you? Strong stuff, this good news!

Seventh Sunday in Ordinary Time
Spanish Springs Presbyterian Church, Sparks, Nevada
February 18, 2001
Genesis 45:3–11, 15
1 Corinthians 15:35–38, 42–50
Luke 6:27–38

"Like Parent, Like Child"

I REMEMBER WONDERING WHAT parenthood would be like. Once upon a time, it was sort of a theoretical question, but then came the day when I realized that I had something less than nine months to prepare for it. And then it finally happened, and I quickly learned that it really is not something that can be scripted according to one's own expectations or preferences. For instance, I had always supposed that people would comment on how much my child looked like me—that others, even perfect strangers, would be able to detect this feature or that of their father in my children's faces. And then came reality. Of all the many folks who have commented one way or the other, I don't think that more than three people have ever said to me that my children look like me. They look a lot like each *other*—people *do* say *that*. But the far more common statement is how much they look like their *mother*. It's so usual now for people to see the resemblance to her that, if anyone were to say otherwise, I wouldn't believe them anyway. O, vanity! O, pride! O, genes that couldn't stand up to the competition!

Of course, there's still hope when it comes to *other* characteristics. And, after all, when the subject is parenting, perhaps those are really the more important areas where we hope that our children will take after us—at least our better habits and qualities—and not simply adopt the ways of the world around them. Mothers and fathers can't do much about the mysteries of how *physical* traits are passed on to the next generation. But we *can* influence character and interests and aptitudes by modeling behavior and vocabulary, by fostering attitudes such as kindness and generosity, by nurturing self-esteem and faith. In the long run, is it more satisfying for us to notice that our children have inherited our height or our hair color or the shape of our nose, or that our children have inherited our inquisitiveness, our compassion, or our respect for others? And, as Christian parents, surely the highest compliment we could receive from another person would be the observation that our children have inherited our abiding trust in God and our profound gratitude toward God and our steadfast love of God.

The words of Jesus that we read last week about who is blessed and who is cursed in life and the implications of all of that shook us up a bit, I think, judging from comments after the worship service. What *Jesus* said isn't the way that *we* *normally* think about life and its fortunes and misfortunes, but it worked a great reversal of the world's wisdom about what constitutes the good life. As Jesus continued his teaching that day, he continued to shock his hearers, and he continues to shock us readers two thousand years later with *further* reversals of worldly wisdom and human custom. Even the holiest of religious leaders in Jesus' time would not have taught their followers to love their *enemies*, to do good to those who *hated* them, to bless those who *cursed* them, to pray for those who *abused* them, to respond to the pain and insult of being struck on the cheek by offering the *other* one, to respond to the demand by another person to surrender one's coat, in debtor's court or otherwise, by giving up one's *shirt* as *well*, to give to every beggar who holds out his or her hand as we're walking along the street minding our own business, not to pursue a thief or a debtor by suing or otherwise. In a single paragraph, Jesus managed to offend every popular conception of justice, to contradict every conventional wisdom, to disembowel every iota of pride, some would even say healthy self-respect.

At first, we might think Jesus hopelessly idealistic—or just plain foolish. Who would ever so subject her- or himself to such humiliation? Who would ever show such weakness? Who would ever think so little of his or her own humanity—or indeed, of the image of God in which we were all created? And then we remember that Jesus, the Son of God, the greatest teacher and healer that ever was, said these words as he was traveling from Nazareth, where he had been cast out of the synagogue, to Jerusalem, where he was going to be executed by the civic and religious leaders after being rejected by the mob. And we remember that the very same person who taught us never to respond to violence with violence, never to answer hate for hate, never to cling to our possessions or our breath, willingly surrendered to the cross, forgave those who were killing him, and poured out his own blood for our salvation. And, suddenly, we understand that his entire life was a lesson as profound as his words: "If you love those who love *you*, what credit is that to *you*? . . . If you do good to those who do good to *you*, what credit is that to *you*?" (Luke 6:32a, 33a NRSV). Even *sinners* do *that* much. "But love your enemies, do good, and lend, expecting nothing in return. Your reward will be great, and you will be children of the Most High; for he is kind to the ungrateful and the wicked. Be merciful, just as your Father is merciful" (Like 6:35–36 NRSV). As your *heavenly parent* is, said Jesus, so must *you* be.

No matter how many sermons we have sat through, no matter how many Sunday school lessons, the values and judgments of the world are so strong that a lot of us probably still, when we picture the majesty and power and greatness of God, do not think in terms of what *popular opinion* would classify as *weakness*—things like mercy, things like tenderness, things like blessing one's enemies. It would be interesting, wouldn't it, for Luke to have given us some idea of how the *crowd* reacted to what Jesus said that day? I suspect that they, too, were used to thinking of God in terms of earthquakes and thunder and commandments on stone—the God who is majestic enough to create a universe to offer its praise, the God who is powerful enough to flood the entire earth, the God who is great enough to topple kings and empires and destroy their armies. *That* accords more with the *popular* measure of *strength*.

We like action heroes. Election after election shows that we prefer tough-talking leaders. Poll after poll shows that we want our presidents to retaliate for every threat and snub and insult. Politics, both here and abroad, has long recognized that people vote primarily on the basis of self-interest and fear, and, frankly, it seems that the more candidates talk about so-called Christian values, the more selfish our voting patterns have become. An eye for an eye! And so, for instance, violence escalates in Israel, where neither Jew nor Arab can let *any* insult go unnoticed, can let *any* violence go unanswered. More for me! And so, for instance, can you imagine any candidate ever being elected who says that taxes ought to be raised in order to make sure that no one's child goes hungry?

Jesus, by the way, *wasn't* teaching his followers to be *passive* in the face of hatred or violence or theft or abuse. What he was saying was that his disciples must *respond* to their mistreatment, but *not* with selfishness or ill will. The strength of a *Christian* is not demonstrated in *retaliation*. Giving and forgiving, loving indiscriminately, treating everyone as a neighbor— that is responding assertively and positively and with the force of right to *undermine* hostility and violence, and it constitutes God's own judgment on wrongdoing and abuse. It is what Jesus did. And Jesus was the full and complete revelation of God. Like parent, like child. And by *loving* our enemies, by doing *good*, and by *lending* without expecting *anything* in return, Jesus said, *we* will show *ourselves* to be children of God as well. "For he is kind to the ungrateful and the wicked," Jesus told those who would follow him. "Be merciful, just as your Father is merciful" (Luke 6:35c, 36 NRSV).

If God is our Father, as Jesus repeatedly said—if *God* is *truly* our *parent*—it isn't simply a matter of expecting God to indulge us with presents and make sure that we have a roof over our head and food on our plate, though God faithfully does those things, daily and many times a day. If God is our Father, as Jesus repeatedly said—if *God* is *truly* our *parent*—it *also* means that *we* resemble *God*, if not in physical appearance, then surely in attitudes and outlook, interests and manners. The very beginning of the Bible says that we were created in God's image. Does that mean with red hair? Or does it mean with the capacity to love without calculation and without reservation and without discrimination? Does that mean with blue eyes? Or does it mean with a kind and generous and forgiving spirit? Does that mean every man six feet tall and 160 pounds and every woman five foot seven and 125 pounds? Or does it mean praying for the welfare of and actually doing good for those who wish you harm and have caused you injury?

Think of the poor showing of gratitude that even the most pious of us makes for the constant loving care that God showers upon us all, even the wicked. And yet God does not turn off the sun, does not hurl the earth out of its orbit off into oblivion. Think of how we can never repay God for a fraction of God's blessings, much less pay them back with interest. And yet God does not evict us from the earth we have been given for our home, does not demand offerings of jewels or sacrifices of our children. Think of how God came in Jesus Christ who did not draw a sword against his enemies, but gave himself up to their abuse and their injustice. And yet in the very death of Jesus his Son, God forgave us and embraced us to himself forever, and *guaranteed* that parental love by raising Jesus from the dead to live forever as our advocate and sent the Holy Spirit to us to abide forever with us as our comforter. Like parent, like child. How can any of us ever refuse to give to someone in need? How can any of us ever plot retaliation and revenge or any other harm against even our worst enemy? How can any of us ever refuse to forgive someone who has wronged us, even wronged us over and over again? "Do to others as you would have them do to you" (Luke 6:31 NRSV), said Jesus. "Be merciful, just as your Father is merciful" (Luke 6:36 NRSV). If we do these things, all people will know whose children we are, because the resemblance will be so close. We will be known as children of the Most High, not because, like God, we can raise mountains with a finger and destroy mighty armies with a word, but because, like God, we are kind and generous and merciful even to the ungrateful and the wicked.

Well, my mother says *she* can see my features in my children. And I have a cousin who said that she could see that baby Christi had the Taylor toes, whatever that means. As time goes by, other physical resemblances may become more apparent. But I've gotten past some of those expectations and desires; as my children grow older and interact more with others in school and at play and in society at large, it's *other* things, not so much physical appearance, that I hope I have been able to pass on in my better moments, perhaps even through sermons that they have had to sit through and listen to each Sunday, since I can't be there each evening to discuss everything personally. Faith, hope, love, kindness, generosity, forgiveness, compassion—they won't inherit those things from the world. Which means, of course, they won't inherit them in any perfect form from *me*; to the degree that they demonstrate those qualities, it will be more because of their *heavenly* parentage than any *human* lineage. Like parent, like child. "Do to others as you would have them do to you. . . . Love your enemies, do good, and lend, expecting nothing in return. Your reward will be great, and you will be children of the Most High" (Luke 6:31, 35a-b NRSV).

Transfiguration of the Lord
Spanish Springs Presbyterian Church, Sparks, Nevada
February 22, 2004
Exodus 34:29–35
2 Corinthians 3:12—4:2
Luke 9:28–43

"On to the Cross"

ONE OF MY BIGGEST mistakes in ministry—at least, one of the biggest ones that I know about—occurred at a synod youth conference held on the campus of the University of Texas at San Antonio in the summer of 1987. It was during my first pastorate—I was an associate pastor at a church in the Dallas area—and I had been invited to be a leader for one of the dozens of discussion groups at a gathering of high school-aged Presbyterians from all over Texas and Oklahoma and Louisiana and Arkansas. An associate synod executive thought that the experience would broaden my exposure to different age groups in the church and to other ministers in the synod. In preparation for the task, I, like the several other discussion group leaders, had been supplied with a fistful of photocopied articles and lists of questions related to the theme of the conference and directed to use them to stimulate the kids to plumb the depths of whatever topics were being presented in the plenary sessions.

It was not a good week for me. I was not at all excited about being in San Antonio in the heat and humidity of July walking back and forth across a college campus for a week to begin with, when I really wanted to be working at finishing my doctoral dissertation during the summer months when not much was going on at the church, and *then* it turned out that I was *also* responsible for making sure that the kids turned the lights off in their dormitory rooms and went to sleep by eleven o'clock each night and *kept* them off and *stayed* asleep (which meant that *I* wasn't getting to sleep until long past midnight each night). On top of that, it ended up being the week that my first child took her first step, and that was in Dallas, and I was in San

Antonio, and I felt much deprived of one of the milestones of parenthood. In fact, it *still* upsets me to think that I missed Christi's first step.

The week did not go well. Several of the kids despised me for somehow being personally responsible for what they considered to be an unreasonable curfew. Most of them were completely uninspired by the conference presentations that they were supposed to sit through in the morning sessions and discuss again most of the afternoon. And all week long, one of the girls in my group, between her junior and senior years of high school, refused to answer my greeting or acknowledge me in any way when we passed in the cafeteria or on the sidewalk during the course of the day. Finally, on the last full day of the conference, she burst out in tears during our closing discussion session and complained bitterly that I had robbed her of the wonderful experience she had expected to have—the opportunity to talk about all of her many problems just like she had been able to talk about all of her many problems in her discussion group when she had come to the conference the year before. Instead, I had wasted her time with all of the boring discussion questions and irrelevant materials that I had been given and told to cover in the discussion sessions. The whole experience had been spoiled for her because it hadn't been exactly like the experience she had had at the conference the previous year, and the quality of her spiritual life was now in serious jeopardy because I hadn't led the discussion group like *last* year's leader had done.

Whatever I mumbled at that point was patently unhelpful—probably something about my having simply followed the directions I had been given—as every other kid in the room looked at me reproachfully with an expression that said, "How *could* you?" and implied, without actually speaking the words, that I was a cad of monstrous proportions. The week ended not a day too soon, and I asked the associate synod executive if I couldn't serve the synod in some *other* way the *next* year.

Clearly, the previous year's synod youth conference had been a mountaintop experience for the girl who was now so very unhappy. Like many of us who have had some insightful or thrilling experience in life, she had returned to the place where it had happened, expecting the same thing to happen all over again. But subsequent visits to Disneyland are never quite as magical as the first.

We come to church hoping for such mountaintop experiences, and expect them, especially at Christmas and Easter. Some churches virtually *promise* them, as if they can be manufactured by human agents at will (and if they *can* be manufactured, then we have to wonder whether they are genuinely *spiritual*). For some people, induced perhaps by advertising, spiritual highs are the *goal* of church attendance—theologically, a major misunderstanding of what worship is about. Such experiences can and do come to us as we participate in the life of the people of God, reviving us, making us feel good. But, in the church, if such experiences don't serve to *transform* the days and events that come *after* we have been to the spiritual mountaintop, then, no matter how momentarily thrilling they might have been, no matter how awe-inspiring, they really weren't all that important to us in the *long* run.

I hope that the girl has forgiven me, or, if she never forgave me, that she has *forgotten* me and the conference that proved to be such a disappointment for her. But I also hope that, by now, she has integrated that *earlier* conference experience into a mature faith that recognizes such mountaintop experiences not as *destinations*, but as memorable milestones along the *way*, not as goals in themselves, but as unique once-in-a-lifetime blessings that prompt a harvest of faithful discipleship throughout life.

In the Gospel of Luke, the mountaintop episode of Christ's transfiguration stands midway through the story of Jesus' journey from the manger to the cross, at the close of his ministry in Galilee and the start of his journey to Jerusalem. *Before* the transfiguration, Luke reflects the many questions that people were asking about who Jesus was and what Jesus was doing. *After* the transfiguration, in Luke's Gospel, the speculation about Jesus' identity ceases. In the Christian year, the transfiguration stands at the midpoint between the celebration of Jesus' *birth* and the observance of Jesus' *death*. With the transfiguration of the Lord, we close the period of scripture readings that reveal that Jesus was the Son of God. *After* the transfiguration of the Lord comes *Lent*, which shows us what being the Son of God *required* of Jesus. There, on the mountaintop, the cloud of God's presence appeared, and a voice from the cloud proclaimed Jesus to be God's Son, God's chosen, along with the command, "Listen to him!" (Luke 9:35c NRSV). *Before* the transfiguration, Jesus had gathered the twelve disciples and had taught them and commissioned them to cast out demons and cure the sick and proclaim the kingdom of God, and they had rejoiced in the miracles they worked by his authority. *Beyond* the transfiguration lay the passion—the rejection, the mocking, the scourging, the torture, the death. And there, on the mountaintop, where the three disciples saw Jesus talking with Moses, the teacher of the Law, and Elijah, the great prophet, speaking to Jesus of his departure—his death, "which he was about to accomplish at Jerusalem" (Luke 9:31b NRSV)—and saw his glory, Peter voiced a suggestion and a desire: "'Master, it is good for us to be here; let us make three dwellings [or tents, or booths], one for you, one for Moses, and one for Elijah,'—not knowing," Luke tells us, "what he said" (Luke 9:33b NRSV).

Peter was expressing his very natural desire, respectful in intent and pious in sound, to freeze the moment of Jesus' visible glory. Jesus' appearance had changed while he was praying—his face looked different, somehow, his clothes became "dazzling white" (Luke 9:29 NRSV), and Moses and Elijah had appeared, talking to him in some way that it was apparently clear to Peter and John and James who they were. Surely, Peter thought, such an unusual sight that focused on the importance of Jesus deserved to be enshrined, to be memorialized, to be made permanent. Peter didn't have a *camera*, but he did blurt out an *observation*—the equivalent of "Master, it's a lucky thing that we were here to see this so that we can tell others all about it." And then he had an idea that later caught on in churches in a big way: essentially, "Let's put up some plaques."

But Peter was wrong in thinking that the moment *should* or even *could* be *frozen*. Moses and Elijah had been talking with Jesus, Luke tells us, about his *departure*—his death—which was about to occur at Jerusalem. They were talking about his continuing on to the cross. And it was in association with that conversation, in response to the confirmation of that destiny, that the cloud of God's presence appeared and overshadowed or enveloped them and the voice said, "This is my Son, my Chosen; listen to him!" (Luke 9:35b NRSV). And the very next day, Jesus and Peter and John and James were again down from the mountain, were again pressed upon by crowds, were again approached by someone who wanted Jesus to perform a healing, and Jesus again cast an unclean spirit out of a lad and restored him to health and, in the poignant words of Luke, "gave him back to his father" (Luke 9:42c NRSV). "And all were astounded at the greatness of God" (Luke 9:43a NRSV).

We don't know exactly *why* the transfiguration occurred, much less *how*, but it bears all the appearance of a pep talk—two great biblical spokespersons for God—the greatest biblical figure associated with the Law, and a great prophet—speaking with Jesus about his impending death, and then God voicing approval of Jesus and confirming Jesus' Sonship. Whatever the reason for the transfiguration, clearly, it was not a *goal*. It was a waypoint on the road to the *cross*. It was a private moment of divine communication, far from the eyes of the crowd, taken at divine initiative, which three of the disciples were privileged to witness and then kept to themselves until after the resurrection. And, clearly, it was not something to be clung to, it was not something that could be repeated, it was not something that could be scheduled as a regular event on Jesus' itinerary. It had happened about a week after Jesus had fed five thousand hungry people. It happened the day before Jesus healed yet another victim of demons. Faithfulness required that Jesus must *continue* on his journey of healing and feeding and forgiving and proclaiming the kingdom of God, not staying on the mountaintop. Faithfulness required that the disciples must *follow* him to the cross, not build a monument on the spot where the transfiguration took place. And, fittingly, not one of the Gospels names the mountain on which the transfiguration occurred or identifies its location.

There are a lot of interesting details in the story. Like Moses after talking with God in the cloud on Mount Sinai, the brightness of Jesus' appearance confirmed that he had been in God's presence. Like Moses who appeared with him, Jesus by now had demonstrated his mastery over the sea and had fed a multitude in the wilderness. Like Elijah and his successor, Elisha, Jesus by now had multiplied loaves and had cleansed lepers and raised the dead. Like the other occasions on which God spoke approval of him, Jesus once again had been praying. But all of these things weave the transfiguration into the Bible story that was still leading, all along, to the cross.

With millions of Christians around the world and throughout history, we acknowledge the transfiguration as a feast day of the church. But our celebration, our piety, our understanding, will not be true and faithful if we linger on this or any other mountaintop of spiritual experience. The destination is not the mount of the *transfiguration*, but the mount called *Calvary*. The journey's conclusion lies on the far side of Lent, and it involves *us* in Jesus' continuing ministry of lowly servanthood to the sick and the hungry and the oppressed and the sin-burdened—a journey that wins us no spotlight, but focuses *our* attention on Jesus, aglow with the holiness of God that shines even brighter with each miracle of healing, with each gift of bread, with each word of encouragement, with each promise of forgiveness offered by *him*, and offered by *us* in *his* name.

Faithfulness isn't about *revisiting* those spiritual high points in our life. Faithfulness is about trustful obedience *today*. Our spiritual mountaintop experiences are *gifts*, not *goals*. The wondrous majesty of the transfiguration might have been a proper ending for a *fairy tale*. But the story of the *gospel*, the good news, is that, the *next* day, Jesus healed the sick son of a desperate father, and kept journeying on to the cross.

Ash Wednesday
Spanish Springs Presbyterian Church, Sparks, Nevada
February 25, 2004
Isaiah 58:1–14
2 Corinthians 5:20b—6:10
Matthew 6:1–6, 16–21

"The Christian Nation"

VARIOUS EVENTS IN THE headlines over the past several months have ignited once again the debate of whether the United States is a "Christian nation," one based on "Judaeo-Christian" values. There are those who argue that, obviously, several of the American colonies were founded specifically as places of religious refuge and that, obviously, the writers of the Declaration of Independence and the framers of the Constitution presumed and anticipated that Christianity *was* and *would be* the nation's religion. Then there are those who argue that the Declaration of Independence calls for *freedom* in religious matters and that the Constitution does not specify a religious preference and in fact guarantees freedom *from* religion *altogether* for those who want it.

    Be that as it may, since this is an election year, we must anticipate once again in 2004 a contest between candidates and their supporters over who is the most "Christian" candidate. Often, these debates—more usually waged by surrogates than by the candidates themselves, though their campaign offices are of course actively involved—center around who prays the most, or how frequently they quote the Bible, or positions they take on abortion and prayer in public schools, either publicly in the halls of government or just as publicly in the conventions of various organizations. Judging from recent trends, the debate in 2004 will be louder than ever, more caustic than ever, and, since some of the debates regard it as moral warfare, it will likely leave the country more divided and antagonistic than it was before. I cringe at the prospect, both for the nation and for the church. Any partisan attempt to co-opt Jesus as the mascot of a political party or political campaign, I think, is an abomination, and something that I personally find deeply offensive.

More fundamentally problematic, though, is the notion that the Christian character of a society is to be measured in terms of church attendance or references to God in speeches and on statues. Of course, Christian faith presupposes Christian worship. And, of course, a person of faith cannot separate God's commands out of any part of his or her life, public or private. The allegiance we profess on Sunday morning is the allegiance that we should honor the other days of the week. Singing hymns about loving thy neighbor in worship, and then on Monday morning declaring that "business is business" or "war is war" or "the locker room is the locker room" is so patently hypocritical that it would be comical if it were not so tragic.

But Jesus had some rather stiff things to say about *parading* our piety, about *advertising* our righteousness, even when it involves otherwise pious and righteous duties. In the Sermon on the Mount, Jesus warned, "Beware of practicing your piety before others in order to be seen by them" (Matt 6:1a NRSV). Any reward of praise or admiration that we receive from the people around us or even a pat on the back from our own conscience will reduce whatever reward we would have gotten in heaven, Jesus said—we can't have it both ways. "So whenever you give alms, do not sound a trumpet before you, as the hypocrites do in the synagogues and in the streets, so that they may be praised by others. Truly I tell you, they have received their reward. But when you give alms, do not let your left hand know what your right hand is doing, so that your alms may be done in secret; and your Father who sees in secret will reward you" (Matt 6:2–4 NRSV). It doesn't sound, does it, like a candidate for public office should make or allow his or her Christianity to be a campaign issue? Nor should *any* of us draw attention to our religious practices, for if we *do*, then we are taking *pride* in them, and that is totally opposite of what Christ is about, and certainly contrary to the model of humility that Jesus gave us. "Whenever you pray, do not be like the hypocrites; for they love to stand and pray in the synagogues and at the street corners, so that they may be seen by others. Truly I tell you, they have received their reward. But whenever you pray, go into your room and shut the door and pray to your Father who is in secret; and your Father who sees in secret will reward you" (Matt 6:5–6 NRSV).

It isn't a matter of *not doing* these things that people of faith do, or not doing them openly and without apology. The problem lies in doing them in a way that draws attention to ourselves, and thus compromises the purpose of doing them at all, whether it be giving alms, or praying, or fasting—something that many Christians do, especially during Lent. Jesus took for granted that *all* people of faith would do *all* of these things, and not just once a year—give to the poor, pray, *and* fast as a sign of repentance; he didn't say *if* you do these things, but *when* you do these things. "Whenever you fast, do not look dismal, like the hypocrites, for they disfigure their faces so as to show others that they are fasting. Truly I tell you, they have received *their* reward. But when *you* fast, put oil on your head and wash your face, so that your fasting may be seen *not* by *others* but by your *Father* who is in *secret*; and your Father who *sees* in secret will *reward* you" (Matt 6:16–18 NRSV). Give to the poor, pray, yes, and fast. Attend worship, study the Bible, observe the sabbath. But do so out of love and gratitude and obedience to God, not out of love and gratitude and obedience to other people's opinions, or even your own opinion of yourself.

That does not mean, of course, that we should abandon our Christian faith in the voting booth or in the council chamber or in political office. There is not too *much* Christianity reflected in American political life, but too *little*, starting with campaign ads that accuse and ridicule and distort and slander. How could any Christian justify setting aside his or her convictions of faith when it comes time to vote in an election, or propose and vote on legislation, if those convictions have been prayed about, if the positions of the candidates have been considered from the perspective of God's intentions for humankind, if those bills have been discussed with other people of genuine good will who are concerned about all of the effects of this or that policy, not only on the nation in general but on the whole world and on the life of each individual, not only on the human scale but on the entirety of God's creation, not just for immediate political advantage but for the permanent public good? How could any Christian rationalize surrendering his or her convictions of faith to a particular ideology or party line or economic theory or polling trend, if those convictions are grounded in having been baptized into the death and resurrection of Jesus Christ and the yoke of humble servanthood that draws us toward the cross, regarding *others* as *better* than *ourselves* and *every bit* as deserving of God's blessings as *we* are and recognizing that *none* of us has *earned* those blessings but that they come *solely* on the basis of God's *grace* and are given for the purpose of being *shared*? Republican, Democrat, liberal, conservative, moderate, independent, Libertarian, Reform, Socialist, or Green—not one of those labels is superior to the allegiance required by God, and not one of those labels is synonymous with it. And although professing one's faith and worshiping God is an indispensable part of Christianity, the Christian character of a nation cannot be measured by labels or by church attendance any more than it can be measured by mottoes on money or statues in courthouses.

About twenty-five hundred years ago, a nation founded on faith in God, a nation that recognized as its basic law the commandments that had been handed down from God to the people through Moses, was collectively scratching its head in bewildered puzzlement. Judah had been through hard times—it had been invaded by the armies of pagan Babylon, its cities had been destroyed and its farmlands had been ruined and its leading citizens had been carted off into exile and then had been allowed to *return* to Judah and *rebuild* the cities and *restore* the farms. And along with that, the people had once again resumed their religious life of worship in the newly-reconstructed temple. Remembering that the destruction of their nation had been a *judgment* upon their *sin* and a *punishment* for it, now they were repenting by even fasting each year on the dates that commemorated the beginning of the siege of Jerusalem and the capture of Jerusalem and the destruction of Jerusalem and the burning of the first temple and the assassination of Gedaliah the governor. Still, the nation had not returned to its former prosperity. Still, the nation had not regained its former glory. Still, the nation was mired in a spiritual malaise. Its citizens were performing all of the rituals. They were telling themselves that they were a religious people. They spent a lot of effort, apparently, taking their spiritual pulse. "Yet day after day they seek me and delight to know my ways," God said in the book of Isaiah,

> *as if* they were a nation that practiced righteousness
>   and did not forsake the ordinance of their God;
> they ask of me righteous judgments,
>   they delight to draw near to God.
> "Why do we fast, but you do not see?
>   Why humble ourselves, but you do not notice?" (Isa 58:2–3a NRSV)

the people complained.

"Look," God answered, "you serve your *own* interest on your fast day, and oppress all your workers" (Isa 58:3b NRSV). What was happening, in essence, was that the *executives* were going to church on the sabbath, but making their employees *work* on the sabbath. The captains of industry were practicing their piety in the temple, saying their prayers, giving their alms, and observing their fasts, even as they were forcing their employees to work longer and work harder. So the more they pointed to their own piety, the less faithful they were being. The more holy days they celebrated, the greater was the actual distance between their religious observance and the things that were pleasing to God. The more they *gave* to charity, the more their workers and their tenants *needed* their charity.

> Is such the fast that I choose,
>   a day to humble oneself?
> Is it to bow down the head like a bulrush,
>   and to lie in sackcloth and ashes?

> Will you call *this* a *fast*,
>> a day acceptable to the Lord?
> Is not *this* the fast that *I* choose:
>> to loose the bonds of injustice,
>> to undo the thongs of the yoke,
> to let the oppressed go free,
>> and to break every yoke?
> Is it not to share your bread with the hungry,
>> and bring the homeless poor into your house;
> when you see the naked, to cover them,
>> and not to hide yourself from your own kin?
> *Then* your light shall break forth like the dawn,
>> and your healing shall spring up quickly;
> your vindicator shall go before you,
>> the glory of the Lord shall be your rear guard.
> *Then* you shall call, and the Lord will answer;
>> you shall cry for help, and he will say, Here I am. . . .
> If you offer your food to the hungry
>> and satisfy the needs of the afflicted,
> then your light shall rise in the darkness
>> and your gloom be like the noonday. (Isa 58:5–9a, 10 NRSV)

But the darkness continued, and the gloom persisted.

The measure of a nation's faithfulness is not how many of its people, or how many of its leaders, *say* they *believe* in *God*, or attend worship weekly, or pray daily. The more accurate gauge of whether a nation is being faithful, the prophets said, is how many of its people are hungry and homeless, the disparity between the rich and the poor, the care given to the young and the old and the sick and the widowed and the orphaned, the hospitality shown to the stranger, the fairness and dignity accorded to the worker. And,

> *if* you refrain from trampling the sabbath,
>> from pursuing your *own* interests on my holy day;
> *if* you call the sabbath a delight
>> and the holy day of the Lord honorable;
> *if* you honor it, not going your *own* ways,
>> serving your *own* interests, or pursuing your *own* affairs;
> *then* you shall take delight in the Lord,
>> and I will make you ride upon the heights of the earth;
> I will feed you with the heritage of your ancestor Jacob,
>> for the mouth of the Lord has spoken. (Isa 58:13–14 NRSV)

God is not impressed by increasing economic productivity if the workers are in poverty or are too busy or too tired to honor the sabbath. Jesus condemned worship that draws attention to the worshiper, and the prophets before him condemned worship that is considered a substitute for treating workers with respect and dealing justly with the poor, but neither Jesus nor the prophets denied the *importance* of worship; quite the opposite.

Various events in the headlines over the past several months have ignited once again the debate over whether the United States is a "Christian nation," one based on "Judaeo-Christian" values. And, since this is an election year, we must anticipate once again in 2004 a contest between candidates and their supporters over who is the most "Christian" candidate. The answer will not be found in counting the number of people who walk in and out of churches, or the number of times the candidates sprinkle their speeches with references to God. Such statistics do not interest God; sitting in a church pew does not make a person a Christian, and those campaign speeches are for the purpose of reaping an earthly reward. I encourage you to use this Lent as a time for prayer, for study, for worship, for repentance, for daily activities that *reflect* our faith and respond to *God's* measurement of our faith. God sees faithfulness in such basic things as keeping the sabbath holy and sharing what God has generously given us to feed the hungry and house the homeless and clothe the naked, and *not* for *human praise*, but because that's what a *Christian*, and a Christian *nation*, does.

First Sunday in Lent
First Presbyterian Church, Dodge City, Kansas
March 5, 1995
Genesis 2:4b–9, 15–17, 25—3:7
Romans 5:12–19
Luke 4:1–13

"Living in Sin, Living by Grace"

IN MY LAST FEW months as associate pastor at another church, I served with an interim pastor as head of staff, a balding, white-haired man about six foot four, a progressive individual with a down-home wisdom which he sometimes expressed rather bluntly. One day near the end of my tenure at that church, I received a telephone call from a young woman requesting a meeting to discuss becoming a member of that congregation. Since I was only going to be working there for a short while longer, I suggested that she come to the office to meet not just with me, but also with the interim pastor, who would be remaining at the church for a few months more. When she arrived for the meeting, the three of us sat in the pastor's study—the interim pastor nearing retirement, this very attractive college-age woman, and me—and we discussed some of the beliefs of the Presbyterian Church and the Reformed faith. Eventually, she disclosed that she was living with a man who was separated from his wife, and with the man's young child, and asked us, "Do you accept into membership people who are living in sin?" Our interim pastor looked at her and responded, "Young lady, you were living in sin long before you moved in with your boyfriend."

The point that the interim pastor was making was twofold: the human creature is sinful, regardless of the particular ways in which sin is manifested; and that sinfulness is with us throughout life, infecting all our thoughts and relationships. He was not condoning her living arrangements. He was disabusing the young woman of any suggestion that one particular act had made her a sinner in need of God's grace. For she was not a sinner simply because of her sexual activity. According to scripture, we are, all of us, living in sin.

We have a tendency to regard sin as a particular sort of action, a certain habit or deed, something that we can easily identify in the life of another person, something that we are perhaps less willing to acknowledge in our own life. It's rather convenient to be able to classify actions, to label this person's behavior as "sin," and label that person's behavior as "not sin." There is an attractive neatness about such precision, and a sort of personal pride and self-confidence that if we can refrain from certain acts, then we will be innocent of the charge of being a sinner. If we can just master our behavior, we tell ourselves, if we can refrain from a particular activity, then we are free from sin. The Bible includes several catalogues of behavior which it condemns as sinful, although none of them is intended to be an exclusive listing. But Paul shows in our reading from Romans, and the same point is made clear in the second and third chapters of Genesis, that sin is not merely something done or left undone. Even if we refrain from certain specific actions, there is no way that we can save *ourselves* from sin and the consequences of sin.

There *is* no other reference to the story of the garden in Eden in either the Old Testament or in the teachings of Jesus. Through the centuries, it has been interpreted as standing for many doctrines which are in fact nowhere mentioned in Genesis, all the way from the inferiority of women to the evils of sex, from the reason for death to the concept of "original sin." But a close reading of the text discloses that the *point* of the story is clearly *not* that women are subordinate to men, or that sex is intrinsically bad, nor even that we are sinful because somebody *before* us was sinful. The point of the story is that humankind, created in God's own image, created to live in harmony with and obey the Creator, has an inveterate tendency to listen to the heart's ambition to go its own direction, and this rebellious way has an evil end.

In the paradise of which Genesis speaks, humankind had received all that it needed from the caring and gentle hand of God. God had asked only that they care for the garden, and had instructed them not to eat of the fruit of but one single tree—a tree purporting to offer wisdom about what is and what is not beneficial to humankind. But when men and women accepted the suggestion that they could *transgress* God's limits with *impunity*, when they began to assume that they could know for *themselves* what was best, rather than trusting *God*, the end of paradise was in sight. For failure to trust God with our lives leads to death, which is separation from God. Presented with the possibility that they might seek a wisdom *equal* to that of God, that they might make their *own* rules for living, humankind confused trust in God with ignorance, and obedience to God's will with bondage. We still do that, each of us, in various ways. The disobedience of Adam and Eve discloses the fatal truth that we human beings are continually disobeying our

Creator and rejecting any limits on our thought and speech and behavior; we challenge our calling to till and keep the garden, we show ingratitude for the invitation to enjoy the earth, we transgress the boundaries which God has established. And then we wonder why we are so often in such misery and why we cause others so much pain.

Life can be blessed only where it is lived in accordance with God's will. The writer of this part of Genesis discerned through faith that the destiny of the human creature is to live in *God's* world, not in a world of our own making. It is to live with God's creatures, which we are to rule but also to care for. And it is to live according to the terms which God, in divine wisdom, has established, content with what God has given us and thankful for it. The story is that Adam and Eve quarreled with the world as they found it, quarreled with the restrictions which God placed on their freedom. They wanted to remake creation in the image of their *own* desires, rather than accept gratefully the world as God ordained it.

Scripture declares that we were made in God's image, to operate in God's world in accordance with God's will. That's paradise—not these popular notions of a place where the fruit falls off of the tree into our hands, where gluttony is a virtue, where we are free to do as we want whenever we please, regardless of how it affects others, regardless of the damage done to the rest of creation. Paradise is not a place; it is the state of living in harmony with God and with God's creation, living according to God's will as we fulfill our vocation and enjoy God's invitation and respect God's boundaries. But *we* want to reach out and grasp the fruit of the tree of knowledge and become our *own* gods, *equal* to our Creator. What Adam and Eve are said to have done is what *we* want to do, and at its very core, that is to worship and obey *another* god than the God who created us. What we really want is to idolize ourselves.

The moment that we rebel against God's rule, the moment that we assert our own self-importance, the moment that we pursue our own ungoverned desires, in that instant is paradise lost; in that instant are we living in sin. And life breaks up into little egocentric fragments and we fall into anxiety and discord and bondage—anxiety in the doubting of God's providence, rejecting God's promise of care, thinking that we must guarantee our own well-being, as if there could be *any* security apart from God; discord in our alienation from God, an alienation which taints all of our relationships with suspicion and distrust and self-centeredness; bondage in the irony that, for the sake of *freedom*, we imprison the soul in the chaos of our conflicting desires. So we amass our fortunes, and build our bombs, and crave our pleasures; we erect altars to our egos and manipulate others and even try to deceive God, and all the while, sense that paradise is slipping even farther away.

We run from God ashamed, lonely, and frightened, pitiful little creatures who were *designed* to be the crowning glory of God's creation and the supreme object of God's love. When God finally hunts us down, we make excuses that it was all a mistake, someone else's doing—"It was the woman—she gave me the fruit of the tree." Ultimately, we complain that it was really God's fault all along—"The woman whom *you* gave to be with me" (Gen 3:12a NRSV). We protest, "Why did *you*, God, create us to be *subject* to temptation? And knowing that we *could* be tempted, why did you ever choose to put us in such a perilous garden?" Well, we might wish for a garden without such dangers, but that isn't the way it is, for whatever reason. The real problem remains not the world in which God has *placed* us, but the twisted perspective that we share with Adam and Eve, that obedience to the law of God is merely an *option*, and that God is an obstacle between what we *have* and what we *want*. And so, we begin to regard God as someone to be circumvented rather than obeyed. It is just as true of Pharisees as of libertines, really. By what right has God forbidden us anything that looks appetizing and beautiful—anything that we think might make life more enjoyable and more fulfilling? Surely we are just as capable, perhaps more so, of deciding for ourselves; certainly we would do better as our *own* authority than being obedient to God. We begin to believe, as the serpent suggested, that God's judgment is an idle threat. Perhaps God is simply an *imagined* Creator, only a paper tiger.

Adam and Eve desired to be "like God" (Gen 3:5 NRSV). That is not an unreasonable goal *if* it means being like God in character, *if* it means bending to God's will. But the serpent's suggestion in the story, and the human desire throughout history, is that we can take God's place. And so we violate God's prohibitions, we pervert God's gracious invitation, and we neglect the vocation of stewardship which God has given us, as we focus our interest on ourselves and on the freedom that we claim. The forbidden fruit brings us knowledge indeed—knowledge that there is no real security apart from the Creator whom we have rejected and obedience to him. We discover our nakedness before the dispassionate eyes of the universe and our nakedness before the cold winds of a life without God. And we discover the loneliness and terror that come with it.

The apostle Paul understood very well that sin is alienation from God, and that sin sends out ripples in all directions that eventually become tidal waves capsizing our feeble efforts at self-salvation and crashing upon the shores of our relationships with friends and family and sweethearts and fellow workers. Paul knew that sin is not merely specific identifiable actions and inactions, but something that permeates all of human life. He realized that the sacrifice of God's Son was not simply for the purpose of smoothing over our moral slip-ups. He understood that even our attempts to *overcome* our sin are the products of supposing that by "trying harder" we can bring about our own reconciliation with God, supposing that our final hope for redemption lies *not* in *God*, but within *us*.

But the effects of sin are so great that only *God* could overcome them. And the gospel is the proclamation of God's powerful resolve to repair the alienation between humankind and himself, to *redeem* his beloved creation, to *correct* the effects of our idolatry, to *rescue* us from the death that we have chosen in the name of freedom. And *this* he has *done* by sending his own Son, who resisted the temptation to serve himself, who resisted the temptation to rule his life by any other standard than God's will. Jesus trusted totally in God's own gracious care, and, by doing so, accomplished what neither Adam nor we *could* accomplish: saving us from ourselves and from our readiness to serve one *other* than God.

We live in sin—each one of us. And not even by "trying harder" can we bring about reconciliation with our Creator. Our habitual disobedience to God *should* move us to *penitence*. But how much more should we *praise* God for the abundant grace showered upon us in the gift of his *Son*—grace which buries our sin under an avalanche of forgiveness! God's undeserved love has given us new hope in Jesus Christ. We live *in sin*. But we live *by grace*.

Second Sunday in Lent
Spanish Springs Presbyterian Church, Sparks, Nevada
March 11, 2001
Genesis 15:1–12, 17–18
Philippians 3:17—4:1
Luke 13:31–35

"Beyond Touch and Sight"

"Almighty God, in Jesus Christ you promised many rooms within your house. Give us faith to see, beyond touch and sight, some sure sign of your kingdom, and, where vision fails, to trust your love which never fails."[1] So reads the prayer of supplication in our Presbyterian service of witness to the resurrection—the order of worship for funerals and memorial services. I think the phrase "beyond touch and sight" well captures the essence of faith, and also suggests why some people find it so difficult to *develop* faith. And here, I do not speak only of non-Christians and people outside the church, but even quite a few folks who identify themselves as Christians, people who may be regular in worship attendance and who are avid readers of the Bible, even people who are generous contributors to the church mission budget and who freely offer themselves to serve on this committee and that. Many people have strong beliefs and convictions which yet never attain to the level of faith; they have mastered the vocabulary and the piety, perhaps, but they have never made the leap of trust beyond the alarming headlines and the discouraging ledger sheets. Faith involves more than reciting stories from scripture and drawing moralisms from them; it requires learning to trust God's promise.

The words "beyond touch and sight" are particularly appropriate for funerals and memorial services, when reality all seems grimly colored with the shadow of death—when disease or accident or depression or rage has left an empty shell, cold and motionless, sterile and senseless, where a

---

1. *Book of Common Worship*, 922.

unique and vibrant personality used to be. Scientific instruments and hospital monitors only confirm what our own touch and sight have already told us—the life of our parent, our spouse, our child, our friend, is gone. All the physical evidence points to the same conclusion.

But all the physical evidence somehow cannot take away our protest that something so good as life should not simply end, nor can it abrogate the word of the very one whom we believe first brought that life into being. Death is a deceiver; in spite of appearances, it is beyond comprehension that something so real as human life can come to an abrupt and total conclusion. And so, in the face of death, we ask God to help us discern a reality truer than what our senses tell us, a reality beyond touch and sight, a reality which conforms to the promises that we have heard about God's love and about God's care and about God's being in control, a reality for which we have never felt the need to hope so keenly. And when the assurance overtakes appearances, when the hope becomes mightier than the grief, when the peace becomes stronger than the pain, when the eternal promise becomes truer for us than the sorrow of the moment, then we know that the faith for which we prayed has blossomed. Then we become aware of a reality more genuine even than the one we can handle and see.

We live in a time that in many ways is unique in human history—not the least so because of the emphasis it places upon the human senses. About two hundred fifty years ago, more or less, human fascination with the scientific method launched Europe and eventually the entire Western world into what historians refer to as "the Enlightenment." With roots in the discoveries of Galileo and Newton, the laws of motion and gravity, the way in which people looked at the world around them and thought of the created order changed radically as all of nature came to be tested by human reason and yielded predictable results. Suddenly, the human eye and the human ear and the human finger and the human mind became the chief authorities in the task of defining reality. Our thought patterns and categories of experience were fundamentally and forever changed by the principles of scientific observation.

It is not evil, and, in any case, there is no going back to the pre-scientific age. It is not anti-Christian—in fact, Newton regarded his scientific discoveries as a defense of the Christian faith. And, although they may rage against the claims of science, fundamentalists and even the so-called "creationists" are as inescapably children of modern science as anybody, and they now advance their arguments in the language of scientific method and observation. Humankind has always been inclined to make itself the standard by which all things are measured. But during the last quarter millennium, the observations of the human senses and the conclusions of the human mind have become the standard for perceiving and testing God's creative and redemptive reality, rather than permitting God's creative and redemptive reality to govern our human perspective and test our human reason. So it has become more difficult for us to trust to a reality that cannot be touched and cannot be seen, but not because that *reality* has changed. So it has become more difficult to have faith in the promises of God, but not because the *promises* have changed.

The Bible speaks of many people who came to faith and acted upon faith—people faced with the appearance of bleakness but finding a reality of hope, people practiced in despair but discovering joy. For several, the journey was made long by their own stubborn skepticism and doubt. For some, the first springs of faith broadened quickly into oceans of blessing. For others, steadfast and unwavering faith yielded what, by the reckoning of scientific observation, seems but a paltry return for long years of expectancy. But for all of these people, faith brought a life-transforming change in perspective and values, and a new reliance on divine promises over human judgments. No longer were the world and all its ambiguities their primary source of data, but heaven. No longer were fickle human expectation and limited human experience the ultimate test of reality, but God's steadfast purpose. "Our citizenship is in heaven," Paul reminded the faith-full Christians in Philippi, "and it is from [heaven] that we are expecting a Savior, the Lord Jesus Christ" (Phil 3:20 NRSV). The permanent address of people of faith, the home office to which they report, is the realm where God's promise is the peerless truth, where reality is measured not by the dimensions of the human mind but by the dimensions of God's heart, where the stubborn facts of human experience are no match for the stubborn fact of God's love.

Once, in a far more primitive time, a nomadic shepherd heard the voice of the Lord speak to him. "Go from your country and your kindred and your father's house to the land that I will show you. I will make of you a great nation, and I will bless you, and make your name great, so that you will be a blessing" (Gen 12:1b–2 NRSV). And he went as the Lord said, taking his wife and his whole household into the land which the Lord showed him. But the years went by, and he and his wife grew old, beyond the age when a woman is able to conceive and bear children. It seemed as if the promise had failed, for how could the man's name be great or his people become a nation if he should die childless? From his human perspective of observation and experience, the thing was hopeless. The Lord spoke to him again.

> "Do not be afraid, Abram, I am your shield; your reward shall be very great." But Abram said, "O Lord God, what will you give me, for I continue childless. . . . You have given me no offspring."

> ... But the word of the LORD came to him, ... "Your very own issue shall be your heir." He brought him outside and said, "Look toward heaven and count the stars, if you are able to count them." Then he said to him, "So shall your descendants be." And [Abram] believed the LORD; and the LORD reckoned it to him as righteousness. (Gen 15:1b–2a, 3a, 4–6 NRSV)

By and by, Sarah his wife did conceive, "and bore Abraham a son in his old age, at the time of which God had spoken to him" (Gen 21:2 NRSV). And the descendants of Abraham grew in number and became a great nation, all despite the very persuasive *human* evidence which argued that the promise of God was foolish, that it was impossible.

The story of Abraham and Sarah is one of faith in the faithfulness of God—of trusting God's promises and acting upon them. At first, Abraham resisted coming to faith. All the evidence seemed against the promise—all those years, Sarah had been barren, and now the two of them were so far beyond being able to conceive a child! The fruitful promise of God stood over against the discouraging bleakness of the landscape. There was not the slightest glimmer of hope on the horizon, but there were stars in the sky. "Look toward heaven," God had said to Abraham. "Look at the stars, how many there are. I am the LORD who brought you from Ur of the Chaldeans, to give you this land to possess. My promise did not fail you then. And if I can make stars without number, do you not suppose that I can cause a son to be conceived in your barrenness, and so fulfill the promise that I have made to you that your name shall be great and you shall be the father of a great nation? Fear not. Those stars in the heavens shall be a sign of my pledge to you. Have faith to see beyond touch and sight. Trust in my promises. Risk on my promises. Rely upon my promises. And you will discover blessings more numerous even than the stars. And you will be a blessing for countless others."

So the God who made the stars beyond number also gave this barren family a son so that they might possess the land and become a great nation, and we understand no more about the one than about the other. Having repented of his doubt, Abraham trusted the promise, risked all the future on it, and had faith that God really *is* God, who brought creation into being out of nothing, who brings hope into being out of despair, who brings joyful blessings out of discouraging facts, who brings life into existence where there was no life before. And every moment of life is blessed with the potential of being a genesis, a beginning, a new thing born in the creative medium of God's redemptive purpose. Flesh and blood, touch and sight, had not revealed God's reality to Abraham, but *faith*.

What hopeless barrenness is haunting your life, robbing it of the fullness of joy which is our inheritance as God's creation? Is it a rebellious child, whose destructive behavior no amount of human reason can seem to penetrate? Is it an alcoholic spouse, whose downward spiral no amount of human pleading can seem to arrest? Is it the threatened loss of a job, which seems to be the end of any security and the end of any self-esteem? Is it a financial crisis, expense upon expense, which seems to have no possibility of solution? Is it a death or a divorce, which seems devastating to your ability ever to cope again with the task of living? "Fear not!" God's word rings through the pages of scripture and into every broken relationship and into every discouraging circumstance. "Fear not!" God's word embraces every sigh and every tear. "Fear not!" God's word reaches into every cold heart and every cold tomb. "Fear not!" God says to us. "There is a truer reality beyond what you are able to touch and beyond what you are able to see. It is the reality of my redeeming love which will not let my creation be destroyed and will not let my purpose be defeated. Do not lose hope, but trust, risk, and rely upon my promise. Have I not created every star in the heavens, stars beyond number? Did I not open Sarah's womb even in her old age, as I promised? Did I not deliver my people up out of slavery in Egypt and bring them into a land where they multiplied and prospered, as I promised? Did I not send to you my anointed one, my Messiah, as I promised? And did I not raise him from the dead to new life in the resurrection? My reality stretches past human senses and human reason," says God. "It reaches even beyond bolted doors and sealed graves. Stand fast against the hopelessness and despair of death. Trust in my promises of life. For your citizenship is in heaven, which lies beyond the limits of touch and sight."

Faith is the conviction of the goodness of God's promise in spite of the way the world is. It does not ignore present conditions, it does not dismiss physical needs. But it discerns in the purpose of God how out of place are human sorrow and brokenness, illness and death, disappointment and despair. Almighty God, in Jesus Christ you turned the deep darkness of our longest night into the brilliant brightness of a new day. Give us faith to see beyond touch and sight some sure sign of your kingdom, and, where vision fails, to trust your love which never fails. Amen.

Third Sunday in Lent
Spanish Springs Presbyterian Church, Sparks, Nevada
March 14, 2004
Isaiah 55:1–9
1 Corinthians 10:1–13
Luke 13:1–9

"Water for the Spirit, Bread for the Soul"

IT WAS PERHAPS THE most notorious case of abduction since the Lindbergh kidnapping. Wealthy heiress, college student Patty Hearst, was taken from her apartment by a radical organization that called itself the "Symbionese Liberation Army." The story dominated the news for weeks in the late winter and early spring of 1974, exactly thirty years ago. The nation was incensed, outraged, stunned that such a thing could happen, even as it exposed what was then a still uncommon living arrangement between the attractive young coed and her college instructor boyfriend. He, and her parents, pleaded for Patty's safe return as reporters informed the country about the nefarious doings of the shadowy SLA. And then, one day, there was a bank robbery, and the surprise of seeing Patty Hearst caught on a bank surveillance camera, holding a rifle, and then the taped statement from the daughter of one of America's most famous capitalists denouncing the American economic and political system.

Speculation ran rampant about how she had been forced to participate in the bank heist, how she had been coerced into making such a public indictment of the very culture that had bestowed upon her such privileges. "Threatened," many people said. "Brainwashed," many other people concluded. But as the tale unfolded, the nation learned some things about the psychology of captivity—how people who are abducted and held against their will oftentimes come to identify with the logic of their abductors, how those who have been captive frequently end up adopting the values of their captors. And so, in the end, Patty Hearst was not *freed* by the police, she was *arrested* by the police, along with others of the revolutionists, whose crimes by then included murder.

Something like that seems to have happened to some of the captive Israelites in Babylon. At first, they mourned the destruction of their homeland and grieved their captivity far from the promised land, far from Mount Zion, far from the temple which now was in ruins. They wondered how they could worship the God of their ancestors Abraham and Sarah, Isaac and Rebekah, Jacob and Rachel, in the land of King Nebuchadnezzar. They were distraught and chagrined that their nation had been conquered and they had been taken into exile and that prophets were saying that it was all God's judgment upon their faithlessness. Nothing was good about where they had been taken, and what they had lost was suddenly dearer to them because they had been deprived of it.

But over time, something happened, to many of them, at least. We don't have a written history of the Babylonian exile of the Jewish people, but the evidence in the scriptures suggests that, over the years, many of the captives must have adapted to their new situation. A new generation was born in exile that had not experienced a land of their own, that had never worshiped in the temple, for whom Israel was not a personal memory but an inherited story. And some of their parents, even, seem to have *cooperated* with their captors to the point that they were permitted to open shops, to engage in business, to own homes, to amass fortunes.

Worse than that, in the opinion of the *prophets* among them, they had forgotten that the God of their *ancestors* was the only *true* God, that the *purpose* of God was their only *legitimate* destiny, that the *worship* of God was the only *acceptable* homage, that the *commandments* of God were the only *right* way to behave. The gods of Mesopotamia were only idols carved from wood and chiseled from stone, the decrees of Nebuchadnezzar were not the blueprints for their future, the religion of their Babylonian captors was to be shunned as rank disloyalty to the God who had graciously led them from captivity in Egypt to freedom in their promised land, the immoralities of their abductors were poison to their soul. They were abandoning their allegiance to God and surrendering to the fleshpots of Mesopotamia, valuing their economic interests over their spiritual welfare, bending their national aspirations to political expediency, trading the convictions of their souls for the pleasures and comforts and amusements and conveniences of a culture built on the foundations of war and lust and conquest and greed.

From *outside* the walls of Babylon, they had recognized it for what it truly was—tyranny, lewdness, falsehood. From *inside* the walls of their prison, some of them came to think it was paradise. If you just had money enough, and power enough, Babylon offered anything that the flesh craved, and no contrition required. Perhaps they thought, some of them, that the old rules of Israel no longer applied to them in a foreign land—"What happens here, stays here," as one modern chamber of commerce sells its city, rather appallingly. But in the long run, the prophets knew, the experience of exile in Babylon was having a corrosive effect upon a people who had sworn allegiance to the God who refused to coddle them with frivolous luxuries, but dependably provided all their necessities; the God who had not made them a mighty empire, but had long protected them against all their foes; the God who denied them license to satisfy their lust and greed, but had steadfastly tutored them in the ways of personal righteousness and communal integrity.

> Ho, everyone who thirsts,
>   come to the waters;
> and you that have no money,
>   come, buy and eat! . . .
> Why do you spend your money for that which is *not* bread,
>   and your labor for that which does *not* satisfy? (Isa 55:1a, 2a NRSV)

The Israelites in exile were working hard, and some of them, at least, were living the Babylonian dream. But the Babylonian dream was not God's purpose for them. There were vendors in the streets selling everything that a person could possibly want, wine and milk, perhaps peddling even water and bread from carts. These were good things, and necessary for living. But the seductions of a material, consumerist culture were pulling the Israelites away from God, and away from the destiny that God had appointed for them many centuries before when he summoned Abraham to a journey of faith, when he liberated the people from slavery in Egypt, when he fed them in the desert, when he gave them the commandments to live by, when he settled them in a land that was fertile and secure, when he blessed them with enough—not excess, but enough—and told them to rely on his loving care and provision and not run after riches or hoard food but to share it all with each other and even foreigners, and especially the poor, because God could be depended upon always to provide sufficient for everyone. The living God had promised these things, and now the people whom the living God had made a nation for his own glory were forgetting the temple and bowing down to the Babylonian deities, not only the statues and the idols, but the goals of wealth and the dictates of the senses. And they were undoubtedly discovering that the more wealth they accumulated, the more they wanted. And the more they gave themselves to physical pleasure and comfort, the more they craved. For when such things become one's ambition, one's reason for living, then one's appetite is never satisfied; the thirst is never quenched, the hunger is never filled. The focus shifts from pleasing God and caring for others, and settles on "me," and our gods become whatever promises to make "me" richer and prouder and more thoroughly self-indulged.

Our Old Testament reading this morning is a plea to God's people not to surrender to the ways of Babylon and lose their souls in a spiritual wasteland. And the irony of it was that so many of them were fretting away their lives in Babylon striving for bigger cars and bigger houses, while God stood anxiously ready to fulfill the promise of caring for them by providing all they needed back in Judah if they would set their hearts not on acquiring things but abiding in God, not on living "the good life" but on living rightly and *doing* good. Had they forgotten that they had been taken *captive* to Babylon, that for all the material things they had *acquired* there, it was still a *prison* for their *bodies*, and was now becoming *perdition* for their *souls*? When they were first brought to Babylon, their bodies were prisoners but their spirits were still free. But the more they bought into Babylon's culture of *things*, the more their spirits were becoming bound with chains of pride and lust and greed. When they were first brought to Babylon, their thoughts and yearnings were all for returning to Israel and the God whom they wished they had never disobeyed. Now some of them no longer cared. The ethics of self-advancement and self-assertion threatened to replace the ethics of grateful devotion and humble obedience, and while some of them had never had it so good, measured in terms of bulging bank accounts and overflowing pantries, for that very reason their souls had never been in greater jeopardy.

God's call through the prophet was gracious but urgent. It was not too late, but almost. Their surrender to the habits of materialism and the worship of things was not complete, but it was far advanced.

> Seek the LORD while he may be found,
>   call upon him while he is near;
> let the wicked forsake their way,
>   and the unrighteous their thoughts;
> let them return to the LORD, that he may have mercy on them,
>   and to our God, for he will abundantly pardon. (Isa 55:6–7b NRSV)

How had things come to that state? How had the people of God become so distant from God's purpose? We can judge the seductive enticements of Babylon as ungodly much more easily in retrospect than the people could identify them at the time. No doubt they were only subtle little compromises with the culture at first—a little jealousy of the neighbor's this or that, a little concern about what might happen if business fell off a bit that prompted putting away a little something for a "rainy day," a little immodest experiment with dress. And as more and more people made the little compromises, things that didn't seem to matter much, some started compromising more, and so on, until the old ways of Israel seemed quaint and the worship of Israel's God seemed old-fashioned and the very purpose for Israel's *being* gradually became irrelevant in the exhausting race to *acquire* the most and *eat* the most and *drink* the most and enjoy the most *pleasure,* no matter the cost to *others,* no matter the cost to one's *soul*. What Paul wrote many centuries later to the Christians at Corinth was not far from the sentiment of what the prophet proclaimed to the Israelites in Babylon: "So if you think you are standing, watch out that you do not fall" (1 Cor 10:12 NRSV).

No one should waste their lives running after that which does not quench our deepest thirst, that which does not satisfy our greatest hunger, that which is unwholesome and, in the end, is useless. Yet so many people in our time and place do just that, and it is almost always the case that the more we run after such toys, such frivolities, such pleasures, to stake our claim on them, the farther we eventually find ourselves away from God, even in some faraway exile that we are busy convincing each other is paradise when in fact it is a prison. And some of us may even begin to doubt that God is important, that God's promises are true, that God's commands are for our own good. In Jesus Christ, God has given most abundantly what God has offered all along—water for the spirit and bread for the soul that don't *have* to be *bought,* in fact *can't* be, and that don't *need* to be *hoarded* and *shouldn't* be, for they are always available and are given to make us more generous and more trusting. The more we *acquire,* the more we think we *need*; the more pleasures and comforts we *get,* the more we think we *deserve*; the more we think we have found *paradise,* the more deeply *imprisoned* we have become—to greed, to pride, to lust, to debt, to economics that cannot save and politics that cannot redeem and a culture of things that cannot fill the empty places in our soul that are yawning bigger with every vain attempt to stuff them. The prophet testifies, it's not a matter of money; it's not a question even of our deserving.

> Why do you spend your money for that which is *not* bread,
>   and your labor for that which does *not* satisfy?
> Listen carefully to me, and eat what is good,
>   and delight yourselves in rich food.
> Incline your ear, and come to me;
>   listen, so that you may live. . . .
> Seek the Lord while he may be found,
>   call upon him while he is near;
> let the wicked forsake their way,
>   and the unrighteous their thoughts;

> let them return to the Lord, that he may have mercy on them,
>> and to our God, for he will abundantly pardon. (Isa 55:2–3a, 6–7 NRSV)

Don't confuse your prison with the promised land. Don't mistake your captivity for freedom. Remember the only one who provides water for your spirit and bread for your soul. Come to the Lord.

Fourth Sunday in Lent
Grace Presbyterian Church, Plano, Texas
March 9, 1986
Joshua 5:9–12
2 Corinthians 5:16–21
Luke 15:1–3, 11–32

"Return from a Far Country"

THE STORY OF THE prodigal, or prodigals, is perhaps the most vividly dramatic parable in the Bible. It is one of the so-called "parables of the lost" that make up the fifteenth chapter of Luke, told by Jesus in Jerusalem, where the final act of his earthly ministry was to be played, and God's plan of salvation was to be accomplished. Jesus had *already* been rejected by the religious leaders. By restoring sight to the blind, he had angered those who could *see*, yet had no *vision*. By healing the sick, he had offended those who were *healthy* in *body* but whose *souls* were in need of a *physician*. By fulfilling the *law*, he had *judged* those who pridefully kept its *letter* but stifled its *spirit*. Jesus was aware of what it was to be weighed on a human scale and be found wanting. In a few days, he would know the full measure of society's condemnation and wrath, the result of human pride, jealousy, and fear.

But there were some who listened with hungering soul to what Jesus said in those final days—not to catch some misstatement to justify charges against him, not to prove him an enemy of Israel. They listened to find solace, to restore hope, and to receive good news. They came to hear Jesus not because they thought themselves smarter than those who rejected him, or because they were more holy. They came for just the opposite reasons—because they were needy, powerless to make themselves right in the eyes of God. They came because they recognized that they were sinful, broken, and estranged from the source of life. They came because they knew that they were lost.

Many of us, when we read or hear the world "lost," think immediately of the word "found," as when we have located something that we have misplaced. But the word "lost" has another sense, a more subjective sense, meaning the opposite of "where we belong." This is the meaning for the *person* who is lost—one who is miles away from those who care the most and from the warm familiar surroundings, one who is without bearings, confused, fearful, perhaps panicked, one who just wants to come home.

We are aware of the problem of lost children in our country. Some of them, we know, have been removed from their homes against their will. Many more, we have learned, have left home on their own. Some are fleeing the cruelty or neglect of parents. Many are trying to escape personal troubles. Others are answering the call to adventure, what we used to call "running away to join the circus," only now it often revolves around sex and drugs. By the time they learn the harsh truth of the emptiness of such a life, these children are frequently too scared to return home, afraid that only judgment and condemnation await them. Perhaps more than that, embarrassed by their own behavior, they are too ashamed to face their families.

Many of you know how necessary it is in developing human character for parents to maintain that tension between guidance and freedom—the need for a parent to show approval of accomplishment and acceptance of failure, to correct misbehavior while continuing to be affectionate, loving as a parent should love. Jesus most often referred to God as "Father," and just as his life revealed new depths of the meaning of sonship, so his teaching about God offered new breadth of meaning for fatherhood.

By Jewish custom, the younger of two sons could expect to inherit one-third of his father's possessions, while the older son would receive two-thirds. Jesus told of a young man who asked for an accounting of *his* share of the inheritance while the father was still alive. That was not unusual, and it does not suggest any discord between father and son. A few days later, the son left and journeyed into a far country, away from the familiar comforts and restraints of home. He wasted *his* share of his father's estate in "loose living." When he had spent it all, a great famine came abroad in the land, and the boy was in want. All that he had bought, all the delights of the far country, left him empty and unfulfilled.

Destitute, he hired himself out to feed pigs—the lowliest of occupations, and the ultimate indignity for a Jew. Pigs were physically and ritually unclean; to care for them was to break Jewish law. Gladly he would have eaten animal fodder. But the carob pods were for the swine; nobody gave him anything. After a while, he "came to himself"—he saw the seductions of the far country for what they were, and he remembered the joys and security of home. He resolved to confess his sin against God for his lawless immoralities, and to confess his sin against his father for squandering his estate. He would not ask and could not have expected to be taken back into the family on the old basis. He would request only that he might toil as a hireling to earn enough to eat. So he arose and went to his father.

"But while he was yet at a distance"—before he had fully reached home—"his father saw him and had compassion, and ran and embraced him and kissed him" (Luke 15:20b–c RSV). According to Jewish practice, the son should have walked all the way towards the father. But, ignoring custom, the father took the initiative and ran toward his boy. "And the son said to him, 'Father, I have sinned against heaven and before you; I am no longer worthy to be called your son.' But the father said to his servants, 'Bring quickly the best robe, and put it on him; and put a ring on his hand, and shoes on his feet; and bring the fatted calf and kill it, and let us eat and make merry; for this my son was dead and is alive again; he was lost, and is found'" (Luke 15:21–24a RSV). So the boy's father had not forgotten him during his long absence, nor his love for him, even when he was off in a far country, dissipating his inheritance with indifference and ingratitude.

We can read into the story no apathy on the part of the father toward his son's wastefulness. But so overriding was his love that when he saw his son making the effort to come back home, he was filled with compassion. He ran toward the boy not to scold or rebuke or berate or condemn, but to embrace him and to kiss him tenderly. The father was aware of the submergence of pride and self-centeredness required for the child to take the first few steps that would eventually bring him home. He ignored the boy's request to be treated simply as a servant. Even before his son returned, the father had been ready to receive him as an honored guest and restore him to the family. The boy had come back to himself, and so had come home. He realized his foolishness, and returned to the source of his existence, daring to hope only for his father's undeserved mercy, receiving instead unanticipated generosity. Placing faith in his father's compassion, he found that it represented but a fraction of the new life awaiting him.

The story of the prodigal speaks forcefully. It tells of the depth and breadth of God's love for us—how much God wants us to come to ourselves and return home—not to be condemned and treated like a slave, but to be welcomed joyfully into the fold of the family, as one who was dead in spirit—dead to everyone and everything but self—but who now is alive to the fullness of life for which God created us—enjoying a relationship with God as children with a parent. This is the heart of the gospel: our salvation is based solely on the grace of God. Our hope rests not in our ability to *earn* God's approval, but only upon the dependability of God's love for us—love so great that he sacrificed his *own Son* for our sake. God has *already* answered our sin by opening the door to his house. We have but to enter. Even before we had returned to him, while we were still in the far country, "while we were yet sinners" (Rom 5:8 RSV), as Paul says, God had compassion, and did all that was necessary to restore our place in the family. "In Christ God was reconciling the world to himself, not counting their trespasses against them, and entrusting to *us* the message of reconciliation" (2 Cor 5:19 RSV).

This reconciliation—this bridging the chasm between God and us—reached its climax at Jesus' crucifixion. God looks at *us* and sees *Christ*, and *his* perfect obedience, even unto death on the cross. It is as though our sins had never been committed. Whether we accept God's offer or not, the truth of it remains. By the will of God, Christ identified himself so completely with sinful people—standing in our place, sharing our burdens, ministering to our needs—that he became involved with our sins while yet knowing no sin himself, all for the sake of us, the sinners. And now we and all sinners are enabled to become the righteousness of God, receiving it as a free gift. The distance *to* the far country may be great indeed, but the distance back home again is not nearly so far. By our response to what God has already done, we can again be united as parent and child.

For some people, this is too easy. Those who spend their lives trying to *earn* salvation, and expecting privilege for their efforts, regard God's indiscriminate love as anything *but* good news. The story of the prodigal really speaks of two truths—God's compassionate love, and the dangers of legalism. Recall that Jesus told this parable as the Pharisees and scribes were murmuring against him for receiving sinners. The Pharisees and scribes were the separatists, the legalists, the self-righteous of Jewish society. The parable is a judgment upon such arrogance and a warning against monopolizing the grace of God. When the elder son, who had stayed home and worked obediently for his father, heard the sounds of merriment, he asked one of the servants about it. He learned that his father was preparing a feast for his younger brother, who had returned safe and sound, and he became angry and refused to go in. His father came out and begged him to join the party, to share in the joy of his brother's return. But he answered his father contemptuously: "Lo, these many years I have served you, and I never disobeyed your command; yet you never gave me a kid, that I might make merry with my friends. But when this son of yours came, who has devoured your living with harlots, you killed for him the fatted calf!" (Luke 15:29–30 RSV). The elder son seethed with resentment because he had not been rewarded for doing what was his duty, while the wastrel, finally come to himself, was being feted.

The older son obviously loved neither his brother nor his father. He had felt neither his brother's suffering nor his father's grief. He responded with jealousy, self-pity, and self-righteousness. His world was centered in himself and his own wants and desires, every bit as much as the world of his younger brother had been. Comfortably secure, assured of his father's bounty, he looked out upon a world which failed to meet *his* code of rewards and punishments and pronounced it "Unfair!" He was as distant from his father in spirit as his brother had been in body. *Each* was a prodigal, wasting his father's goodness and love. And to the older boy, the father said, "Son, you are always with me, and all that is mine is yours. It was fitting to make merry and be glad, for this your brother was dead, and is alive; he was lost, and is found" (Luke 15:31–32 RSV).

Apparently, Jesus' telling of this story did not move the Pharisees and scribes. But if the scribes and Pharisees of Jesus' day were oblivious to his message, we today in the church of Jesus Christ must not be. It is our duty of discipleship to go into the world and proclaim that God has already reconciled himself to humanity—God has already sought and found us, God has already bridged the chasm between us in the life, death, and resurrection of Jesus the Christ. God does not, we do not, excuse the *sin*. But God *forgives*, and *we* must forgive, the *sinner* and welcome that person home. The cross has made all *human* measure of men and women artificial and obsolete. Race, birth, nationality, money, position, all are irrelevant in the light of the truth that we are all sinners, that we are all loved by God, and that in Christ, God calls us all into God's family. There is no human honor that can exempt us from the judgment of the cross. But there is no measure of estrangement from which we cannot be restored into fellowship with God. Each person is a sinner. And each person is a brother or sister for whom Christ died.

Are you exiled in a far country? Do you know others who are distant from home? The message of the cross is that amnesty has been declared, that you and I and all people are welcome to return to the family, where a place of honor is waiting. That is good news for us. And it is good news that we must proclaim to others, not only in word, but in deeds that remove whatever obstacle is keeping them from claiming *their* place as sons and daughters of the most high.

That means pointing people not only to reconciliation with God, but with each other, dismantling the instruments of war and forging bonds of peace; denouncing oppression and injustice, and insisting on compassion and dignity; being willing to sacrifice our pride and even our worldly security to the God who has already sacrificed so much for us. The cross is God's deed of reconciliation. The cross is the welcome sign hung on the door, beckoning us to return from the far country. The cross is our guarantee that God will wipe away our tears of confession and shame with kisses of compassion and joy. The cross is God's message to us and our message to all people: *God loves like that*. Amen.

Fifth Sunday in Lent
First Presbyterian Church, Ponca City, Oklahoma
March 13, 2016
Isaiah 43:16–21
Philippians 3:4b–14
John 12:1–8

"What Are You Giving Up for Lent?"

MESITA ELEMENTARY SCHOOL IN El Paso was a marvelous place to experience the religious and cultural mix of the largest city on the border of the United States and Mexico. In addition to classmates named Carlton and McNeil and Robbins, I had classmates named Torres and Salazar and Roybal. I also had classmates named Goodman and Leavitt and Aaronson. Located on the Rio Grande, El Paso had attracted a large number of Jewish families to the import and export business and the garment industry. My family lived not very far from an enormous synagogue—Temple Sinai, high up on the slopes of Mount Franklin. Jewish children were excused from public school classes for high holy days of Yom Kippur and Rosh Hashanah and for Hanukkah and Passover, which seemed eminently reasonable, since Christmas and Good Friday were respected on the school calendar, and of course there was no school on Easter, being on a Sunday.

On the Christian side, Protestants and Roman Catholics, whether Anglo or Hispanic or otherwise, pretty much observed the same holy days, as far as I was aware, except that most Protestants didn't seem to pay much attention to Lent, whereas it seemed to be a big deal among my Catholic friends. Later in life, I learned that that was an omission on the part of a lot of modern Protestants, not an invention of the Roman Catholics. But there was a lot about Catholicism that seemed very mysterious and arcane to a young Presbyterian lad. Much of it was surrounded by ritual that I had no idea was rooted in ancient theological beliefs that are our *common* Christian heritage. The one thing that I knew about Lent was that it had to do with giving something up in the weeks before Easter. I had probably already noticed that the school cafeteria never served meat on Fridays anyway, but a lot of my friends seemed not to eat meat *anytime* during Lent.

I think it was in third grade that one classmate of mine, Patricia—"Patti"—was absent from school one day, and our teacher told us that Patti's father had died of a heart attack. I knew that her family was Jewish; they attended Temple Sinai, where many of my other classmates worshiped. I wondered what Patti thought about her father dying, since I had been told that Jews did not believe that Jesus was raised from the dead. It wasn't long after Patti returned to school that she began wearing a cross on a necklace. When some of us remarked on it, she proudly announced that she and her sisters had become Catholic (I suppose that her mother might have been Catholic before her marriage; or, maybe at that time, they felt the need for the Christian hope of the resurrection). This amazed me. The possibility of switching one's faith had never occurred to me. I was Presbyterian, just like my skin was a particular color and I had a certain name, and I supposed that people remained what they were all their life.

I remember that it was just before or during *Lent* when all this happened, and Patti was rather public about her process of deciding what she should *give up* for Lent. I don't remember what she finally settled on—Lent might have been over by the time she made up her mind. But it got all of us thinking about what *we* might give up for Lent. It turned into a sort of a contest, which of us would be willing to make the greatest sacrifice, and of course we trivialized the whole concept by our pride and valor in giving up a favorite cartoon show or chocolate candy, though, truthfully, even *we* suspected there was nothing genuinely heroic involved in giving up things like liver and lima beans. All of this was taking place just as the Second Vatican Council was meeting, which altered a whole lot of traditions and rituals, and understandings about them. Maybe Patti never *did* have to give anything up for Lent. But I am grateful that, at an early age, I was daily in a setting that exposed me to people of different religious and ethnic and cultural backgrounds and that encouraged me to respect them and that made it easy to cultivate friendships among them.

Whatever basis there was in Roman Catholic teaching *before* Vatican II for giving up something during Lent, there has never been any doctrine in Protestant teaching that *requires* symbolic denial for a season. Those Protestant churches that have rediscovered Lent in the years after Vatican II, or that haven't *had* to rediscover something they never forgot, acknowledge that Lent is traditionally a time when people *adopt* some spiritual discipline, but such discipline is something that should *add to* our lives rather than *taking away* from them—for instance, the discipline of daily Bible reading, if we are not already in the habit, or a new intensity in prayer. Fasting has lost much of its meaning for modern Christians in Western culture, who are perpetually trying to lose weight and find it hard to distinguish fasting from dieting. Lent is not about shedding a few pounds or lowering our cholesterol level. Fasting is to make us more prayerful and more aware of God's presence, not more prideful and more conscious of our stomachs. Besides, good Protestant teaching, like good Catholic teaching, encourages us to give up things that are harmful to us and to others year-round, not just at Lent and certainly not just *during* Lent. As so often happens, when expressions of faith become ritualized and encrusted with tradition, we have to work harder to remember the meaning—in this case, to make sacrifice genuine, and to offer our sacrifice gratefully as a gift that we are *privileged* to *give*, not begrudgingly as an *obligation* we are required to *endure*.

One of the most important passages in the Bible about giving things up in proper spirit is our epistle reading for this morning from Paul, the Pharisee-turned-apostle. He was a Jew from birth, not a late convert, born into a Jewish family, keeper of the Jewish tradition, his body bearing ritualized evidence of his faith. He could trace his lineage to one of the tribes of Israel. As to the law of Moses, he was totally dedicated to it. As to defense of his faith, he had been an ardent persecutor of Christianity, which he had once thought posed a serious threat to the people of God. In his obedience to all of the details of the law, all of its commands, both positive and negative, he was impeccable. He could be proud, and *was*, of his religious achievements and his spiritual discipline. He was as close to perfect in God's eyes as a person could make himself or herself, except, of course, that in his very zeal for perfection, Paul had killed and harassed many who had vowed to be faithful to God's own Son. But we should not assume that it was at all easy for someone who was so spiritually sensitive as Paul, so zealous to do what he thought God required of him, to set out on a new course that would put him diametrically at odds with all his inherited attitudes about the law, all his acquired opinions about Christians. "Whatever gains I had," Paul wrote to the church in Philippi—a mainly Gentile congregation in a Gentile land, the first church that Paul had organized in Greece—whatever gains he had from all his scrupulousness, all his learning, all his heritage, all his pedigree, "these I have come to regard as *loss* because of *Christ*. More than that, I regard *everything* as loss because of the surpassing value of knowing Christ Jesus my Lord" (Phil 3:7–8a NRSV).

You could not put a price on what Paul *had* regarded as valuable in those years before encountering the risen Lord on the road to Damascus. But compared with Christ, it was all as nothing. Paul had not come to Christ out of despair for his deep flaws, his many inadequacies, his inability to discipline his flesh. Paul had always considered himself blameless, and, apparently, under the *law*, he *was* blameless. Paul's problem *wasn't* that he couldn't *keep* the commandments. Paul's problem was that his faith was all about the fact that he *had* kept the commandments. His *confidence* was in his *own* righteousness. His *trust* was in his own commendable *discipline.*

But then, he came to know Christ Jesus as his Lord, and no personal achievement, no physical purity or spiritual perfection, even, could compare with finding his righteousness in *Christ*—theologians call it "justification by faith." Ironically, everything that the *world* thought of as valuable—possessions, reputation, a settled home life—Paul had cast aside in his work as an apostle, but more dear to him yet had been his earlier reliance upon his blamelessness before the law. "For his sake," said Paul,

> I have suffered the loss of all things, and I regard them as *rubbish*, in order that I may gain Christ and be found in him, not having a righteousness of my own that comes from the law, but one that comes through faith in Christ, the righteousness from God based on faith. . . .
>
> Beloved, I do not consider that I have made it on my own, but this one thing I do: forgetting what lies behind and straining forward to what lies ahead, I press on toward the goal for the prize of the heavenly call of God in Christ Jesus (Phil 3:8b–9, 13 NRSV).

And that is a prize to which none of us can lay claim by our being good, or by our being successful, or by *our* being anything else at all, but only by our having *faith* in Jesus Christ—faith that he is the Son of God, and that his death on the cross means that we need not try to buy salvation with sacrifices or earn salvation with our obedience to the law, as indeed we cannot; rather, we are finally free to make offerings out of pure thanksgiving, and to follow God's commands out of sheer love.

Of all the many things to which we can attach ourselves, and have difficulty prying ourselves away from, beyond wealth and fame and reputation even, are surely self-centeredness, self-interest, self-reliance. In an act of pure selflessness, pure love, pure dependence, a woman named Mary once gave up what was very likely the most precious thing she possessed to honor Jesus—a costly pound of rare and fragrant ointment. Some thought it a silly act, or an extravagance, or a waste. But it was the most sacrificial gesture that she could make. Mary, the sister of Lazarus, set a standard for the disciples' devotion, and for the disciples' surrender of all they considered precious for Jesus' sake and because of the surpassing value of knowing him as their Lord. Success in life—even successfully resisting temptations to sexual immorality, successfully resisting temptations to cursing, successfully resisting temptations to hatred—may be our greatest obstacle to having faith in God through Jesus Christ. The more we think we have *made* it, or *can* make it, by our own purity, by our obedience, by our perfection, by our strength of character and our firmness of will, the further we push ourselves away from everything that the cross stands for. Strength of character and firmness of will are certainly not bad; neither were Paul's Jewish identity and upbringing bad, and his obedience to the law was certainly very commendable by anyone's standard. But all that spiritual success did not even *begin* to compare with the *righteousness of Christ*, and it is *Christ's* righteousness that saves us, *not our own*.

Life in Christ Jesus is not self-improvement, not a dressing up of the old you and me. It is a transformation to eternal life that only the death and resurrection of Christ Jesus can accomplish, *does* accomplish, has *already* accomplished, *totally apart* from however righteous we have managed to be on our own. It is only by the grace of God in Jesus Christ that you and I are free to give *ourselves* up and welcome the life that God has in store for us in all its transforming power, and it is only by *giving ourselves up*—our own efforts, our own achievements, our pride and our plans—that we can be raised with Christ to eternal life. Christianity is not a moral code. We cannot will or work or earn our way to salvation. We cannot be our own redeemer, no matter how hard we try. Jesus Christ is all in all. And alongside him, *everything*—cars, houses, stock portfolios, family name, nationality, even moral purity—is as nothing.

What are you giving up for Lent? There may be good and sound and wholesome reasons for abstaining from sweets or from meat or from sex or from alcohol or from smoking or from buying clothes or from whatever. Giving up one of these things may even help us concentrate on the riches of the Spirit, help us focus on the sufficiency of God. Certainly, taking on a new spiritual discipline of prayer or studying the scriptures or being more faithful in worship or more free in offering our money and time and concern to people in need will help us appreciate better the meaning of Lent as a season of preparation by repentance and reflection and self-denial. But surely most in keeping with Lent, as we accompany Jesus on his way to the cross, is giving up any trust in our own ability to save ourselves, giving up any righteousness of our own, whether it comes from the law or our own imagining, and instead to find *our* righteousness, and our salvation, in the surpassing value of knowing Christ Jesus our Lord.

Palm/Passion Sunday

First Presbyterian Church, Dodge City, Kansas

April 12, 1992

Isaiah 50:4–9a

Philippians 2:5–11

Luke 19:28–40

"Conversation in a Workshop"

HAND ME THAT TOOL over there, will you, my friend? No, the other one. Thank you. . . . My son Elias? He's gone down to the market to help out my cousin for a few days—you know, with the Passover crowd in the city, there's so much more business at the market. So, here I am to do the work around the shop myself, and at my age! . . . Alright, alright, so I'm younger than Uncle Mordecai who still works by himself, but he doesn't have this many mouths to feed, does he, eh? Please to hold that crosspiece steady for me for a moment. . . .Yes, it's a little job for the governor. . . . Listen, I will work for *Satan* even, if he pays me fairly. Times are hard. This soldier comes this morning banging on my door, says it's a rush job and I've got the sturdiest timber in Jerusalem. So, he shows me the money, so I get to work. Everybody's mind is on celebrating the Passover, not carpentry, so I welcome the work, even with Elias gone.

So, what's new with you? Your brother's wife had another child, did she? Boy or girl? . . . Ah, I thank you, God, that you made me a man. . . . A parade? No, I know nothing about a parade. When? . . . No. What was it about? Have the Romans blessed us with another garrison? . . . A Jew? . . . From Galilee? And what might a Galilean have done to deserve a parade? . . . Oh, another miracle worker, is he? We've had enough of them lately—curing the same cripple in every town, restoring sight to the same blind man every day, not a one of them able to work a real miracle and make the tax collectors disappear! . . . You say he has tax collectors among his *followers*? *I want no part of him, then.* What could he possibly do miraculous enough to turn a tax collector from his rolls, anyway? . . . Well, that's a new one, I must say! In Bethany, was it? And not just sick, but really dead? . . . Four days in the tomb? . . . Bless me, this one must be bold indeed. I suppose that *would* draw something of a crowd. . . . They did *what*? Laid their clothes down on the road in front of him? . . . That's a fine way to treat a good garment, letting a donkey walk on it!

. . . "Blessed is the King who comes in the name of the Lord! Peace in heaven and glory in the highest!" Quotes the Psalms, does he? He'll soon find himself an enemy of Herod *and* the Romans if he's calling himself a king. . . . Alright, then, even if he allows his *followers* to call him "king"—they'll see it as a threat just the same, and even more so, if the crowd shows any sign of disorder. If Pilate can kill a bunch of Galileans quietly making their sacrifices in the temple, he can easily enough kill a single Galilean inciting a riot! . . . Yes, well, your Galilean may well *talk* peace, but it takes Pilate very little threat of disobedience to react with an iron fist. If you ask me, he likes nothing more than an excuse to crack down on the Jews. And Herod—Herod will brook no rivals to his pomp and his wealth. . . . You say this one seeks no riches? Since when did a king not covet money and jewels? Even David had his palace! If this man would be a king, surely he has no aversion to power and prestige and an army to guarantee it all. . . . Not that kind of king? Then *what* kind? . . . A kingdom in heaven? . . . Give all you have to the poor? Forgive your enemies? Bless those who curse you? This sounds like no king I have heard of! More like a fool, or a dreamer. Well, it sounds like he's harmless after all. Few enough people will really be willing to follow a revolutionary who promises his supporters poverty and tells them to be humble.

So what sort of people were there at this parade for a king with no kingdom—the city rabble and ne'er-do-wells? . . . All the way up from Jericho, eh? Well, I suppose if they were *responsible* folk, they'd have plenty of work of their own to do instead of hanging around the latest celebrity. Hold that still, now. . . . You think they were sincere, then, do you? And did you see this man of miracles yourself? What did you make of him? . . . I think you get carried away too much with the emotion of the crowd, my friend! Be careful—the next thing you know, *you* will be a follower of this Galilean, praying for poverty and learning to be humble!

So what has become of him since he came to the city? . . . At the *temple*, was he? . . . No, I have heard nothing—I mind my own business and my customers mind theirs, what few customers I have had this week. I am a carpenter, not a gossip. Mind you, I could tell you all sorts of things about my neighbors and my customers, but I say nothing! I knew about the scandal of your sister for days before I heard it from the butcher, did I not? And even then I did not tell anyone but my family and my closest friends whom

I could trust to keep quiet, as you know. So, tell me about this Galilean at the temple. . . . He did *what*? By what authority did he drive them out? . . . Ha! He has a strange way of impressing the officials, this Galilean whom people call "king." True enough, those thieves in the temple should have been thrown out long ago. But no, no, this Galilean of yours goes too far! There must be order, especially in the house of God.

. . . What? He dared to go back to the temple and teach after all that? . . . You heard him, then? And a large crowd? . . . And what did he say, this Galilean teacher and man of miracles? . . . You seem quite moved by him, my friend. . . . What? You are considering becoming a follower of his? Are you serious? Leave Jerusalem, leave your family and your job to follow a vagabond teacher from Galilee? Think of your responsibilities, man! Consider your reputation! I admit that, from what you tell me, his words sound very fine, but if the priests do not endorse him and if, as you say, the scribes are unhappy with him, how can what he says be right? And even if he does speak the truth, they are not likely to let him go on *this* way very long. They are powerful men, and learned in the scriptures. They are respected, and they respect the mood of Pilate too well for you to suppose that they will let your Galilean give him any excuse for doing away with their privileges. Mark my words, if this teacher is as popular as you say, and if he is attracting crowds like you say, they will find some way to have him silenced, even if he *is* a Jew, even if he says his kingdom is not an earthly one!

. . . What? You say there is more? . . . The messiah? Who says this? . . . But if he is the messiah, surely the priests and the scribes would be the first to hail him! And even the Pharisees! . . . Well, I am sure that even God himself works through the established channels. The priests and scribes speak for God, do they not? They are intelligent men, are they not? They know his ways, do they not? Surely, God would have the courtesy of informing them if the messiah were coming. Besides, from what you say, this Galilean is hardly what we have been told to expect! . . . A God of love and mercy? What then becomes of righteousness under the law? I spend my whole life doing what the priests and the scribes say to do, I try to live as carefully as the Pharisees, and what is to prevent a sinner from saying, "God, forgive me," and suddenly he is as righteous as I am, who have obeyed the law? Preposterous! This is a far cry, I think, from the messiah. Now, hold this up while I lash it in place, then I will drive these nails in to keep it rigid.

Say, what's all the commotion in the street? You! Boys! What is going on? . . . A crowd at the governor's palace? For what? . . . Pilate might release Barabbas? There's a bad one, if you ask me. That madman Barabbas will bring the death of us all, him and the Zealots. . . . Well, you are a good friend and if you do decide to follow this dreamer and king and teacher and miracle-worker, then God go with you, but if it doesn't work out, don't say I didn't warn you. True enough, your Galilean must be a remarkable man, in his own way. But it seems to me there's danger in it. And even if Pilate and Herod and the priests and the scribes leave him alone, many of his followers will find a life of poverty and humility and forgiveness to be less romantic and filled with more hardship than they may think. But I know you must follow your heart. I suppose that is why I love you as my own brother—and why I am so worried by what you have told me.

Well, that job is done. That soldier should be back for it soon with some of his comrades. Help me to get it out onto the street—I really don't want Romans under my roof, especially at Passover. . . . Yes, I know it's heavy—I told you that I have the sturdiest timbers in town. . . . Thank you for your help, my friend. . . . No, I don't like making this kind of thing. It's certainly not why I learned to be a carpenter. But, as I told you, orders have been slow, and I don't relish the thought of what might happen to me if I defied the request of the governor. . . . I just wonder what poor soul they're going to crucify today.

Maundy Thursday
Spanish Springs Presbyterian Church, Sparks, Nevada
April 12, 2001
Exodus 12:1–4, 11–14
1 Corinthians 11:23–26
John 13:1–17, 31b–35

"What We Do Here"

SOME OF YOU ARE aware that I am an amateur archaeologist. Although I haven't been able to work at it for the past few years, I enjoy nothing more than sitting in a hole with a trowel in my hand and a bucket at my side and a brush in my pocket, uncovering the evidence by which we can learn about the past—what people valued, how people lived. I don't suppose that the people of the Gallina phase of the Anasazi culture in northwestern New Mexico, among whose ruins I have had most of my experience digging, ever considered that they were leaving a trail of clues for later generations when they tossed a cracked cooking pot out onto the trash heap, or added a storage bin on their roof, or left a few corn cobs or beans in the bottom of a jar that later was forgotten and left behind when they moved on to follow the game or find better farmland. But for the archaeologist, even such little bits of information help to paint a picture of what was important to these people—what prompted them to get up from their mats each morning, and what bonded them together as a civilization.

I've also explained to some of you that that is one reason I think it's important to have the Lord's table visible and set for every worship service, even on the occasions when we aren't receiving the Lord's Supper. It should be clear to anybody who enters this place what it is that we do here. And, with an archaeologist's mindset, I think that, if some sudden disaster were to befall us, or if we had to abandon this place in haste, leaving behind the artifacts of the life that we shared here, I would want future archaeologists to have evidence of what we believed, what we held dear, what gave our life purpose and zest, what identified us as a community.

From the very beginning of the Christian church, one activity more than any other has been the central, defining feature of worship. That is the sacrament of the Lord's Supper, the eucharist, holy communion. The very multiplicity of names by which we call it testifies to the richness of meaning that it has for Christians. Over the centuries, styles of music in the church have changed; there was a time when there were no organs, and some people are predicting that the organ will soon disappear. Over the years, preaching has waxed and waned, from very brief comments on the scriptures to sermons that went on for hours. But every Christian congregation, at some time or other, some less often and others more often, have taken bread, blessed it, broken it, and given it to those assembled in remembrance of the crucified and risen Lord Jesus Christ, and in some mysterious way, at a level deeper than words could ever express, they have understood in those simple actions the profound redeeming grace of God.

The importance of what we do here is more than the artifacts of our worship services, though. The importance of what we do here is more than just remembering a bit of historical fact. What happened on a Thursday night in an upstairs room in a building in Jerusalem two thousand years ago, more or less, would not be worth more than an answer on *Jeopardy* if it remained only a matter of history for us. If you have ever attended a Passover meal, as our family was privileged to do last weekend with the Jewish congregation of Temple Sinai, something that becomes clear in the course of the dinner is that the old story of the ancient Hebrews' escape from slavery in Egypt by God's wondrous liberating deed is *present* experience for *modern* Jews in their celebration. They eat the meal not just to remember the *past*, but, in *remembering*, to become conscious of God's powerful liberating purpose in the *present*. In and through the celebration of Passover, God's saving work is experienced ever anew, binding Jews together even today as the community established and redeemed through the exodus thousands of years ago. The message is *experienced* as well as *heard*: it isn't just that God delivered *them*—those people *long ago*—but that God delivers *us, today*. The language of memory, the ritual of remembrance, makes the saving power of the original historical event available to the community ever anew, so that worshipers in every Passover celebration are contemporary participants in God's saving deed: God brought *us* out of Egypt, God brings *us* out of captivity today, God inspires *us* to be doers of liberating deeds in our own time.

In much the same way, you and I who are gathered around this table tonight and other times that we worship—actually, most properly, it should be *every* time that we worship—not only remember the *last* supper that Jesus had with his disciples before his death on the cross, but share a meal with our risen and living Lord *now, today*. His body was broken not only

"WHAT WE DO HERE" 133

for *them*, but for *us*; his blood was shed not just for people of *old*, but for us *today*. And for you and me to take part in this feast tonight, and every time we come to this table, is to proclaim, in our very participation, the meaning of the Lord's death until he returns.

The ancient peoples of northwestern New Mexico, I am sure, took quite for granted their daily routine. They would probably never have explained their life in the language that anthropologists and archaeologists use to describe what the ruins and the potsherds and the pollen samples tell us. And maybe *we* take a bit for granted what *we* do in the Lord's Supper. I don't mean that we forget that it is *related* to Jesus' death for us, but that we might not always consider deeply enough what this shared meal *says* about Jesus' dying for us. Most of us can recite the words that Paul repeated for the benefit of the Corinthian Christians—"that the Lord Jesus on the night when he was betrayed"—the Greek word is actually "handed over"—"took a loaf of bread, and when he had given thanks, he broke it and said, 'This is my body that is for you. Do this in remembrance of me.' In the same way he took the cup also, after supper, saying, 'This cup is the new covenant in my blood. Do this, as often as you drink it, in remembrance of me'" (1 Cor 11:23b–25 NRSV). And that may be what remains foremost in our minds—the fact that the bread symbolizes Jesus' sacrificed body, the fact that the wine symbolizes Jesus' sacrificed blood. But Paul wanted the Corinthians to think about what sort of witness *they* were making by *their participation* in the ritual meal—what they were saying to the *world* about the God who, in Jesus Christ, took the bread and gave thanks for it and broke it and gave it to them, saying, "'This is my body that is for you'" (1 Cor 11:24b NRSV) and what they were saying to the *world* about the God who, in Jesus Christ, "took the cup also, after supper, saying, 'This cup is the new covenant in my blood'" (1 Cor 11:25a NRSV).

"As often as you eat this bread and drink this cup," said Paul, "you proclaim the Lord's death until he comes" (1 Cor 11:26 NRSV). As often as you eat this bread and drink this cup, Paul was asking, are you acting out the compassionate self-giving, the unconditional love, the gracious redemption of Jesus Christ that calls you into covenant with him and with the whole community of faith? Are you witnessing by your own behavior Jesus' death for others, binding yourselves to be responsible to God and to each other, epitomized in the sharing of bread and wine with all, so that none go hungry, so that all are included, just as Jesus lived and died and lives again for all? Hospitality, feeding, the companionship of the table, complete trust in the wondrous love by which God provides daily what we need, and provides for a lifetime and beyond in Christ whose body, broken for us, we are to recognize in the taking of bread, whose blood, shed for us, we are to recognize in the sharing of the cup. Might some future archaeologist detect what it was that we did here way back in 2001—what we believed, what we valued, what we thought our purpose was for being in the world—and perhaps be moved to faith in this Jesus Christ who gave himself up for the salvation of the world and to whom we, by our joyful and generous sharing of this meal, gave clear witness in our worship and in our daily living?

It seems that the celebration of the Lord's Supper in the church at Corinth had deteriorated to the point that it bore *no resemblance* to Christ's gracious love—that even observers of their *own* time could not recognize the Lord's sacrificial death in what the Corinthian Christians did when *they* came to the table. They were greedy, it seems, and gluttonous. The idle rich who could afford to come early took the best seats and grabbed the majority of the meal as soon as it was laid out, leaving literally crumbs for the latecomers, the people who had just gotten off of their shift at work, to nibble on in the back room. "When *you* come together," said Paul to the Corinthians, "it is not really to eat the *Lord's* supper. For when the time comes to *eat*, each of you goes ahead with your *own* supper, and one goes *hungry* and another becomes *drunk*" (1 Cor 11:20–21 NRSV). They were not proclaiming the *Lord's death* in their ritual meal, Paul complained, but their own selfishness that had nothing to do with the *covenant* that *Jesus* had established *with* them and *between* them with his blood. *Their* communion meal had become an occasion for *division* and *self-indulgence*. The Lord's Supper, Paul was saying, should be the best evidence of Christ's gracious sacrifice for the salvation of all—a sacrifice for which we should be so thankful that we are moved to share, graciously, *all* that we have, to give, sacrificially, *all* that we are, so that the world may come to know the saving love that we have experienced in Jesus Christ. They weren't proclaiming the *Lord's death*. *They* were proclaiming their own pride, it seems, and their own assertions of privilege. They were not eating the supper in remembrance of *Christ*. It was not incorporating them into the saving event of the cross. An archaeologist digging up the house-church at Corinth, finding the best china and softest cushions spread out for some guests in the finest room in the house, and the cheap stuff laid out in the dark and stuffy back rooms for the rest, would hardly conclude that this was a banquet to which all were welcomed equally and without qualification, at which all shared alike and at which all found a common bond in a common Lord who gave freely of himself so that *all*, rich and poor *alike*, master and slave, male and female, Jew and Greek, were welcomed as honored guests, so that none should go hungry or homeless or oppressed in the world which God created, and none should go unforgiven or outcast or unloved in the world for which Christ died.

Well, this table, and the way that it is set, is of course not the *only* evidence of what we do here. There is other evidence, too. And as archaeologists dug out away from this place into the rest of our community, that would all come to light—whether what we did here had anything to do with what we did in the rest of our life. For instance, did sharing this meal together make any difference for our neighborhoods—was there a great disparity between the size and comfort of houses in this city; did some live in great opulence while others lived in squalor? Did sharing this meal together prompt us to put public resources toward the most vulnerable of our community—our young and our old, for instance, our sick and our widowed? Was our eating this meal together reflected in not having to have much in the way of courtrooms and police stations and jails, or was that all a major reality in this place, and if so, what were the reasons for theft and burglary and murder and all the rest? Were these people really proclaiming in their public and personal lives a loving and gracious and compassionate and generous and forgiving God? Did sharing this meal have anything to do with what the people of this community did for entertainment? How did they spend their money—did they invest in *things*, or in *people*? Did they trust their *God* to *provide* as they had need, or did they build great storehouses and places to accumulate their money and keep it safe and untouched? Were they more prolific in building *fences*, or in building *bridges*? Were their daily lives proclamations of what they did at this table, and what Christ did on the cross?

What we do here is not just a sentimental device to help us remember an event that happened long ago—Christ's death. What we do here is to proclaim the present-day reality of Christ alive, within us and within our community of faith and, through us, within Sparks and Reno. What we do here is a loud and radical judgment upon all the world's selfishness, upon all the world's greed, upon all the world's fear and jealousy and hatred, upon all the world's classism and sexism and racism and nationalism, all its touting of economies and all its allegiance to political theories and all its idolatries of every sort. And if the archaeologists someday first start digging in some *other* part of town, and discover that all the people in our community were housed safely and comfortably and securely, that our jails had been dismantled and our courtrooms had been turned into nursery schools, that the graffiti on our walls praised God rather than promoted fear or devalued women, that the books in our libraries encouraged faithfulness rather than debased creation, that we had no weapons, but tools for planting and harvesting, medicine for healing, technology for communicating, that our artwork depicted people of every race and condition working and playing side by side, and then at last, they reach *this* place in their digging, and they finally uncover this pulpit and this font and this table, set for a shared meal of bread and wine, they will know precisely what we did here—"That explains everything," they will say. "These people knew and understood about the death of the Lord, and so they proclaimed it until he comes again."

Good Friday
Spanish Springs Presbyterian Church, Sparks, Nevada
April 6, 2007
Isaiah 52:13—53:12
Hebrews 4:14-16; 5:7-9
John 18:1—19:42

"Beneath the Cross of Jesus"

Mary the Mother of Jesus, Her Sister Mary, the Wife of Clopas, Mary Magdalene, and the Beloved Disciple

He was my son, my child, my oldest, the one to whom I was closest. And yet, the one that I least understood, and who, in a strange way, was the most distant from me. You can't imagine the thrill of the thought of life growing inside you, the first movement of a new little . . . well, of course you can, or *some* of you, at least, *women* who are *mothers*. I was so young, though, I didn't know what to expect. I hadn't heard that much about it. But my memories . . . he was such a beautiful child; light just radiated from him. And then he grew up so fast . . . they do, don't they? And then he was off, gone from home. I would hear about him, what he was doing, frequently, and he would come home for family obligations now and then, and then, when I heard that he was going to Jerusalem, I decided . . .

He was always loving, and dutiful, but even as a child he seemed to be listening to another voice, and responding. He saw things a little differently, spoke of things from a different perspective. So he stood out from the other children, and eventually he stood out from other men. And I worried about that. Mostly, I was proud. But I also worried. And, today, my worst fears came true. My son—they killed my son. They were skeptical of him, they were jealous of him, they were afraid of him, though I don't know why. He was gentle. He was fair. He was generous. He was pious. And they killed him.

It always seemed that Jesus could deal with any situation. There was the time at a wedding we went to together when the hosts ran out of wine. I suppose we thought he could deal with *this* situation—many of us sensed that he might be in danger if he came here to Jerusalem. But he was determined. And we had become accustomed to deferring to his judgment. When he spoke, it was always with such . . . I guess the word would be "authority." And people would listen. When people did as he told them, good things happened.

Why didn't *they* listen to him? I mean really listen. *I* did. I learned so much. Not things like you learn from books and in school, but how to act toward others, how to respond, how to see. Usually, it's the *parent* who teaches the *child*, and I *did* teach him many things—or did my *best*. But *I* learned so much more from *him* than he *ever* learned from *me*. He was so special. And I really don't think I'm saying that just because I was his *mother*. So *many* people's lives were better because of him. And now, he's dead.

A *son* should bury his *mother*. A *mother* should not have to bury her *son*. How I wish I had never lived to see this day. And yet, whose arms but these that cradled him so long ago were more fitting to hold him when they lowered him from the cross? My son!

What Mary my sister told you is true. He was special, my nephew. Even as a little boy, we knew it. And, as he grew older, his interest in people—all people, not just us who were his family—was unusually strong, and it motivated him to do extraordinary things, but things that oftentimes upset those who liked to be in charge, those who liked to be in control, and particularly those who liked things to remain the way they were, even if people were being hurt by it. Sometimes, we in the family thought he should spend more time with *us*, care more—I'm ashamed now to say it—care more exclusively about *us*, perform for *us* all those wondrous things he did for *others*. I guess *we* got a little jealous, too. I'm sorry about that now. He didn't belong just to *us*. From early on, I think, we knew that he belonged to *everyone*, and especially to those who were sick or blind or hungry, even those who were shunned and gossiped about. But he didn't deserve this, what happened today. Nobody does. It's terrible. It's barbaric. See how it has broken my sister's heart! Feel how the world is colder, darker, sadder.

I remember when Joseph first told my husband, Clopas, and me that Mary was going to have a child. He was happy, I think—I mean, I *know* that he was, he *must* have been—but he *also* seemed *reserved*, maybe even a little *troubled*. So maybe we always felt something bad might happen to the boy. He never hurt anyone. But these last few years, when he was traveling around Galilee teaching and healing—and sometimes, they say, even on the sabbath—and right here in Jerusalem, we were afraid that he might make some enemies. Especially when he told people that they were forgiven of their sins. To be honest, that even made *me* a little uneasy. Of course, we never imagined that it might lead to something like this. We came up to Jerusalem with him. We were proud of Jesus and wanted to see how people here reacted to his teaching and, well, wanted to encourage him not to get into trouble. But when the priests and the Pharisees heard about Lazarus, who came back to life from the tomb, well, they seemed to become very hostile toward Jesus, and we heard rumors that they were criticizing everything that he did. But what he was *doing* was *helping* people. They should have thanked him! And now . . .

Some men Jesus knew were kind enough to find a burial place, and they said they would prepare his body in the proper way. We are very grateful for that. It all had to be done so quickly. It has been a terrible day. It's hard to see how any good could ever come out of it. I feel so sorry for his mother. The Romans are so . . . I mustn't say exactly what I'm thinking. We don't want any more trouble. It wouldn't help things now, anyway. I guess we should just go home.

No, I can't leave yet. I can't leave him. I must be near him. He has become my life. Without him, I have none. These past few months—it's like I never was really alive until I met him, I heard him, I ate with him. My life before was hardly worth living. Nothing ever went well for me. Everything always went wrong. I couldn't ever do anything right. My family looked down on me, and my friends . . . well, I didn't really have anybody you could call a "friend." And then Jesus came to town. And he became my friend. And I became friends with some of the others who were following him, and, for the first time in my life, I felt like I belonged, that people cared for me, that people valued what I felt and what I had to say, like all the demons that had been tormenting me and making my life miserable had vanished!

Well, I had to be here. I thought it would be so fine to be with Jesus in Jerusalem with all the other people gathered for Passover. When I heard that he'd been arrested, I was so scared, partly for me, but mostly for him. And then I heard they'd taken him to the council, and then to the governor. My heart sank. I thought they might put him in prison. I never dreamed . . . I love him so much. I must stay. After the sabbath, I must see where they've taken him. I must be near him.

I, too, must stay. I've tried to be faithful to Jesus all these months. I won't abandon him now. It's as if I can still hear his voice, speaking to me in his patient way whenever I failed to understand. I must have disappointed him so many times, I just couldn't disappoint him this time. I had to be there beneath the cross.

I'll never have another friend like Jesus. It chilled me to the bone at dinner last night to hear Jesus say that some one of us would betray him. I thought that we were *all* Jesus' friends, that we *all* loved him. But Judas . . . Jesus told us to love one another, said that we were his friends if we did what he told us to do, that he had shared with us everything that God had told him, and then told us that the world would hate us for it. And then he said that he would be leaving us, "going to the Father," he said. But I never really thought he might die.

"Stick together," he said. "Stay united." But the others—where *are* they? They should have been here. I guess I'll go back to where we've been staying here in Jerusalem. Maybe they'll be there, some of them, anyway. I suppose that I can't really blame them. Everything's come so apart in the past couple of days. But first I need to take care of his mother. I promised him that. I won't let him down.

You know, not too long ago, I was just doing what everybody always expected me to do—fishing, selling my catch, paying taxes, not thinking much about tomorrow. I'd heard the baptizer, of course, and thought a lot about what he said. And then Jesus came along and asked me to follow him. Boy, did my life change! The wonders I've seen since then! The good times we've had together! And it all had to do with Jesus. And now he's dead. It's not fair. He didn't deserve that! We, perhaps, but not him. He was always so good and kind and understanding. And I . . . I haven't been any of those things, not really. I can't help thinking that it's for people like me that he died.

The Resurrection of the Lord (Sunrise)
First Presbyterian Church, Ponca City, Oklahoma
March 31, 2013
Acts 10:34–43
1 Corinthians 15:19–26
John 20:1–18

"God's Flower Has Shattered the Stone"

HAVE YOU EVER THOUGHT about how persistent life is? In the middle of the most barren desert, if you take a little sample of the sand or soil and put it under a powerful microscope, you will discover that, even there, there are small organisms, even tiny creatures. In the frigid and windswept Antarctic, scientists find the same thing. Life is stubborn. Life is tenacious. Life is triumphant.

    I grew up in the West. Throughout my youth and most of my adulthood, I have lived in the sight of mountains, with their vast masses of exposed rock, solid-looking, unyielding, sterile. One summer, in my early twenties, I worked in an old gold mine near Death Valley, all day, underground, chiseling out samples of rock with a geology pick—a slow, backbreaking, shoulder-straining process. Building roads through the mountains and tunnels under them requires tons of dynamite. And yet, if you're out hiking or perhaps just driving along a mountain road, it's not unusual to notice narrow crevices and cracks and joints where little seedlings are growing—little oases of life that, over time, will send out tender roots that slowly wedge the crevice wider and deeper and finally split the rock open. John Jarvis and Joe Henry once captured the truth of that phenomenon and made it a parable for the inexorable work of love upon the human heart in a song sung by John Denver, titled, "The Flower that Shattered the Stone." Something so tender and fragile ultimately proves to be more powerful than the hardest substance we can think of. True of geology, it is also true of personalities. Both are miracles. Life where, according to all logic, there should be no life. A force powerful enough to break open what is cold, hard, stubborn, unyielding. Impossible?

Once, in a country where the landscape is largely barren and dominated by rock all around, a man who had been unjustly charged with being a criminal was executed. Unfortunately, there was nothing unusual in an execution. There probably wasn't even anything particularly unusual about executing someone who was innocent. But this victim had been loved by many people, because he himself had shown great love to many people. A few days after his body had been buried, a woman came early in the morning to the tomb where it had been laid. The landscape spoke of nothing but death, for it was a cemetery full of tombs carved into a limestone cliff. And death was all that she was expecting. But when she arrived, she saw that there was a gaping hole in the rock. The stone that had been rolled in front of the tomb had been removed. A fresh sharp edge was added to the grief that she was already feeling. "They have taken away my Lord," she said, for she had been one of those who was devoted to the man she had seen put to death on a cross, "and I do not know where they have laid him" (John 20:13b NRSV). Thus she explained to two figures clad in white, sitting where the body of the man had been laid, when they asked why she was weeping. Another figure, standing behind her, asked the same question: "Woman, why are you weeping?" (John 20:15a NRSV). She turned and, supposing him to be a caretaker in this garden of death, asked where he might have taken the body of her friend. When he spoke her name, she immediately knew that, miraculously, it was the very one whose dead body, as she thought, had been taken out of the tomb. "I have seen the Lord" (John 20:18b NRSV), she later explained to the man's disciples.

"Whom are you looking for?" (John 20:15b NRSV) Jesus, alive and standing behind her, outside the tomb, had asked her. Certainly, what she had been looking for, what she had been expecting to find, wasn't life burst forth from *rock*, Jesus *alive* again and standing outside the tomb! But what seems totally impossible, from all that *human logic* tells us, is possible with God, whose purpose for creation will be fulfilled despite every obstacle. Didn't the angel say that very thing to Mary back even before Jesus was born to a virgin, before John was born to Elizabeth, who, for many years, had been barren? The Bible and our own experience both make clear that God's love is powerful to break the walls of prisons and the walls of exclusion and the walls of pride and the walls of division. Stone upon stone, God works tirelessly to dismantle.

But can even *God* break open the sealed tomb? Can God bring forth any kind of life from the stark reality of death? Anything hopeful? Anything promising? Anything eternal? Can God break apart the most stubborn stone of all?

It doesn't take explosives to break open rock, it turns out. It only takes a seed. And the most stubborn and unyielding of natural phenomena breaks, eventually crumbles, finally becomes nothing more substantial than sand, while God's marvelous miracle of life triumphs over every impossibility, finally, even, triumphs over the most intractable of all. Life burst forth from rock. Jesus risen from the tomb. The stone rolled away, never again able to limit or contain God's greatest gift to the creation that he will not allow to be destroyed, God's greatest gift to the human creatures with whom God wants to spend eternity. Alleluia. Amen.

The Resurrection of the Lord
First Presbyterian Church, Norfolk, Nebraska
March 31, 1991
Isaiah 25:6–9
Acts 10:34–43
John 20:1–18

"Whom Do You Seek?"

How glorious Palm Sunday had been. The crowd of followers had hailed Jesus as he entered Jerusalem riding on a donkey. They spread their garments out and laid palm branches down on the road before him in sign of welcome and respect. But by Good Friday, the crowd around Jesus had dwindled to just a few. The respect and welcome had given way to jeers and mockery. The garments and the branches had been replaced by a robe and a cross. The festal banners were gone, and in their place was a wooden shingle sarcastically lettered, "The King of the Jews." In the short space of a few days, triumph had turned to tragedy, and the one who had been greeted with the words, "Blessed is the one who comes in the name of the Lord—the King of Israel!" (John 12:13b NRSV) was made to wear a crown of thorns. On Friday afternoon, only a few dedicated relatives and friends were still close to Jesus. The cries of "Hosanna!" were now but a muffled memory. Their joy had turned to tears as the incredible chain of events had led from a celebrative parade to a criminal's execution.

According to the Gospels, one of those who stood looking in dismay and grief at the dying form of their Master on the cross was Mary, from the town of Magdala on the western shore of the Sea of Galilee. The Bible gives us very little clear information about Mary Magdalene. We do not know when or under what circumstances she first met Jesus—only that, according to Mark and Luke, she had been healed when seven demons had gone out of her, and that she contributed to the financial support of Jesus and his company. There has been much speculation throughout history whether she were the harlot whom Jesus forgave, but the Bible is silent about this. Some have suggested that Mary Magdalene was the Mary that lived in Bethany with her sister Martha, but this seems unlikely. What we do know is that she was among the most faithful followers of Jesus, that she accompanied him on his final journey to Jerusalem, that she was present at the crucifixion, and that on the Sunday following Good Friday, she discovered the empty tomb.

Perhaps she had been attracted to Jesus for the same reasons that many others were attracted to him. For some people, he was a novelty, a celebrity in an out-of-the-way land at a time before there were movie stars and rock singers. For some people, he was a miracle-worker—he caused things to happen that defied common experience. For some people, he was a healer—those who were ill called on him, and their diseases and afflictions were no more. For some people, he was a restorer of vision; on one occasion, at least, he even brought vision to a man who asserted his preference to remain blind, for his blindness had become comfortable to him. For some people, Jesus was a teacher—as he had opened the eyes of the blind, so he opened people's minds and hearts to the nature and will of God, with a fresh authority which the chief priests and scribes did not possess. For some people, he was a prophet—in his last days at Jerusalem, he dramatically denounced the oppression of the poor and the commercialization of the Jewish faith, and on occasion he seemed to speak of the end times. For some people, he was a friend—someone who listened intently, who beheld life situations with unique perception, who encouraged society's unlovables and ne'er-do-wells to dare and succeed, and who embraced them with a nonjudgmental love.

How it must have hurt them to see Jesus tried and convicted and scourged and mocked, hanging on a cross like a criminal. How it must have hurt Mary Magdalene. Was she the one who, just days before, had graciously ministered to Jesus and to his other disciples? Now she could at least perform one last act of ministry for her friend; she could anoint his dead body, in the customary and respectful manner of the Jews. So, on the first day of the week, Mary came to the tomb early, while it was still dark. But she was alarmed to discover that the stone used to seal the tomb had been rolled away.

> So she ran and went to Simon Peter and the other disciple, the one whom Jesus loved, and said to them, "They have taken the Lord out of the tomb, and we do not know where they have laid him." Then Peter and the other disciple set out and went toward the tomb. The two were running together, but the other disciple outran Peter and reached the tomb first. He bent down to look in.... Then Simon Peter came, following him, and went into the tomb. He saw the linen wrappings lying there, and the cloth that had been on Jesus' head, not lying with the linen wrappings but

rolled up in a place by itself. . . . Then the disciples returned to their homes.

> But Mary stood weeping outside the tomb. As she wept, she bent over to look into the tomb; and she saw two angels in white, sitting where the body of Jesus had been lying, one at the head and the other at the feet. They said to her, "Woman, why are you weeping?" She said to them, "They have taken away my Lord, and I do not know where they have laid him." When she had said this, she turned around and saw Jesus standing there, but she did not know that it was Jesus. Jesus said to her, "Woman, why are you weeping? Whom are you looking for?" Supposing him to be the gardener, she said to him, "Sir, if you have carried him away, tell me where you have laid him, and I will take him away." Jesus said to her, "Mary!" She turned and said to him in Hebrew, "Rabbouni!" (which means Teacher). (John 20:2–7, 10–16 NRSV)

"Whom are you looking for?" (John 20:15b NRSV); "Whom do you seek?" (John 20:15b, RSV) Jesus asked. Mary was seeking Jesus the miracle-worker, the healer, the teacher, the prophet, the friend—Jesus, who had been executed and laid in the tomb. She was seeking a dead man—a lifeless body, the way that all bodies are lifeless when they die. But there *was* no dead body. She could not find what she was looking for, because what she was looking for did not exist. She had seen, with her own eyes, the lifeless form of Jesus placed in the tomb. Now, on the third day after the *crucifixion*, she failed to recognize the risen Christ, because she was expecting only a dead man.

Finally, when she heard him speak her name, she recognized her master. Surely, her first word of recognition—"Rabbouni," which means "teacher"—was too modest a title for the Christ of God. But she began to understand that the earthly Jesus was now the risen Lord. And when she joyfully told the disciples of what had happened, she did not say that she had seen merely the miracle-worker, or the healer, or the teacher, or the prophet, or even her friend. "I have seen the Lord" (John 20:18b NRSV).

Easter Sunday is the high festival of the empty tomb. The empty tomb is what made the Christian church, for it is the *resurrection* that transformed a huddle of dispirited and frightened people into a valiant band ready to dare anything. It is the empty tomb which is the center of the biblical faith—not the manger of the baby Jesus, despite the halos that countless artists have painted around the baby's head. In fact, without the empty tomb, even the cross is an incomplete symbol of the biblical faith. It was outside the empty tomb where the true character of Jesus was revealed unequivocally and the *present life* and activity of Christ is attested. The manger symbolizes the birth of the earthly Jesus—a soft radiant baby (but other babies are soft and radiant); a beautiful and winsome child (but other children are beautiful and winsome); a perceptive and inquiring youth (but other youth are perceptive and inquiring). As an adult, he attracted followers when he worked miracles, but there had been other workers of miracles. He healed the sick and even raised the dead, but the Bible tells of others who healed the sick and raised the dead. He prophesied, proclaiming God's truth, but others had prophesied before him, proclaiming God's truth.

The cross symbolizes Jesus' sacrificial death and the depth of God's love for us. It is a strong and poignant reminder of a man who responded to God by living for others and who was put to death for doing good. Many people are attracted to the cross as a sentimental token of a great philosopher and teacher and a man who had deep compassion for suffering humanity. But to seek in Jesus *only* a miracle-worker or a teacher or a healer or a prophet or a compassionate friend is to seek someone other than the Lord of creation and the Lord of one's own life. It is certainly to miss the climax of God's story. Jesus was all of these things during his earthly ministry—miracle-worker, teacher, healer, prophet, friend. But the empty tomb confronts each of us—you and me—with the profound truth that he was much more. The empty tomb proclaims that Jesus was the very Son of God, and that *he* is the *risen Christ*, the *living Lord of all*.

To seek the *Christ* for any purpose *less* than as Lord of all creation and Lord of your every thought, word, and deed is to go to the tomb looking for a dead man—the Jesus of two thousand years ago, the Jesus of pleasant memory, the quotable Jesus—and nothing more. Perhaps we would actually prefer to find the body still there in the tomb, for that would make Jesus more manageable for us. It would enable us to treat his teachings simply as the wisdom of a philosopher—some words from which we are free to pick and choose in order to help us through trials, perhaps, but which make no ultimate demands upon us of obedience and loyalty. It would enable us to regard Jesus' actions as the actions of any other doer of good deeds—an admirable example of positive thinking and helpful living, perhaps, but one which places no claims upon the *way* we live *our* lives, and which requires few changes in our attitude and our behavior. An entombed Jesus permits us to *deny* that we have any obligation toward other people, and allows us to *ignore* their needs. If Jesus is still in the tomb, we can leave the emotionally wounded in our families and the physically wounded in South Africa to their hurts; we can let the children of Northern Ireland and the West Bank and Watts feed on hatred and suspicion; we can turn our eyes from the homeless in Central America and the starving in Ethiopia and the unlovely in our own community. If Jesus is still in the tomb, we can dismiss AIDS as a fitting judgment on perversion and promiscuity, and we can turn our backs upon its victims as people reaping deserved consequences; we can excuse all manner of oppression and we can rationalize all manner of injustice. If Jesus is still in the tomb, we can provide excuses for nursing our cherished grudges and fueling others' fears.

But if Jesus has *burst forth* from the tomb, if he is now *free* of the chains of death and the limits of time and space, if he now has not only a place in our *memory* but is actively present *here*, *today*, if he is now the *risen* Christ *alive* and *at work* in the world, then what he taught was not just another opinion from another philosopher; it was God's truth. His good deeds were not soft-hearted sentimentalism; they were models of how God expects us to love one another. His ministry to the sick was not simply a trick to win followers, but was a devotion to suffering people which plunges his disciples headlong into the thick of others' pain, whatever its cause. His instructions were not just suggestions for happy living, but the very commandments of God. His call to repentance was not merely psychological therapy, but a prescription for eternal life with our creator. Suddenly, God must matter to us, and every other person in the entire world must matter to us, because every other person in the entire world matters to *him*.

That being the case, we might expect that the news of Jesus' resurrection would have greatly distressed Jesus' disciples; the obligations and responsibilities imposed by a living Christ might well have seemed an overwhelming burden. But *no*—the followers of Jesus rejoiced exceedingly. Why were they joyful? The resurrection means that Christ yet *lives*—that Christ is still working miracles, teaching, healing, making plain God's will, befriending the friendless. He is still interceding with God on our behalf. He is still calling us to repentance. He is still praying for us. Joy! The tomb is empty! Evil has no future! Death has been overcome! Christ has been glorified and reigns in power! Our Lord lives! What *good news* to disciples!

Is it good news for *you*—you who have come to look into the tomb this Easter morning? That depends upon your purpose for being here. Whom are you *seeking*? If you are looking for someone to insure against rough times in your life but who will not demand your loyalty and obedience, then an empty tomb is not very good news, for you seek not a living Lord, but a magician. If you are looking for someone who will comfort you in your affliction, but who will never call you to risk yourself in advocacy for the oppressed and for victims of injustice, then an empty tomb is not very good news, for you seek not a living Lord, but a hypocrite. If you are looking for someone who will answer your *prayers* but will be *silent* about how you spend your money or cast your vote or pass your leisure time, then an empty tomb is not very good news, for you seek not a living Lord, but a deceiver.

But if it *is* a living Lord, the risen Christ, the Son of God, that *you* seek, then the empty tomb is good news indeed—the *best* news. God's promises are true! His purpose will not be defeated, not by hatred, not by fear, not by indifference, not even by death! Hallelujah! Christ is risen! *Our Lord* is *alive*!

Second Sunday of Easter
Spanish Springs Presbyterian Church, Sparks, Nevada
April 18, 2004
Acts 5:27–32
Revelation 1:4–8
John 20:19–31

"Stubborn Faith"

EARLIER THIS WEEK, AS I reread John's account of the resurrected Jesus suddenly standing among his followers in the room where they had locked themselves because of fear, it occurred to me that the episode includes at least two miracles. First, the miracle that Jesus, who was crucified on Friday, on Sunday night *appeared* to the disciples. Second, the miracle that Jesus, who was crucified on Friday, on Sunday night appeared to the *disciples*.

The resurrection itself, of course, is a miracle beyond comparison. That God brings Jesus to life again from the dead is the remarkable climax of each of the four Gospels—God vindicated in the most dramatic way the one whose goodness and love and mercy and truth had led the self-righteous and the powerful and the privileged to conspire to bring about his condemnation and execution, and, in the same instant, God broke the finality of death. But it is no *less* a miracle, I think, every bit as extraordinary as the resurrection itself, that Jesus, once *raised* from the dead, should seek out and spend the evening with his *disciples*—most of whom had abandoned him in his hour of greatest need, one of whom had denied ever having known or associated with him in order to save his own neck, all of whom, simple and rustic and unpolished, seem less suitable company for the risen Lord of all than the angels and archangels who inhabit their heavenly courts, or even the kings and princes who inhabit their *earthly* courts.

Our first reaction might be, "Well, of *course* he appeared to the disciples; he'd spent three years with some of them." But now, free from the limitations of time and space, apparently able to appear at will even inside locked rooms and to *dis*appear at will, too, Jesus could have had any audience that he wanted, could have kept company with Israel's "beautiful people" or skipped the earthly scene altogether. But in each of the Gospels that reports the appearances of the resurrected Christ, the accounts place him among those to whom he had ministered before the crucifixion, those with whom he had shared meals and adventures, those whom he had taught and encouraged, those whom he had told that the Son of man must be killed and then, three days later, rise again. There was no necessity for the risen Christ, who was entitled to judge all people and inherit all authority in heaven and on earth, to return to the same group that had been so fickle in their loyalty and so uncomprehending in their understanding. Surely, the risen Christ could do *better*. Jesus had certainly *deserved* better. Why, one of them *still* didn't believe in the resurrection even after the others told him Jesus had appeared to the rest of them in his absence—he insisted that *he* wouldn't believe unless he could examine for himself and even touch the wounds in Jesus' hands and Jesus' side. That would be proof, to Thomas, that the person who had appeared alive to the others was indeed the same Jesus who had been crucified.

Frankly, if *I* were Jesus, I think I might well have ignored the disciples as unworthy of my company. *I* would have *given up* on them, with a large dose of resentment, even. But, in fact, it was to the *disciples* that Jesus, raised from the dead to life again, beat a path. "When it was evening on that day, the first day of the week, and the doors of the house where the disciples had met were locked for fear of the Jews, Jesus came and stood among them and said, 'Peace be with you'" (John 20:19 NRSV). His words to them weren't even words of anger or chastisement or revenge, but a greeting such as friends customarily exchanged, and one intended to put the disciples at ease. "After he said this, he showed them his hands and his side. Then the disciples rejoiced when they saw the Lord. Jesus said to them again, 'Peace be with you. As the Father has sent me, so I send you.' When he had said this, he breathed on them and said to them, 'Receive the Holy Spirit. If you forgive the sins of any, they are forgiven them; if you retain the sins of any, they are retained'" (John 20:20-23 NRSV).

And here is a third miracle: not only did God raise Jesus from the dead, not only did the risen Christ then appear to the disciples who had repeatedly let him down, but he commissioned them and empowered them with authority to be his representatives, doing the work that he authorized, and even giving them the control of other people's destinies before God by *forgiving* them their sins or *refusing* to forgive their sins. What had the disciples done to earn such a privilege? What had they done to deserve such a commission? What had they done to show they were responsible enough to exercise such authority?

Throughout the *Old* Testament, God had chosen people to perform great and important roles in the cause of salvation whom you and I might never have selected—Abraham, who had some startling lapses of moral judgment, Jacob, the opportunistic schemer and deceiver, Moses, the reluctant liberator whom God sought out while he was hiding from the authorities who wanted him for murder, David, whose zeal for the Lord was matched by his adulterous love for Bathsheba and his blind indulgence of his treasonous son Absalom. In the *New* Testament, Jesus, God's Son, made some surprising choices of friends and helpers, too—tax collectors, harlots, people whose lives had been all boats and nets. And, on his way to his heavenly throne, Jesus returned to them to greet them, to comfort them, and to give them a measure of his power and authority. Remarkable!

In the Gospel passage for today, our attention usually falls on Thomas, so stubborn in his lack of faith that he has been dubbed "Doubting Thomas" by generations of Christians and others, too. The words of Jesus echo comfortingly down through the centuries of believers who have not had the opportunity of seeing the resurrected Christ standing before us: "Blessed are those who have not seen me and yet have come to believe" (John 20:29b NRSV). But consider how this passage is a witness to the stubborn faith of *Jesus Christ* in his *disciples*—not just those *first* followers of Jesus, but his *later* followers who were not present that night in that room.

Peter is not the only follower of Christ ever to have misunderstood, to have been impetuous, to have denied friendship with Jesus when he felt threatened, subject to ridicule, confused by the turn of events. Thomas is not the only follower of Christ to have been absent when Christ came calling, to have demanded proof before believing, to have scoffed at reports of a miracle. The most devout Christian must admit episodes of disloyalty and occasions of doubt. But Jesus Christ's faith in his followers, his faith in his church, is so *stubborn* that *despite* all the times throughout history that the church and individual believers have been unfaithful, have been an enemy of the poor and the oppressed, have kept silence in the face of absurdities and atrocities, have sat by while the truth of the gospel was being distorted and compromised, have worshiped ideologies and creeds and rules rather than the living God, have sought public approval over costly discipleship, he *still* sends *us* as the *Father* sent *him*, and *continues* to breathe the Holy Spirit upon us and entrust us with the care of human souls. Perhaps the reason that his faith in us is so stubborn is that his love for us is stubborn, too.

Most of us, when we learn that someone has put their trust in us, try to rise to the occasion. We sacrifice something of our own wants in an effort to respond to the other person's needs. We reach down within ourselves to tap our reserves of courage and compassion to try to be as good and trustworthy as the other person thinks we are. Thomas was skeptical, perhaps not so much of *Jesus* as of the other disciples' report of having *seen* Jesus. At any rate, as soon as he *saw* Jesus alive again, his faith leapt beyond all the others' to make an offering of himself to Christ with the exclamation, "My Lord and my God!" (John 20:28 NRSV). Apparently, he didn't in fact have to touch the marks of the nails and the sword, as he had earlier insisted. And, according to legend, he traveled farther than any other of the original disciples, taking the good news of Jesus Christ and his resurrection all the way to the shores of India. The apostles faced extraordinary challenges with extraordinary courage, ministered in extraordinary circumstances with extraordinary compassion. The same Peter who, trembling with fear, denied ever having known Jesus on the night of his arrest, days later fearlessly defied the orders of the Sanhedrin not to preach the gospel of Jesus Christ.

> The high priest questioned [Peter and the other apostles], saying, "We gave you strict orders not to teach in this name, yet here you have filled Jerusalem with your teaching and you are determined to bring this man's blood on us." But Peter and the apostles answered, "We must obey God rather than any human authority. The God of our ancestors raised up Jesus, whom you had killed by hanging him on a tree. God exalted him at his right hand as Leader and Savior that he might give repentance to Israel and forgiveness of sins. And we are witnesses to these things, and so is the Holy Spirit whom God has given to those who obey him." (Acts 5:27b–32 NRSV)

"Peace be with you. As the Father has sent me, so I send you" (John 20:21 NRSV). Christ has chosen us, you and me and the church. In spite of our failures, our faults, and even our doubts and our denials, Christ has *chosen* us, has dared to *trust* us and to have *faith* in us, to preach and teach accurately and precisely and scrupulously, to pray and discern fervently and with understanding, to heal and comfort with confidence and compassion, to feed and clothe graciously and generously, to confront and rebuke boldly and uncompromisingly, to worship and give praise authentically and gratefully, to repent of our own sins and to forgive the sins of others. We may not *recognize* such qualities in ourselves. Without the Holy Spirit breathed upon us and Christ alive within us, indeed we would not be capable of a *single one* of these things that Christ expects of us and has commissioned us to do. Gifted with the Spirit, we could still refuse, could still resist, and sometimes we do. But Christ's faith in us is more stubborn than our disobedience. Christ's love for us is more stubborn than our love of self. And so, when God raises him from the tomb, he immediately seeks out those he loves, to comfort them, to give them companionship, to assure them, and to rejoice that, alive forevermore, not even death will separate him from us or us from him.

What deeds of faith does *Christ's* faith elicit from *you*? What has the breath of Christ upon *you* given you the Holy Spirit's power to accomplish? What reversal of timidity or fear or irresoluteness is being worked in your life by Christ's stubborn faith in you? The same Peter who drew near to the soldier's campfire as his Master was being arraigned and who disowned his friend and teacher became a bold preacher and Christ's agent in performing many mighty miracles. The same Thomas who refused to accept the testimony of the *other* disciples was the first to acknowledge the full truth of Jesus' identity and courageously proclaimed it in pagan lands despite threats and dangers. "As the Father has sent me, so I send you. . . . Receive the Holy Spirit" (John 20:21b, 22b NRSV). See what faith Christ has in his church to minister in the name and manner of our Lord and our God!

Third Sunday of Easter
Spanish Springs Presbyterian Church, Sparks, Nevada
April 18, 2010
Acts 9:1–20
Revelation 5:11–14
John 21:1–19

"On the Other Side of Healing"

ONE OF THE WONDERFULLY unique things about the Bible is that we are never done with it, and it is never done with us. Most books can be read and set aside; we have gleaned from them the information that we sought, or we have been entertained and now want to move on to the *next* entertainment. Even the reference books and novels that we *return* to for data or pleasure are either consulted again to retrieve facts or reread to capture again an earlier experience of enjoyment. But for the person of faith, the Bible remains always fresh, and close to the heart of the meaning of "inspiration" is the fact that each time we open its pages with believing eyes and receptive spirit, we find a new facet to this precious gem of a book. Often, the discovery is aided by someone else sharing *their* observations in a sermon or a Bible study or a piece of sacred music, perhaps.

As I was reading a recent commentary on our Acts passage for today, it dawned on me, as it had never done before, that the story of the conversion of Saul, starting with his being blinded after the risen Lord encountered him in a flash of heavenly light while Saul was on the road to Damascus to persecute Christians, is a *healing* story—one of several in Acts. So crucial, in Luke's telling, is Paul's conversion and his mission work to the story of the spread of the gospel and the growth of the church that it is his *conversion* that had always grabbed my attention in this episode. Some of us even suppose that Saul's experience is the sort to which we should *all* aspire, or by which we measure our *own* coming to accept Jesus Christ as Lord and Savior. But Saul's experience is only one of *several* different conversion experiences that are related in Acts, and, in any event, neither *Saul's* nor anyone *else's* conversion is an end in *itself*. And when Ananias, the disciple who had just a few qualms about going to visit the very man who had been doing evil to the saints in Jerusalem and had come to Damascus with authority from the chief priests to bind all who invoked Christ's name, submitted to the Lord's instruction and went to the street called Straight, to the house of Judas, to find the great persecutor of the church and lay hands on him so that he might regain his sight, the result was that "something like scales fell from [Saul's] eyes, and his sight was restored" (Acts 9:18a NRSV). It is a *healing* story—never mind that it was apparently the risen Christ *himself* who had just *blinded* Saul with a heavenly light, so that, at Ananias's touch, he could be made to *see* again. And when the Bible recounts the story of a healing, there is a purpose to it. As far as Jesus was concerned, for instance, the man in the Gospel of John was born blind so that God's works might be revealed in him.

Like some other healings, this one occurred when Ananias the disciple laid his hands on Saul—the very person who had been on his way to Damascus with the intention of laying *his* hands on followers of Jesus like *Ananias*, not for the purpose of *healing* them, of course, but to bind them and haul them before the authorities back in Jerusalem! *Saul's* intention had been to *destroy*. *Ananias's* intention had been to *restore*—not just to allow Saul to *see* again, but to be brought back into a right relationship with God so that he might become God's instrument for restoring *others* to a right relationship with God and with each other. We can't know for certain what quality it was in Saul that drew the Lord's attention; maybe it was mainly the Lord's own desire to move him from the column marked "enemy" to the column marked "friend." At any rate, when Ananias points out to the Lord that the person to whom the Lord wants to send him is the *very* one who has been so zealous to *destroy* the *church*, the Lord responds that Saul is the one whom the Lord has chosen for the task of spreading the gospel in foreign lands and before foreign leaders and before Israel, as well. And the rest of the story we know about.

Every healing story has another side to it—beyond the healing *itself*, there is the matter of what happened *next*. As good and compassionate as healing might be, the instances of healing in the *Bible* open up possibilities of a *consequence*. Naaman the Syrian general comes to understand that there is only one God, and *that* one is the God of Israel. The Gerasene demoniac tells people that Jesus has freed him from the unclean spirit, and everyone is amazed at Jesus. Peter's mother-in-law is healed of her fever, and she serves the disciples. (Women may think that there should have been some *better* consequence than *that*.) As a *healing* story, the restoration of Saul's sight had a consequence, too—"he got up and was baptized" (Acts 9:18b NRSV), took some food (was it the eucharist, the Lord's Supper?), regained his strength, and began proclaiming Jesus in the synagogues, saying, "He is the Son of God" (Acts 9:20b NRSV).

The whole subject of divine healing is one that raises questions in our minds: Why are some healed and others aren't? What sort of faith is required for healing? Exactly how does divine healing happen? We can't answer those questions with certainty. But *those* aren't the questions that the Bible is interested in answering, or even wants us to raise. The Bible is more interested in *our* amazement—our *response* to the healing that Jesus does. Saul was *converted*—transformed—not just in an instant, but over the course of the rest of his life. His *healing* cleared the way for and made possible his baptism and his preaching and his mission of evangelism, and his continuing growth in Christlikeness. The emphasis of the book of Acts is not concerned so much with Paul's *conversion* as with his *vocation*, his *calling*, his faithful assumption of the work that God now put before him as a genuine follower of Christ. It is not just that "he once was blind but now he sees." Rather, "he once was a *persecutor* of the church and now he risks *being* persecuted for the *sake* of the church." As one commentator puts it, in the book of Acts, personal transformation never collapses into sanctified self-absorption.[1] Rather, conversion prepares the believer to perform concrete tasks in the service of God. On the *other side* of healing, there is *ministry* to be done.

Peter was in need of healing. His spirit was low after he had failed Jesus by denying him three times. We can well imagine that he was sick with self-reproach. Perhaps that is why his vision of the new reality inaugurated with Jesus' resurrection was so cloudy. All he could think to do after the resurrected Jesus came to the disciples in the upper room was to go fishing—to try to get back to the "normal" that had been suspended for three years. The other disciples followed suit. But the resurrection had changed everything from "normal." While they were out on the lake, a man standing on the beach called out to them and asked how the fishing was—seemed to know, in fact, that they had caught nothing. The man told them to cast their net on the starboard side of the boat. It turned out to be the "right" side—the fishing net filled so full that they had difficulty hauling it in. The man now called to them to come and join him for breakfast. By that time, they had perceived that it was Jesus. The disciples accepted the invitation, and, when breakfast was over,

> Jesus said to Simon Peter, "Simon son of John, do you love me more than these?" He said to him, "Yes, Lord; you know that I

---

8. Wall, "Acts of the Apostles," 155.

> love you." Jesus said to him, "Feed my lambs." A second time he said to him, "Simon son of John, do you love me?" He said to him, "Yes, Lord; you know that I love you." Jesus said to him, "Tend my sheep." He said to him the third time, "Simon son of John, do you love me?" Peter felt hurt because he said to him the third time, "Do you love me?" And he said to him, "Lord, you know everything; you know that I love you." Jesus said to him, "Feed my sheep." (John 21:15–17 NRSV)

And then Jesus told Peter that he was going to die for his loyalty, and concluded their conversation by saying to Peter, "Follow me" (John 21:19c NRSV). And Peter became an evangelist, and a leader to whom other leaders of the early church looked.

This, too, is a healing story—the story of Jesus' healing the relationship between himself and Peter, a relationship that was broken not from Jesus' side but from Peter's. "'I will not deny you'" (Mark 14:31b NRSV), Peter had objected when Jesus had said that he would be unfaithful. But of course, he *did* deny Jesus. And this episode at the end of John's Gospel fits the pattern of healing stories. The threefold questioning of Peter's love for Jesus matched and counter-balanced Peter's threefold denial of Jesus on the night of his arrest. Their unity and intimacy and mutuality were now restored. Peter's spirit was healed, having been assured again of Jesus' acceptance of him. And Peter was now capable of doing the work that Jesus set before him: "'Feed my sheep'" (John 21:17c NRSV). And, as the book of Acts bears out, Peter rather miraculously began to see things quite differently from the way he had seen them before—was converted, we might say—transformed from an unimaginative legalist into a compassionate shepherd, from someone who had thought that life was all about the *law* into a person who came to understand that custom must yield to life-giving *gospel*. Though he had denied knowing him, Peter had never stopped loving Jesus. But Jesus' healing power now translated Peter's love for him into love for Christ's church—for the entire flock Jesus would call to himself and who would need caring and compassionate leaders, shepherds. With the words "Follow me," Peter was being called not just to believe in Jesus in a general way, but to be so faithful that he would willingly face martyrdom and death. "'Very truly, I tell you, when you were younger, you used to fasten your own belt and to go wherever you wished. But when you grow old, you will stretch out your hands, and someone else will fasten a belt around you and take you where you do not wish to go.' (He said this to indicate the kind of death by which he would glorify God)" (John 21:18–19a NRSV). According to early Christian writings, Peter *also* was crucified. On the other side of healing, Peter would lay down his life in love.

Healing and conversion are closely related in the New Testament. But, like the Bible itself, we should focus not so much on the speculative features, but on the purposeful consequences. And if we wonder what all this has to do with *us*, if, for instance, we have never *had* a great illness of which we needed to be healed, it may be useful to remember that the same Greek word that we translate with the English word "healing" can *also* be translated with the English word "salvation." What is the consequence of *your* salvation? What is Jesus Christ calling you to do, now that you have been saved, now that you have been healed?

Fourth Sunday of Easter
First Presbyterian Church, Dodge City, Kansas
May 3, 1998
Acts 9:36–43
Revelation 7:9–17
John 10:22–30

"Nothing Will Ever Be Quite the Same"

THE BOOK OF ACTS, it seems to me, is one of the most under-attended parts of the New Testament. Naturally, we are drawn to the *Gospel* stories of Jesus. And the letters of Paul are extremely important to understanding the significance of Christ. And the Revelation to John is . . . well, the Revelation has gotten a lot of attention, and it will probably be receiving even *more* as we approach the millennium. But *Acts* tells us how the *power* of the *risen Christ* infused the world through the *church*, and how the world was never again quite the same. The Acts of the Apostles was not written simply as ancient history. The Acts of the Apostles was written to tell the church who it *is* and what it is to be *about* in every age. The episodes in this book are *our* story, the *church's* story. Do we recognize ourselves in it? Do we see our own struggles, our own victories, our own faith mirrored in the witness of the ancient saints—a witness that revolutionized the communities in which they lived?

Our passage from Acts this morning is really quite remarkable. Nearly everybody in this room knows what it is like to lose someone who is very important to us, someone to whom we are very close. Oftentimes, the news comes to us in a telephone call, sometimes by mail, sometimes with a personal visit. We hang up the phone, we lay down the letter, we close the door, and we grieve. But not *one* of us, no matter how much we might wish it, has ever received a *second* phone call or a *second* letter or a *second* visit delivering the news, "Your loved one has miraculously come back to life again!" In *our* experience, such things don't *happen*. And we don't *expect* them to. But if you and I are honest with our trust in the scriptures, and if you and I truly believe that *we* are a marvelous continuation of the great parade of saints and martyrs and their stunning deeds of faith, then we must admit to wondering why no one seems to have the power to bring the dead back to life *today*. Not even the most earnest television evangelists have been able to work *that* miracle, and I don't suppose that even their most ardent followers truly *expect* them to. Is there any particular reason that modern disciples should not be prepared and able to do what *Peter* did of *old*? *Our* relatives are every bit as dear to *us* as *Tabitha* was to *her* family. *Our* leaders are just important to *us* as *Tabitha* was to *her* congregation. Wouldn't we like to know *how* Peter brought her back to life, so that we could do whatever *Peter did*?

But Luke is not interested in *explaining* Tabitha's return to life. He just tells the story. A disciple named Tabitha lived at Joppa, and she was devoted to good works and acts of charity—much like a deacon. It seems that she had a special concern for the *widows* in that Christian community; she *sewed* for them, making sure that they had clothes to wear. It was a great loss to the church when Tabitha died, not only in the way of fellowship with her, but with regard to practical concerns of what she did for the needy. So they notified *Peter*, who was in a nearby town only a few miles away. Perhaps he could say a word of encouragement to the congregation. Perhaps he would lead them in giving thanks to God for her exemplary life. But when Peter came, and heard how beloved she had been and saw how significant her ministry was to that congregation, he asked them all to leave the room, and he turned toward the body and said, "'Tabitha, get up.' Then she opened her eyes, and seeing Peter, she sat up. He gave her his hand and helped her up. Then calling the saints and widows, he showed her to be alive. This became known throughout Joppa, and many believed in the Lord." (Acts 9:40b–42 NRSV). Jesus once said that his *followers* were to do even *greater* things than *he* had done, and two of the things *Jesus* did were to bring back to life a friend and a little girl. Already, Peter had healed people who were sick, and that had become known, but in spite of Jesus' promise, none of the apostles had ever brought *anyone* back to life from the *dead*. So the Christians at Joppa must not have *expected* Peter to do anything of the sort. But when Peter assessed the situation, he did what must have seemed to be most helpful. And the result was that "many believed in the Lord" (Acts 10:42b NRSV).

This was *not* a *resurrection*—there is only *one* case of resurrection in the Bible, and that is of Jesus himself, raised from the dead to everlasting life by God. The episode with Tabitha was a *resuscitation*—a temporary restoration to earthly life, so that Tabitha's ministry might continue for a while longer, not in a *resurrection* body, but in the very *same* body she had *always* had. Eventually, Tabitha died again, as *all* people die, and presumably, no one tried to bring her back to life yet once more. Death is normal.

"You are dust," God said, "and to dust you shall return" (Gen 3:19b NRSV). Still, *many* of us wish that we might have our loved ones back, if only for a little while longer, though it would mean the pain of dying and parting a second time. We have unfinished business with them, or we think that they have unfinished business with us. Many of us wish that we might have the visionary and courageous leaders of old back to guide us again, if only briefly, hoping to learn better this time what they tried to teach us, though it might have the effect of encouraging us not to *excellence* but to *complacency*. But death *does* come. Death is *normal*. It is a fact of existence. The younger generation must succeed the older. Things cannot remain the same, nor should they. And life is sweeter for it. Luke does not explain Tabitha's return to life, and neither can we. For God's own inscrutable purpose, Peter was inspired and enabled by the Holy Spirit to work this mighty miracle, and the result was that Tabitha's ministry continued, and many people believed in the Lord. But, like Jesus, Peter did not spend all his time bringing back to physical life all of those who had died, not even all the believers. There was other ministry to do, too, every bit as necessary to God's purpose, every bit as urgent to God's kingdom.

But the story of Peter and Tabitha is remarkable for some other reasons, as well, not the least of which is mentioned in the very first sentence: "Now in Joppa there was a *disciple* whose name was *Tabitha*" (Acts 9:36a NRSV). In Joppa, there was a *woman* who was a leader of the congregation. In Joppa, there was a *woman* who administered a welfare program for the poor. In Joppa, there was a *woman* who held a place of high responsibility in the church, whose skill and experience were deemed irreplaceable. For over four decades now, the Presbyterian Church (USA) has insisted that *all* offices of the church shall be open to both men and women, including the ordained offices of deacon, elder, and minister of word and sacrament. I hope that that is not a strange notion to us. It is based on the scriptural testimony about the ministry of Jesus and about life in the early church. Some modern Christians still refuse to admit women to the highest offices of the church. But if some *Christians* in our late *twentieth* century have problems with women in leadership, imagine what a *radical* notion it was among *Jews* in the early *first* century! A woman just didn't *do* that sort of thing, not even among the *Gentiles*! But through Tabitha's work in the church, God was *overturning* old notions of authority, and God was establishing a new configuration of power. In Jesus Christ, God took what was lowly and despised in the world to bring to naught the mighty and the privileged. God is totally free to upset the customary and to defy the expected.

And the story of Peter and Tabitha is remarkable for *another* feature. You and I might not have thought anything about the comment that Peter, while he was in Joppa, stayed for some time with a certain Simon, a tanner. But no scrupulous Jew would ever have considered lodging in the house of a tanner. To treat leather—animal hide—was immediately to open oneself to suspicion of violating the laws about how animals may be killed and prepared, about what is clean and unclean. On his visit to Joppa, Peter was crossing all sorts of boundaries, ignoring all kinds of time-honored taboos, acknowledging all manner of new possibilities. Then, finally, in the very next chapter, while he was still at the house of Simon the tanner, Peter received a strange vision about eating forbidden food. Suddenly, he was summoned to the house of Cornelius the *Roman centurion*, and he realized that no one should call *anyone* unclean, consider *anyone* beyond God's love, or declare *anyone* out of the reach of God's grace. The revolutionary nature of the New Testament had reached its zenith. The phrase "conservative Christianity" became forever a contradiction in terms.

The Christian faith is where things that aren't *supposed* to happen, happen *daily*. *Slaves* sit at table with their *masters*. *Jews* eat with *Gentiles*. *Women* lead *congregations*. Even the *dead* can be brought back to life! In Christ's new community, the church, *no one* stays in his or her place, because Christ is the head of the church, and among his people there is neither slave nor free, Jew nor Gentile, male nor female, nor any other distinction. Despite our attempts, *we* do not define who can be visited by the Holy Spirit and how. *We* do not limit who can be saved and how. *We* do not even grant that death will have the final say. Any widow was considered as good as dead herself; according to custom, her only significance in life had been as some man's wife. It was to such lowly, poor, and despised that the Holy Spirit had led the disciple Tabitha to give them life, to raise them up from the social ladder's bottom rung and endow them with a dignity beyond any that the culture recognized. Their coats and garments were proof of the ministry that Tabitha had offered. Her death plunged the community of faith into crisis. Who, now, would care for the widows? Who, now, would honor the radical hope to which they had been lifted? Would they simply fall back down into the place society had customarily put them—on the margins, unimportant and unacknowledged?

The story of Peter and Tabitha is testimony that there is a power loose in the world—a power which is able to break open the last vestiges of the *old* order, self-absorbed and self-congratulating. In God's new creation heralded by the church, widows will not be abandoned. Jesus Christ reigns. And the name of Jesus Christ means life, every bit as much as the word of God means life. "The Father and I are one" (John 10:30 NRSV), Jesus declared to the guardians of the old order—the old order that thought *it* could dictate where widows belonged, *and* the sick, *and* the poor. "I give [my sheep] eternal life, and they will never perish" (John 10:28a NRSV). "*I declare who they are, and no one shall ever take that identity from them, not by social convention, not by common wisdom, not by worldly schemes.*" And immediately they took up stones with which to stone him. Eventually, they crucified him. But death *did not win*, and death *has not won*. "Tabitha, get up, rise, and defy every unredeemed expectation and embolden every feeble hope with the power of the risen Lord Jesus Christ"—the risen Lord Jesus Christ who transforms every arrangement and every order, who changes them from evidence of death into testimony to life! Even the poor are no longer on the margins; they are the very center of God's attention. Never again need anyone resign him- or herself to the station and role that *others* have appointed for them—not fisherfolk, not widows. The power of Christ is loose and at work, and no *inherited order*, no accustomed understanding, no self-serving truism is safe from its revolutionary impact. The *only* truth is the life-giving, life-restoring, life-transforming word of God, *and it will have its way*. And you and I are *stewards* of that word, that promise, that power, for you and I are the church of Jesus Christ that began with the apostles, that worked wonders of old, and that still exists today to work miracles. New life, people rising above the dead staleness of their old selves, overcoming fears and anxieties—those are the marks of the church of which the risen Lord Jesus Christ is head. Evangelists and prophets, we, who look upon every appearance of death and hopelessness, misery and despair, and say, "Get up! Rise!" No hunger! No thirst! No tears! And *nothing* will ever be quite the same again.

Fifth Sunday of Easter

Spanish Springs Presbyterian Church, Sparks, Nevada

May 2, 2010

Acts 11:1–18

Revelation 21:1–6

John 13:31–35

"Revelation"

Deborah had always known that there was something different about her son. She was no expert on child behavior, but from an early age, Michael's interaction with girls and boys had not been what she would have expected of a boy of his age. Her husband, Jake, had also noticed, and had increasingly blamed her for turning him into a "mama's boy," though she had always encouraged Michael to do things with his father, and to play with other children in the neighborhood and school. And eventually, when the differences took on a more recognizable nature, Jake's criticism of her became more emotionally abusive and he increasingly ignored his son, seldom speaking to him after he once called him a "sissy," leaving the room when the boy would enter it.

Deborah had sometimes considered seeking help—going to a psychologist or a counselor—but always ended up feeling too embarrassed to do so, and, in truth, afraid of what she might learn. Instead, as Michael grew older, she would ask whether he wouldn't like to invite a girl over to the house, or to go to a movie, perhaps. Sometimes, in the beginning, Michael would just turn away. As he progressed through his teens, such conversations sometimes ended up in shouting matches, Deborah arguing that his lack of interest in girls wasn't normal, Michael responding that he should be allowed to live his own life. Then, one day, their confrontation had led to tears, a slammed door, and the sound of the boy's uncontrollable groaning and sobbing from behind it. Once, Deborah had considered talking with the minister about Michael, but then he had preached a sermon on the abominable sinfulness of people like Michael, and how they were destroying the country's moral fiber, and she had abandoned the plan. It was shortly after that that Jake had left her and Michael, saying that her coddling of the boy had deprived him of the son he had wanted and expected and deserved.

As Deborah turned from closing the front door behind the two men who had been in her living room for the past twenty minutes, with despair and shame and anger competing for supremacy within her, she saw Michael standing at the head of the stairs above the entryway. His face showed profound sorrow. She wiped her eyes and sniffed, and then said in his direction, "Two of the elders."

Michael responded, "I know." Then he added, "I heard."

Anger was now in the ascendancy within Deborah's heart, and her face was turning red. She looked toward the living room and away from the child she had carried within her for nine months, whose diapers she had changed, whose fevers she had worried over, whose behavior she had agonized about, and for whom she had prayed daily since even before the doctor had confirmed that she was pregnant.

"I can't help it, Mama," Michael said in a voice twisted with pain over the pain that his *mother* was feeling. "I'm sorry."

Tears now flowed freely down Deborah's cheeks. She shook her head, though neither of them knew exactly whether it was in anger at the visitors or in dismay at the situation or in rejection of the apology or in denial that any apology was necessary.

Michael walked down to the landing. "I'll leave and go somewhere else to live if you want," he said limply. "I don't want to cause you any more trouble."

Deborah turned to look at her son, and her tears became a convulsion of grief—grief, mainly, at the thought of losing her boy.

"I love you, Mama," Michael said, tears now trickling down *his* cheeks, too. Deborah climbed the stairs and put her arms around her son as he put one arm around her waist—the first time in many months that they had touched—and they stood there on the landing for several minutes, both continuing to cry, neither knowing what more to say. The grandfather clock below them at the foot of the stairs chimed seven thirty.

"Hadn't you better get to class?" the mother said to her son, more telling than asking. They both knew that he didn't feel like driving to the college campus for his night class in English literature.

"Yes, I guess so," he answered weakly.

"Are you coming home afterward?" Deborah asked. "Or . . .?"

Michael pursed his lips. He considered for a few seconds, but then said, "I'll be home about ten."

The telephone rang a few minutes after Deborah heard Michael driving off down the street. "Mrs. Simms," the voice on the other end of the phone began. Deborah recognized it as belonging to Margaret Durkin, the woman who chaired the ladies' guild at the church and who once had been Michael's Sunday school teacher and had advised that she didn't think he was yet ready for baptism. "I know you signed up to bring a casserole to our lunch next week. But I really think it would be best if you chose not to come. I know that you had a visit from George Haines and Cleve Barker tonight, so I'm sure that you understand." Deborah replaced the receiver without responding. For the time being, there were no more tears left in her. She simply sat in her chair at the kitchen table, hardly thinking, little aware of the accustomed surroundings. In front of her was a short stack of mail, mostly junk solicitations, addressed to Jake, that had been accumulating until, as usual, she would bundle it into a large manila envelope at the end of the week and send it to his apartment address.

She was still there at the table when, two hours later, Michael said, "I'm back." Although she had not been conscious that he had come into the house, she was not startled. Her back was turned to him, and he could hear only a quiet reply to his greeting. After a few seconds of waiting to see whether she had anything else to say, he went upstairs to his room. Deborah continued to sit at the table long into the night.

Deborah had never warmed to her coworkers. In part, she feared what the office gossipers would do if they knew about her family and home life, so she had seldom spoken at work about Michael and, in the last couple of years, less and less about her husband. Today, she was grateful that much of her work was routine and rather mechanical; she was not in the mood to do anything that required much concentration. It was unusual for her to take a break from her work, although that morning she had brought a section of the newspaper with her from home to read over again a notice that she had seen under the listing of church events. She could not easily set aside her lifelong habit of attending worship and being moderately involved in other congregational activities. The latter practice had waned as tensions had increased at home and nearly stopped altogether when Jake left. But she had recently started to participate in the ladies' guild—a group to which, it now seemed, she was no longer welcome.

Rather than turning against God, she had decided to investigate other churches, sad as that was for someone as sentimental as herself, and so had looked over the newspaper that morning before leaving for work. Under the listed events for one church—a congregation belonging to a denomination that she had frequently heard denounced by people in her own church as "liberal"—she had noticed the mention of a support group for parents and grandparents of gays and lesbians. A few years earlier—even a few *weeks* earlier—she might have considered the notion of a church hosting such a group as strange or even shameful. But her experience over the past several months, culminating in the visit from the elders and the telephone call from Margaret Durkin, had produced a change in her outlook—those things, and the fear that she might lose contact with her son, whom she had always loved even though she could not always understand. Indeed, one of the things she had thought about long into the night, sitting at the kitchen table, was Michael's words, "I love you," and how, for too many months now—or was it years?—she had been unable or unwilling to say the same thing to him.

She found again the church listing and noted the time and day of the meeting—Tuesday at 8:00 p.m. It was now Friday morning. She resolved to go to the meeting. No one would know her. After all, she was quite certain that she didn't know anyone who had a homosexual child or grandchild. But could she really bring herself to attend that other church on Sunday? For years, she had lived in dread that someone would make a comment, that someone would ask a question, that someone would make a doctrinaire statement about homosexuals burning in hell and she would break down uncontrollably and then the secret would be out. And then, after all of her self-conscious caution, Jake had said something to somebody about having moved out and why, and it had gotten back to the church and to the elders and, obviously, to Margaret Durkin. And George Haines and Cleve Barker had been sent to make sure that she was aware that the Bible said homosexuality is a sin. They would be praying for her, they had said, that she would be a good parent and get Michael "straightened out," and that he would recognize and acknowledge and repent of the grave error of his choice. In the meantime, he would not be welcome at the church, and the tone of their visit indicated that everyone would be more comfortable if *she* were not around, either, until the family again followed the ways of scripture.

In the eyes of her own congregation, attending such a church as the one that offered the support group was almost as objectionable as homosexuality itself. But, she told herself as she folded up the newspaper section and put it back in her purse, she was a *Christian*, and Christians needed to worship *God*. If her *own* church would not allow her to fulfill a Christian duty, she reasoned, she would fulfill that duty *elsewhere*. And if there was a church that was willing to help her deal with the circumstances in which she found herself, then she would take the risk of worshiping *there*. She refused to punish *God* for her sorrows. She would even put money in the offering plate, if they had one.

Deborah Simms found a seat near the rear of the sanctuary on Sunday morning—a section of the room that seemed to be particularly popular.

Much about the service was unfamiliar, with music and responses that she had never heard or spoken. There was also rather more scripture read than she was used to, and there seemed to be special attention given to the words and deeds of Jesus. The minister talked a lot about mercy and grace and not so much about judgment and damnation. She herself was focusing on being inconspicuous, and prayed that no one would try to engage her in conversation at the end of the service. Except for the persistent anxiety about the events that had caused her to attend the church in the first place, she was not uncomfortable in the worship service despite the differences from what she considered normal. But toward the end of the service, she noticed a man and woman seated on the other side of the sanctuary and somewhat closer to the chancel than herself. From her angle, they appeared familiar, and when, following the benediction, they turned to greet someone who had been sitting behind them, she recognized Miles and Stacy Harbison, who had disappeared rather suddenly from her own church about two years previously. She slipped out of the sanctuary and into the parking lot without speaking to anyone, although several people tried to offer a word of greeting.

On Tuesday evening, Deborah returned to the church and followed the signs to the room where the support group would be meeting. She was normally early for appointments and events, but, on this occasion, she chose to sit in her car in the parking lot until just a few minutes before eight o'clock. When she arrived at Room 114, there were already about a dozen people present, both men and women, ranging in age from their mid-thirties to their seventies. One woman gestured to Deborah to sit down in the empty chair alongside her. Just as she did, another couple entered the room. Deborah looked at them, and was shocked to recognize the faces of Miles and Stacy Harbison. Before she could feel embarrassed, and before she could formulate a plan to slip out of the room without their noticing, Stacy's eyes met hers. The other woman crossed the room and embraced her. "Deborah! How good to see you. I've missed you since we started coming here."

"Hello, Stacy," was all Deborah could bring herself to say.

"We've been here about two years now," Stacy explained, "and we've found it so warm and accepting. About a year and a half ago," she continued, "we became a part of this group, and now we're leading it, since the original leaders moved away."

By now, Miles Harbison had noticed his wife talking with a new participant, and then, recognizing Deborah, came across the room to greet her.

"A few years ago, we finally acknowledged the truth about our Rachel," Stacy explained.

"I remember Rachel," Deborah said. "She was so beautiful and charm. . . ." Deborah stopped in disbelief. The question escaped from her lips unintended. "You mean that Rachel . . . ?"

"Pastor Blaine said we should disassociate ourselves from her," Stacy said.

"We were always being told to ask what Jesus would do in different situations," Miles took over. "Well, we didn't think that's what Jesus would *do*."

"And, as we've talked with other people in the same situation, we've become convinced of it," Stacy added. "We had some very difficult times. But today, our family is stronger than it has ever been. And Rachel is so happy and doing so well, now that she, now that we. . . ." Stacy's sentence trailed off. Eventually, she added, "There's so much love back in our lives."

Miles spoke again. "We'd better get started," he said. He and his wife sat down together. "Hello, everybody. Let's begin the evening with prayer." Before the meeting was over, Deborah Simms had shed many tears. But, by the end of the meeting, the tears she was shedding were tears of joy and thanksgiving.

When Deborah got home that night, she climbed the stairs and knocked on the door of her son's room. She hadn't told him at dinner where she was going, only that she had a meeting to attend, and he hadn't questioned her about it. "Come in," she heard him say from within.

She opened the door to find Michael rising from his desk and closing a textbook. "Michael, would you come to church with me on Sunday?" she asked. It had been many months since he had attended a worship service. "At the place I went last week," she added.

"Well. . . ." he started.

"Honey, it's different there."

"Yes, I guess so," he shrugged.

Deborah crossed to where Michael was standing and put her arms around him. "Michael, I love you so much," she said to her son. And there were no tears in her eyes.

Sixth Sunday of Easter
Spanish Springs Presbyterian Church, Sparks, Nevada
May 13, 2007
Acts 16:9–15
Revelation 21:10, 21:22—22:5
John 5:1–9

"Water of Life"

WITH AS LITTLE SNOW as we had this past winter, we all know that water is going to be in short supply this summer. Life in our area always exists in precarious balance with the winter snowpack in the Sierra, and most of us already know the days on which we are permitted to water our yards. In most cities in the West, outdoor watering restrictions have become a common thing, even in summers following relatively wet winters. Growing up in Colorado, for instance, as the Front Range rapidly became suburbanized, I cannot remember very many summers when we didn't have water rationing. We were permitted to water only every third day, as here. Each house was designated as a "diamond" or a "circle" or a "square," according to address. I was always a little chagrined that, by virtue of our number on East Lake Drive—1853—year after year we were designated as "squares," allowed to water only on a "square" watering day. In the days before automatic timers, our entire family schedule revolved around our watering periods. During the long, hot months of July and August, the water board even got to the point of sending out a patrol to make sure that people were not violating their appointed times. You could be ticketed for watering on the wrong day. As I recall, the water police even had the authority to turn off your water altogether if you were a repeat offender. People automatically came to associate the words "water" and "restrictions."

Water is precious, as people here know, and as people in the desert Near East know. People have *killed* over water. And the *worst* is *ahead* of us. The day is approaching when the oil crises we have experienced will pale in comparison to a world-wide shortage of clean, fresh water. Just a few years ago, Ontario and Michigan announced a lawsuit against an entrepreneur who contracted to sell and transport water from Lake Superior to Asia. But I predict that before the middle of the century, the thirsty southwest United States will be constructing pipelines to siphon water from northern Canada.

One of the *simplest* phenomena of nature is one of the most *important*. Water is necessary to sustain life. Water is necessary to restore life. In the months *before* we are born, we are *surrounded* by it. In all the days *after* we are born, we are *refreshed* by it. By opening up a way of escape through the waves and then sending them crashing back upon Pharaoh's army, God delivered a people by means of water. A Samaritan woman on one occasion came to the village well to draw water and met a man she did not know who explained to her, "Everyone who drinks of *this* water will be thirsty *again*, but those who drink of the water that *I* will give them will *never* be thirsty" (John 4:13–14a NRSV). And she pleaded with him to give her the water that gushes up to *eternal life*. And shortly thereafter, a royal official came to Jesus asking him to come to his little son who was gravely ill. "Jesus said to him, 'Go; your son will *live*'" (John 4:50a NRSV). And the boy lived, and the man and his whole household believed.

Just after that, Jesus went up to Jerusalem for a festival, probably the Jewish Pentecost. And he was passing by a pool near one of the city's gates, where many invalids lay in the shade of the porticoes surrounding the water—blind, lame, and paralyzed. They believed the legend that some spirit or angel stirred up the pool a couple of times a day, agitating the waters—actually, it was the gush of water from a spring which fed the pond—and that the first sick person to get into the water after the spring had bubbled up would be healed. But it was too hot to sit or lie out in the sun all day waiting for the angel to do its work, so the invalids remained in the porticoes until the rare event occurred. It must have been quite a stampede to the water as soon as someone noticed the bubbling.

Jesus noticed a man lying in the portico—one he discerned had been coming there many years—thirty-eight, in fact. Paralyzed or lame, he was always too late to the pool. Imagine the frustration of praying for thirty-eight long years to be first to the finish line and win the prize, pulling himself forward on his elbows, or clawing his way ahead, or trying to roll down to the pool, hoping not to fall in and drown, always to be pushed aside in the rush of hopefuls, or pushed back, or simply run over. And still he came to the precious water, made even more precious to him because of his great affliction.

"'Do you want to be made well?'" (John 5:6b NRSV), Jesus asked him, without any words of introduction, and without any show of faith on the part of the man—only the obvious *hope* that daily drew him to the water's edge. The man could think of only one thing that would make him well—getting into the water—but that would require finally that someone pick him up and actually carry him through and over and ahead of the crowd. "'Sir,'" the sick man said to Jesus, "'I have no one to put me into the pool when the water is stirred up; and while I am making my way, someone else steps down ahead of me'" (John 5:7 NRSV). Did he hope that Jesus would take pity on him and stay with him until the water bubbled and carry him to the pool? Or was he just explaining why, despite his desperate desire to be well, thirty-eight years later he was still crippled? "Jesus said to him, 'Stand up, take your mat and walk.' At once the man was made well, and he took up his mat and began to walk" (John 5:8–9a NRSV). The man did not need to crawl to the water to be healed. The water of life had come to *him*.

We would be well satisfied if the story ended there. The man, so long paralyzed and lame, was made well by the simple command of Jesus—words that leaped over his frustration and fulfilled his hope. Imagine the man's astonishment and his joy! To walk again! To have purpose in life again! Not having to spend every day lying and waiting, lying and waiting, just to be kicked or shoved or stepped on when the narrow opportunity arrived. There must be a lot of people like that—not just the ones who are chronically sick, but those who feel chronically shut out of society, prevented from making a decent living, lonely, or outcast. We can really stand up and cheer with this man and give thanks to God for the new beginning made possible by Jesus.

But the story also has an ominous side, which our Gospel reading today only hints at in the last sentence: "Now that day was a sabbath" (John 5:9b NRSV). That day was the day on which the law declared that there should be no work—no healing, no curing, no miracles of God, even. And the next part of the story says that the great defenders of the law, those who considered themselves in control, those who loved their authority and enjoyed wielding their power, "started persecuting Jesus, because he was doing such things on the sabbath. But Jesus answered them, 'My Father is still working, and I also am working.' For this reason the Jews were seeking all the more to kill him" (John 5:16–18a NRSV). Rather than allow Jesus to *redefine* God's gracious presence in the world, they decided to *eliminate* Jesus, for he had threatened their conventional order, he had threatened their accustomed authority, he had threatened their beloved power, he had threatened their very perception of the way things are and always should be.

That is what old Jerusalem had become—the holy city of David, the city beloved by God, the city of the beautiful and celebrated temple, was the city where Jesus would eventually be crucified, the center of unbelief and hostility towards the Son of God. God's jewel had become the gate that stood in the way of the healing water, locked against the very people who needed God's mercy the most. And many were like the man by the pool, existing within earshot of God's blessing, straining for it, stretching their arms through the slats of the closed gate, but never able to reach it, and no one was interested in helping them because those who *could* help wanted all of God's mercy for *themselves*.

Come with me now to the last book of the Bible, and God's promise of a *new* Jerusalem coming down out of heaven. There is no temple, no altar to offer sacrifice, no sanctuary for making intercessions to God, for God is not off at a distance, but immediately present, just as God used to walk with first man and first woman in the evening breeze. There is no need for sun or moon; the *true* light shines upon *that* place—the glory of God, and its lamp is the Lamb of God—and there is no night, when fears grow large and shadows threaten. The gates of the *new* Jerusalem will *never* be shut—even kings and nations, the peoples who were once *enemies* of God, will be free to walk in the door, and they will *all* do so, cleansed and made suitable to be in the presence of God. And right through the middle of the city, bright as crystal, flowing from the throne of God and of the Lamb, is the river of the water of life, giving nourishment to the tree of life. And all the servants of God and of the Lamb will worship him and see his face and bear his name on their foreheads.

Some Christians think that the new Jerusalem will be a place for the spiritually elite, for a select few. As time goes on, we hear more and more claims for just who will be citizens of the new Jerusalem, as well as the exact timetable of its arrival. But even Revelation says that the city will be huge, not just a tiny village for the pious few, but a metropolis with room for an uncountable number of the redeemed. The gates, with their one-way flow of traffic from outside to inside, will be kept open permanently—it will be radically inclusive, and shockingly so to anyone who has presumed to be a guardian of holiness. According to Revelation, even the nations and kings that *opposed God's rule* and *oppressed Christ's church* will be redeemed in the end, and welcomed into God's glorious realm of mercy. And all things will be made new. All afflictions will be healed. All sickness will be cured. All sin will be cleansed. And despite every *contrary* appearance, the world is *destined* for the new Jerusalem. Every thought, word, or deed in some direction *other* than the city of God is a wasted move, for it is out of step with God's reality, ultimately futile and unavailing.

The river that flowed out of Eden to give life to the garden, whose branches and rivulets surge through all the history of the Bible, by whose waters God's people were saved long ago and are marked for salvation even today, flows finally from the very throne of God, and of the Lamb, who himself is the very water of life—water not to be hoarded, but which flows freely where it will, refreshing whoever is thirsty and restoring whatever is unclean in God's merciful realm, the gates of which are *never* shut. The church must be the *model* of God's free and merciful grace, never presuming, like the pious defenders of law and order of old, that its job is to *guard* or *restrict* God's grace, never acting in a way that *excludes anyone* from the new Jerusalem, but always *inviting* people—all *sorts* of people—to the water of life, healing, cleansing, refreshing; the water of life, abundant, full, and free. Jesus Christ—the water of life. There is no water rationing here.

Ascension of the Lord
First Presbyterian Church, Dodge City, Kansas
May 21, 1998
Acts 1:1–11
Ephesians 1:15–23
Luke 24:44–53

"Witnesses of Hope"

THIS PAST WEEK, NEWSPAPERS carried one of the most memorable mixtures of hope and despair I can remember. In the same editions, even on the same page, there were stories about a promising new treatment for breast cancer that could be on the market, with few side effects, as early as this fall, and there were stories about India's defiance of world opinion by exploding not one, but several, nuclear devices, and the likelihood that first Pakistan, and then China, and then perhaps Russia and other countries, will throw off restraint and we will be plunged once again into a doomsday spiral. The two greatest fears of humankind, one—the epidemic of cancer—on the way to being eradicated, one—nuclear devastation—intensified.

For every human advancement, it seems, there is always an equal step backward. When unbounded pride in human achievement during the late nineteenth century was followed by the horrors of World War I in the early twentieth century, Europe was spiritually devastated. Progress in medicine, a myriad of inventions that increased productivity and were thought to make life not only *easier* but *better*, campaigns for temperance, even advances in Christianizing Africa and Asia, seemed to be the fulfillment of ancient hopes. But a stubborn reality of human existence—Karl Barth called it "sin"—shadowed our perceptions of progress. A lot of people began to examine the *basis* of their hope and were surprised to discover that we had been building a modern Tower of Babel. The inventions were real. The medicine often worked. The discoveries were important. They promised wisdom. They promised power. They promised wealth and ease and comfort. And that was even *before* "Windows '98." But, a century of inventions and discoveries later, we are plagued with new diseases, poverty is *still* acute and in some ways even *more* acute, and governments pay scientists to come up with ever more lethal weapons. We *want* to *hope*. But every time the news on the *first* page tempts us to hope in *ourselves*, *our* accomplishments, *our* knowledge, the news on the *next* page *jeopardizes* our hope, even makes it seem foolish.

As Christians, we are *called* to be people of hope. "I pray," wrote Paul (or someone using his name) to the Christians at Ephesus,

> that the God of our Lord Jesus Christ, the Father of glory, may give you a spirit of wisdom and revelation as you come to know him, so that, with the eyes of your heart enlightened, you may *know* what is the *hope* to which he has called you, what are the *riches* of his glorious *inheritance* among the saints, and what is the immeasurable *greatness* of his *power* for us who believe, according to the working of his great power. God put this power to work in Christ when he raised him from the dead and seated him at his right hand in the heavenly places. (Eph 1:17–20 NRSV)

Christians *are* called to be people of hope. But we are *not* called to be irresponsibly oblivious to the condition of the world, or to the motives of human beings, which are often dark and at best mixed, or to belief in the inevitability of progress, or even to an attitude of positive thinking. Our hope is not general. It is specific. Our hope is not abstract. It is concrete. It is *the* hope given us by God in Jesus Christ—the hope that God's purpose *will* be fulfilled, is *being* fulfilled, in us and in all creation through Jesus Christ, whose death and resurrection save us to eternal life. Our hope does not rest on any human invention, on any human wisdom, on any human advance. It rests upon the faithfulness of God in vindicating Jesus Christ—his forgiveness, his healing, his love—by granting him a power and authority which can only be described in human words by saying that he has ascended into heaven and is seated at the right hand of God.

Whatever the disciples saw when the appearances of the resurrected Jesus came to an end, they did *not* peer into heaven and see Jesus sitting on a throne. That is a *conclusion* that they reached on the basis of what happened *next*. The authority of the risen Christ is manifested in the *power* that Christ gives to the church through the Holy Spirit, even prompting the church to venture into places where it would not otherwise have gone, doing things *in* which it would not otherwise be engaged, astonished, sometimes, to discover, upon reflection, that it was in fact *not* the church's *own* doing, but that the church was only the agent of the risen Christ. Our technology tempts us to suppose that *we* are masters of all things. On Ascension Day, we remember that it is not a skilled workforce and great academic minds and captains of industry and prime ministers and presidents that God has raised to the position of *heavenly* power and authority. God has raised *Jesus Christ* to the position of heavenly power and authority. As for the first disciples, so for us, that is our *best* hope. In fact, that is our only *true* hope.

There are many outside the church, and even some within the church, who, perhaps never having acknowledged the authority of the risen Christ and perhaps never having sensed his power, might disparage this truth as a prescription for complacency, an excuse to strive for nothing, a justification for leaving things the way they are. "Stay here in the city" (Luke 24:49b NRSV), Jesus told his followers. "Wait." And, indeed, the church, at certain times in history, has been guilty of being a silent accomplice to many sorts of atrocities, a lethargic accessory to many missed opportunities. Even worse, in an effort to save itself or to enhance its prestige or its wealth, the church has sometimes in history increased the burdens of the poor, the powerless, the outcast, perpetuating by a vote or a decree or simply by indifference the despair of the very sorts of people Jesus ministered to in ancient Palestine.

But there are also the times that the church, taking seriously the Lordship of Jesus Christ, has boldly confronted the exploitation of children, has unpopularly given opportunity for leadership to women, has directly condemned racism, has defiantly offered compassionate embrace to people whom society regarded as literally untouchable, has stretched itself to build hospitals to provide curing, has faithfully started schools to counteract superstition. What could two missionaries—one black and one white—do to end slavery on the rubber plantations of the Belgian Congo? By their *own* power, nothing; but through their witness, slavery there came to an end. What could a frail little nun do in the slums of Calcutta to lessen the misery of millions? By her own authority, nothing; but through her witness, the poor are less miserable there now than they were before. What could one priest do to restore faith and justice to the lives of millions of people in Poland and throughout eastern Europe? By his own wisdom, nothing; but, through his witness, people are once again free to worship God and govern themselves in places which for almost fifty years knew only oppression and dictatorship.

In what should we hope? The same printing press that can print a medical encyclopedia makes it cheap and easy to multiply profanity and defamation and pornography. The cotton gin increased human productivity, but it was at the cost of enslaving millions. The most luxurious steamship ever built—even God could not sink it, they boasted—took over a thousand people to a watery grave. The computer has made tedium somewhat less so, and has increased the speed and volume of communicating information, but many people are finding that their economic future and personal life are now ensnared in a world-wide web. Jesus Christ, risen and sitting at the right hand of God, is at work through the church, in small ways and great, to make people sons and daughters of the living God. Our hope is not in a *thing*—an ideology or an invention or an institution—but in a person, and he is not a politician or a scientist or a philosopher or an artist or an entertainer, but the Lord of all. Our hope is not in an abstract progress, but in a concrete promise that millions of Christians over many centuries have experienced as being fulfilled. Our hope is not in a calendar event, but in the culmination of history when everything and everyone is taken up and presented to God, and all creation will be redeemed, and God's purpose will be fulfilled, to which God is calling us to give witness today—witness to hope, witness to *the* hope that God loves the creation so much that God sent his own Son to save it, and that, when creation said "No" to his Son, God put him in authority with power over all—power and authority that he still exercises in mercy and wholeness and compassion.

We are witnesses to the hope that is Jesus Christ. Surely, we are witnessing medical cures, we are witnessing technological advance, we are witnessing globalization of markets. But these events, helpful and interesting as they might be, are not the *source* of *our* hope. *Our* hope is the power and authority of the risen Lord Jesus Christ, and it is as *witnesses* to that hope that you and I have been called by God—witnesses not only in what we *say*, but witnesses in what we *do*, putting our conviction into action that God's forgiveness and peace and wholeness are meant for *everyone*, and they are ratified in the crucifixion and resurrection of God's Son. Jesus said,

> "Thus it is written, that the Messiah is to suffer and to rise from the dead on the third day, and that repentance and forgiveness of sins is to be proclaimed in his name to all nations, beginning from Jerusalem. You are witnesses of these things. And see, I am sending upon *you* what my Father promised."
> . . .While he was blessing them, he withdrew from them and was carried up into heaven. And they worshiped him, and returned to Jerusalem with great joy; and they were continually in the temple blessing God. (Luke 24:46–49a, 51–53 NRSV)

They had become witnesses of hope.

Seventh Sunday of Easter
Spanish Springs Presbyterian Church, Sparks, Nevada
May 16, 2010
Acts 16:16–34
Revelation 22:12–14, 16–17, 20–21
John 17:20–26

"Real Life"

THERE HAS BEEN A lot of discussion in recent years about whether Christianity is still relevant in the modern world, or how, if it is to *remain* relevant, it must *change*. People can't "connect" with the Bible anymore, some people say. It has too much of "this" and not enough of "that." It is ponderous, like history, and most people aren't interested in what happened once a long time ago, even once just a few years ago. The only thing that's important is the *now*, and how it directly affects *me*. All that talk about kings and shepherds and idols and Pharisees and the like—it might as well have happened on some other planet. And, in fact, some churches hardly read from the Bible in worship, seldom quote it in their music, seem not to pattern their prayers upon it. In this age of radical individualism and consumerist values, the common opinion is that the Bible may be the inspired word of God, but it is foreign to who and where people are today, has little to do with real life, especially the fantastic stories that seem to defy what we know of science and human behavior and the laws of nature, even if we find some of them mildly amusing.

Take, for example, this story about a slave girl possessed by a spirit which Paul exorcised from her, and then he and one of his associates ended up in jail for disturbing the peace with their preaching, but an earthquake came and damaged the prison so that the bolts of their chains were loosened from the wall and the doors fell off their hinges, but Paul and Silas just stayed there rather than escaping, which saved the warden's honor and prevented him from having to make a choice between receiving severe punishment and committing suicide, and he was so impressed with their honesty that he asked them how he could be saved, then he took them to his own home and dressed the wounds they had received from their floggings and he and his entire household were baptized and then he fed the men who had been prisoners and now were guests in his house, and wasn't that going to be just about as difficult to explain as if they had escaped? Well, it's an interesting story and all that, most people might say, but what does it have to do with *us*? What does it have to do with *real life*? What do these tales of *old* have to do with the issues that you and I are facing in *2010*? Surely, we're past all that sort of thing in twenty-first-century America. What we *really* need to know is how to pay the mortgage and car loan and tuition statement and orthodontist bill and the internet provider when we're afraid of losing our job any day if we haven't already. Real life in the modern world revolves around economics, national and household, and even our politics is driven mainly by how *this* person's election or *that* person's election is going to affect my pocketbook.

Did you notice that this story in Acts about Paul and Silas has its very *origin* in the realm of economics? In fact, it's but one of *several* stories in the New Testament that began with a dispute about money and the means of making it. Jesus had a lot to say about money and how treasure in heaven is better than treasure on earth and the fact that you can't serve two masters and the futility of hoarding. And you may remember the Gospel account of the pig owner who was unhappy that Jesus cured a man possessed by demons by casting the man's demons into the farmer's swine—animals that were *already* unclean, as far as Jews were concerned. The man's anxiety about his *investment* kept him from doing what people who think that *human beings* are more important than *swine* would know he *should* have done—given praise to God that the demoniac had been *cured*! In another episode, in Acts, Paul upset the silversmiths in Ephesus by cutting into the market for their little statues of the Greek goddess Artemis and threatening the entire tourist industry of Ephesus by preaching that the great temple of the goddess there was a monument to someone who didn't *exist*. Demetrius, one of the silversmiths who made his livelihood by selling little shrines of the goddess, said to his fellow craftsmen,

> "Men, you know that we get our wealth from this business. You also see and hear that not only in Ephesus but in almost the whole of Asia this Paul has persuaded and drawn away a considerable number of people by saying that gods made with *hands* are not *gods*. And there is danger not only that this *trade* of *ours* may come into *disrepute* but also that the *temple* of the great goddess Artemis will be *scorned*, and she will be deprived of her majesty that brought all Asia and the world to worship her" (Acts 19:25b–27 NRSV)

—by which Demetrius meant: brought tourists from all over Asia and the rest of the world to spend their money in Ephesus. It's pretty clear that the honor of Artemis was not his main concern, but the fact that pilgrims from the entire province and throughout the empire came to Ephesus to make sacrifices at her temple and, while they were there, filled the local coffers by spending money at restaurants, bars, shops, hotels, and, shall we say, other places of accommodation. Why, without all those *tourists*, the locals might even have to start paying an *income tax*!

When Paul grew weary of being followed around Philippi by a fortune-telling slave-girl who kept drawing attention to the fact that he and Silas were preaching in the streets about the God of Israel—which was illegal—he finally wheeled around and ordered the spirit of divination to come out of her—the spirit of fortune-telling by which *she* had made a fortune for her *owner*. The entire ethos of the city promoted love of money and condoned the exploitation of one person for another person's benefit. That included turning religion into a business and profiting on people's devotion.

> When her owners saw that their hope of making money was gone, they seized Paul and Silas and dragged them ... before the authorities ... [and] said, "These men are disturbing our city; they are Jews and are advocating customs that are not lawful for us Romans to adopt or observe." The crowd joined in attacking them, and the magistrates had them stripped of their clothing and ordered them to be beaten with rods. After they had given them a severe flogging, they threw them into prison and ordered the jailer to keep them securely. Following these instructions, he put them in the innermost cell and fastened their feet in the stocks. (Acts 16:19–24 NRSV)

And then, about midnight, while Paul and Silas were singing hymns and other prisoners in the place were listening to them, the earthquake struck.

It may be that none of us has ever been arrested and flogged and put in prison with our wrists in chains and our feet in stocks for preaching about God and his Son Jesus Christ. But, if we truly believe in the *authority* of God and the *lordship* of his Son Jesus Christ, we have probably each had the real life experience of being excluded from some group or shunned by peers when we didn't laugh at their ethnic jokes or share their racial prejudices or participate in their promiscuous adventures or condone their dishonest business practices. And maybe that had the real-life impact of costing us a friendship or losing a contract or forfeiting a promotion or missing out on a deal that was really more of a swindle.

The biblical book that we know as the Revelation to John was written in a time when the *cost* of witnessing to the supremacy of God and the lordship of Christ in all matters was more obvious, perhaps, than in our present-day situation, but no different in significance. And, of course, there are places in the world where Christians are being persecuted *today*, even killed, simply because they *are* Christians, believers trying to live out their allegiance to God and to Christ. The language of Revelation is highly metaphorical. Because of the fear of persecution, Revelation is coded in apocalyptic terminology. It may seem strange to us. We may get discouraged when we read the book, written in the form of a long letter addressed to seven churches, including the one in Ephesus where the temple of Artemis was, because the imagery makes it difficult for us to understand nineteen centuries later and half a world distant from the places it was speaking about. Of all the books in the Bible, it probably seems the least like real life. But, in fact, the language about washing our robes in the blood of the Lamb is as relevant, *urgent* even, for us Christians today in modern capitalist, consumerist, pluralistic America as it was for Christians long ago in the Roman province of Asia—the western part of what we know as Turkey. There may not be a law against being loyal to Jesus Christ in our own country with a penalty of fine or imprisonment or execution—although, in fact, even in the United States, following one's understanding of Christ's teachings may indeed mean just that, *has* meant that, for people in some circumstances. But there are *other* penalties to be paid in our culture for witnessing, with our words as well as our silence, with our actions as well as our refusal to act, to the supremacy of God and the lordship of Christ.

This reference to washing robes and making them white in the blood of the Lamb is not as gruesome as some bad hymns have made it sound. It is John's way of reminding his readers and listeners that Jesus was crucified, that he bled, yes, and died for us in a gruesome way, cruel in the extreme, because he was faithful to God, would not compromise his loyalty to God, witnessed with everything that he said and did to the absolute authority of God. And it is John's way of saying that entry into the new Jerusalem that will be inaugurated when Christ returns, entry into eternal fellowship with God in the new heaven and the new earth that Christ has promised, depends upon *our* being loyal and faithful witnesses to the supremacy of God and the lordship of Christ over all things, despite the threats and insults and earthly penalties *we* may face as a *result*. To wash one's robe so that it becomes white, and thus "have the right to the tree of life" (Rev 22:14b NRSV) and be entitled to "enter the city by the gates" (Rev 22:14c NRSV)—in other words, to be able to experience salvation unto eternal life—means to be steadfast in giving witness to God's supremacy and Christ's lordship by resisting every claim of absoluteness that *worldly* authorities, be they governments or employers or cultural icons, make for themselves and expect us to honor. By resisting, by giving witness in our words and our deeds that *God* is supreme, that *Jesus* is Lord, *not* the economy, *not* the boss, *not* Madison Avenue, *not* Hollywood, *not* the values of class or race or clan, *not* even family traditions, but *God* and his Son *Jesus Christ*, in *every* case, in *every* circumstance, not just for one hour on Sunday but all the other 167 hours of the week as well, not just in the church sanctuary but in the marketplace and the office and the workshop and the schoolyard and the courtroom and the voting booth and the bedroom and the locker room and the sporting field and any and every place else we find ourselves, regardless the cost, regardless the threat, regardless the custom, regardless the expectation—*that* is how one washes one's robe dazzling white, like the traditional garment of baptism, answering the invitation for all who are thirsty to come, for anyone who wishes to receive the water of life as a gift.

"The one who testifies to these things says, 'Surely I am coming soon.' Amen. Come, Lord Jesus!" (Rev 22:20 NRSV). The original audience for the letter, having heard those closing words read to them in their worship service, would then have moved straight into the Lord's Supper, of which Paul said, "For as often as you eat this bread and drink the cup, you proclaim the Lord's death until he comes"(1 Cor 11:26 NRSV)—until he comes and inaugurates the new heaven and the new earth, the new Jerusalem into which those who have washed their robes by witnessing to the supreme authority of God and the lordship of Jesus Christ in and over all things are welcome and have a home for eternity.

This is real life we're talking about—the real-life words and deeds of Christians in twenty-first-century America, just as important and urgent as the words and deeds of Christians in first-century Rome. The biblical story did not end with the final page of Revelation. It continues today. *Our faithful response to the gospel in the year 2010, including our witness to the truth of God and Christ and our resistance to the claims of the world even at the cost of suffering and persecution, even death, is the continuation of the Bible's stories of faithful response to the gospel by Christians many centuries ago, witnessing to the truth of God and Christ and resisting the claims of the world.* Their struggles back *then* were no different in kind from our struggles *today*. Their temptations back *then* are still our temptations *today*. And *their* loyal response back *then*, which earned them entrance into the new Jerusalem, makes clear what response is required of *us today* so that *we* will be deemed to have washed our robes and have the right to the tree of life and entry into the eternal presence of God. What the Bible is talking about here is real life.

Appendix

Soon after becoming the Organizing Pastor of the Spanish Springs New Church Development in Sparks, Nevada, the author was invited to become a clergy member of the baccalaureate committee for the joint service held annually at the Nugget Hotel and Casino for the three Sparks-area high schools. In a time when baccalaureate services have largely disappeared from the list of graduation events, I was delighted to participate, and became a perennial organizer of the event which, even in my thirteen years in Nevada, annually saw fewer students in attendance. Although an interfaith event, the gathering of course could not take place on school district property, and thus had long been hosted by the Nugget's owner, John Ascuaga, as a service to the community. Muslim, Jewish, Mormon, Roman Catholic, Protestant, Hindu, and sometimes Native American religious traditions were represented in the leadership and the liturgy, and care was taken to be respectful of the broad range of spiritual beliefs, cautious against religious exclusion or particularism, while avoiding crossing over into the bland safety of a secular observance. The first of my several opportunities to preach at the service, based each time on themes and scripture selections assigned by the committee, came a few months after the United States military intervention in Iraq.

Sparks High Schools Baccalaureate

Rose Ballroom, John Ascuaga's Nugget, Sparks, Nevada

June 1, 2003

Isaiah 55:10–13

Matthew 5:1–12

"Peace . . . Our Hope for the Future"

WHEN I HEARD WHAT your baccalaureate committee decided upon as the theme for this worship service—"Peace . . . Our Hope for the Future"—I suddenly felt a little nervous about my assignment. We have just waged the first war of the twenty-first century. Our nation is divided over the wisdom and propriety of our military action in Iraq—both sides can claim to be patriotic. Most of the international community remains opposed to the American decision to strike Iraq. Peace seems like a ticklish subject just now, one on which I as speaker at your baccalaureate need to be judicious in my address to you. But the words of scripture—the words that we heard read just a few moments ago, the Beatitudes, part of Jesus' Sermon on the Mount in the Gospel of Matthew—would not be nearly so pertinent in times of political harmony and international calm, if young men and women were not in danger of dying on a foreign battlefield. We don't *need* peacemakers when peace is already the condition of the world and the condition of our society and the condition of the soul. The times when the individual and communities and nations need peacemakers are when the task of *being* a peacemaker is just the most *hazardous*, and when being *peacemakers* opens us to the harshest criticism and exposes us to the most biting ridicule, and when taking *risks* for peace is thought to be most unrealistic and naïve. If there *were* no danger in the world, if there *were* no disagreement in society, if there *were* no trouble in individual lives, being a *peacemaker* would be an unnecessary job. But, then, there would be nothing about us that would identify us as "children of God." "Blessed are the peacemakers," Jesus declared, "for they will be called children of God" (Matt 5:9 NRSV).

Christians believe that the person who was preeminently "the child of God," in fact, the one we identify as "the *Son* of God," was the Prince of Peace—the peacemaker whom all other peacemakers should imitate, the one for whom being a child of God was all wrapped up with his being a peacemaker. Yet, his life—and certainly his death—were not what most people would think of as "peaceful." He was rejected by many people because he would *not* take up weapons and use force to bring about God's purpose for humankind. He was hated by people who insisted on retaining their privileges and their prestige, who benefited from keeping things just the way they were. He was killed by people who thought that peace could be achieved by stamping out any dissent or disorder. And yet he told his followers that he would pass on to them his *peace*. Paul, the apostle, told the Christians at Corinth that they were ministers of reconciliation—they were to be peacemakers among people who were at odds with each other and with God—and yet Paul had a very turbulent life, being imprisoned, being stoned, being insulted, finally being executed, we think, because of his faith in the Prince of Peace.

Maybe all this points to the truth that we don't just have peace *handed* to us in this world of pride and envy and prejudice and suspicion. The Bible's promises about peace must have something to do with the willingness of people who *believe* in God to risk themselves in *working* for peace, to swallow injured pride and forgive other people for the *sake* of peace, to trust God's promises to lay aside old feuds and suspicions in *favor* of peace, to live as if God's peace was *already* the guiding vision of the world and of their own lives—a world in which love is our motive and mercy is our method, a world in which the earth's bounty is shared freely so that there *is* no reason to invade and conquer, a world in which trust in God leads to respect for others and there is nothing to "prove," nothing to "gain," no glory to be had by threatening or injuring or killing; a world in which forgiveness is unlimited and love is even more generous than that, a world in which every person is recognized as bearing the image of God and being precious to God, a world in which every person sees in every other person a brother or a sister whose welfare is just as important as his or her own.

Does anyone here know Hebrew? Raise your hand. I'm going to teach you a Hebrew word. "Debar." Can you say that? "Debar." That's the Hebrew word that means "word." So, in the Bible, when you read in the Old Testament the English word "word," the Hebrew letters spell out the word "debar." In the book of Isaiah, in the fifty-fifth chapter, the prophet is speaking God's promise to the Israelite people who are in exile in Babylon, telling them the good news that God is going to bring them safely back to the promised land.

> For as the rain and the snow come down from heaven,
> > and do not return there until they have watered the earth,
> > making it bring forth and sprout,
> > > giving seed to the sower and bread to the eater,
> > so shall my word—

"debar"—

> > so shall my word be that goes out from my mouth;
> > > it shall not return to me empty,
> > but it shall accomplish that which I purpose,
> > > and succeed in the thing for which I sent it. (Isa 55:10–11 NRSV)

Now, that Hebrew word "debar" that means "word" also happens to mean "deed." "So shall my word be that goes out from my mouth; it shall not return to me empty, but it shall accomplish that which I purpose, and succeed in the thing for which I sent it" (Isa 55:11 NRSV). When God declares something, that's the way it is, no matter how long it takes. As soon as God utters it, it is as good as done, so certain is it that the thing is going to come to pass. So when the prophet promised,

> For you shall go out in joy,
> > and be led back in peace;
> the mountains and the hills before you
> > shall burst into song,
> > and all the trees of the field shall clap their hands.
> Instead of the thorn shall come up the cypress;
> > instead of the brier shall come up the myrtle, (Isa 55:12–13a NRSV)

it was as good as done, even though the Israelites could see nothing but desert wilderness everywhere they looked around them. The prophet promised them that God would bring about peace—though they were at that moment still captives in a faraway land—and that they would be led safely home, and even *nature itself* would rejoice and be a part of the peace that God had declared, and so it would be.

Peace . . . our hope for the future. With suspicions about weapons of mass destruction; with American bunker-busting bombs being lobbed into Baghdad, not very far from ancient Babylon; with rumors of terror attacks; with anxiety about the next chapter in your life; with worry about college or getting a job; with uncertainty about the economy and what's going to happen to the friendships you have made in high school, peace may seem nothing more than a wish, a nice thought, a dream. But, for people who have faith in God, peace is a *hope*. A *wish* is nothing more than our own *desire*. A *nice thought* is nothing more permanent than something that makes us feel better for the *moment*. A *dream* has nothing *real* about it. But genuine *hope* is based on *God's promise*, and the recollection that what *God* has *promised*, *God* will *bring about*; the "debar" that God has spoken—the *word* that God has spoken—is the "debar" that God will bring about—the *deed* that God will bring about. And the *way* that God will bring about the deed of *peace* is by the trusting forgiveness, the trusting love, the trusting sharing for the good of others, of people who have *faith* in *God* and the truth and goodness of God's *promises*.

Your learning will continue. Your preparation for a career may shift now into high gear. But something else important within you has prompted you to be here today—to recognize that you want your graduation from high school to be blessed by God, and that you want God to accompany you into the next chapter of your life and to guide and watch over you throughout your days. Do not neglect your spiritual life in the days and months and years ahead. Do not omit being a part of a community of faith. Be bold in your commitment to be merciful and loving and kind and generous, not just to your friends, but to *all* people. Be courageous in your testimony that God's will is peace among nations, peace within our society, peace between individuals, and peace in your own soul. For if you are a peacemaker, you will be known as a child of God.

List of Sources Cited

Book of Common Worship. Louisville, KY: Westminster John Knox, 1993.
The Constitution of the Presbyterian Church (U.S.A.). Part 1: "Book of Confessions." Louisville, KY: Office of the General Assembly, 1999.
Southwell, Robert. "The Nativity of Christ." https://www.poemhunter.com/poem/the-nativity-of-christ/.
Wall, James E. "The Acts of the Apostles, Reflections." In *The New Interpreter's Bible*, edited by Leander E. Keck, 10:155. Nashville: Abingdon, 2002.
Zeffirelli, Franco, dir. *Brother Sun, Sister Moon*. Paramount Pictures, 1972.
———, dir. *Jesus of Nazareth*. TV miniseries. Aired on NBC, starting April 3, 1977.

www.ingramcontent.com/pod-product-compliance
Lightning Source LLC
Chambersburg PA
CBHW062039220426
43662CB00010B/1566